T3-BWP-913

FROMMER'S
1983-84 GUIDE TO LONDON

by Darwin Porter

Copyright © 1977, 1979, 1981, 1983
by Simon & Schuster

All rights reserved
including the right of reproduction
in whole or in part in any form

Published by Frommer/Pasmantier Publishers
A Simon & Schuster Division of
Gulf & Western Corporation
1230 Avenue of the Americas
New York, NY 10020

ISBN 0-671-44794-7

Manufactured in the United States of America

Motif drawings by Paul Berkow

*Although every effort was made to ensure the accuracy
of price information appearing in this book,
it should be kept in mind that prices can and do fluctuate in
the course of time.*

CONTENTS

MAPS

Inflation Alert

It is hardly a secret that a wave of inflation has battered the countries of Northern Europe, and Britain has been hard hit. The author of this book has spent laborious hours attempting to ensure the accuracy of prices appearing in this guide. As we go to press, I believe I have obtained the most reliable data possible. However, in a system that in 1982 alone saw one London hotelier raise his prices twice in one season, I cannot offer guarantees for the tariffs quoted. In the lifetime of this edition—particularly its second year (1984)—the wise traveler will add *at least* 20% to the prices quoted.

The Dollar and the Pound

The currency conversions from pounds to dollars appearing in parentheses throughout these pages were prepared on the basis of £1 = $1.95. That rate may not be accurate by the time you travel, as it varies from day to day, depending on the relative values of both currencies on world markets. Use my currency conversions, therefore, only as a gauge of what you'll be spending—and check with a banker before you leave for England to determine what the actual rate of exchange is at that time.

Chapter I

CITY WITH A PAST

LONDON IS A CITY that has never quite made up its mind about its own size. For the "City of London" proper is merely one square mile of (very expensive) real estate around the Bank of England, inhabited by a few hundred nightwatchmen and caretakers, several score police officers, and innumerable cats.

All the gargantuan rest is made up of separate cities, boroughs, and corporations called Westminster, Chelsea, Hampstead, Kensington, Camden Town, etc., each with its own mayor and administration and ready to fight for its independent status at the drop of an ordinance.

Together, however, they add up to a mammoth metropolis—once the largest on the globe. However, a United Nations survey of global population now places London in the sixth position.

The millions of people loosely governed by the Greater London Council live spread out over 609 square miles. Luckily, only a minute fraction of this territory need concern us—the rest is simply suburbs, stretching endlessly into the horizon, red-roofed and bristling with TV antennas.

But the heart, the brick and mortar core of this giant, is perhaps the most fascinating area on earth. For about a century, one-quarter of the world was ruled from there. And with every step you take, you'll come across some sign of the tremendous influence this city has exerted over our past thoughts and actions —and still wields today.

London is a very old city, even by European standards. The Roman conquerors of Britain founded Londinium in A.D. 43 by settling and fortifying two small hills on the north bank of the River Thames and linking them via a military road network with the rest of the island.

More than a thousand years later, another conqueror turned the city into his capital. This was William of Normandy, who defeated the last Saxon ruler of England, Harold Godwin, in

1066. There isn't much left of the Roman period, but William the Conqueror left his imprint on London for all time to come.

For a start, he completed and had himself crowned in Westminster Abbey. Every British monarch has been crowned there since, right up to the present Queen Elizabeth II. He also built the White Tower, which today forms part of the Tower of London.

William did more than transform London (or rather Westminster) into a royal capital. He and his nobles superimposed their Norman French on the country's original Anglo-Saxon language and thus concocted English as we speak it today. Both the richness and the maddening illogicality of our tongue are direct results of that transplant.

The Normans weren't exactly gentle rulers, but the nation they created did pretty well. No one, for instance, has ever successfully invaded Britain since William's time—unless you count North American tourists.

CROWN VERSUS PARLIAMENT: London, as mentioned before, is a mass of contradictions, some of them dating way back in her history. On the one hand, she's a decidedly royal city, studded with palaces, court gardens, coats-of-arms, and other regal paraphernalia.

Yet she is also the home of mankind's second-oldest parliamentary assembly (Iceland has the oldest). And when handsome and rash King Charles I tried to defy its representatives, he found himself swept off his throne and onto a scaffold long before the French got around to dealing likewise with their anointed monarch.

The huge, gray building that houses the "Mother of Parliaments," with its famous clock, Big Ben, is more truly symbolic of London than Buckingham Palace. For it was there that Prime Minister William Pitt intoned, "You cannot make peace with dictators—you have to defeat them!" at a time when England, alone, stood against the might of Napoleon. And it was there that Winston Churchill repeated these sentiments in even better phrases when England—again alone—held out against Hitler.

It was also in Parliament that "His Majesty's Loyal Opposition" stood up to give a rousing cheer for General Washington's army which had just whipped His Majesty's Hessian mercenaries —whom they detested every ounce as much as did the American colonists.

Nevertheless, London was largely shaped by the monarchs who ruled her—imposingly by the tough Tudors, beautifully by the wicked Georges, clumsily by the worthy Victoria. To get an idea of the taste abyss between the straitlaced queen and her rakish predecessors, look at the classical elegance of Regent Street and then, say, at the Albert Memorial—perhaps the most exquisitely awful piece of statuary extant.

THE FIRE AND THE BLITZ: Much of London is also the result of disasters, both accidental and premeditated.

The first was the Great Fire of 1666, which swept away most of the old wooden Tudor-style houses and resulted in a new city, built of brick.

The cause of the fire—like that of the great Chicago conflagration—remains unknown. Considering the fire hazards of those tightly packed timber dwellings, the remarkable thing is that the town didn't burn down annually.

As it was, the blaze gutted three-quarters of London—about 13,300 homes, churches, and public buildings. But it also gave England's greatest architect, Christopher Wren, the chance to design St. Paul's Cathedral as it stands today, as well as 51 other superb churches, plus the magnificent Royal Hospitals at Chelsea and Greenwich.

The Blitz Hitler unleashed on the city during 1940–1941 also had one beneficial result. Along with beautiful structures, the rain of incendiary bombs demolished vast patches of the pestilential slum areas around Whitechapel in the East End. This region —made equally famous by Charles Dickens and Jack the Ripper —had been London's festering sore, boasting possibly the worst housing conditions in the Western world. With slum clearance courtesy of the Luftwaffe, the L.C.C. rebuilt most of the area into rather drab, but infinitely superior, apartment blocks.

There was something else the Blitz gave London: a world image as the embattled fortress of freedom, caught unforgettably by the wartime news photo showing the white dome of St. Paul's silhouetted against the black smoke of a dozen simultaneous fires.

The postwar building boom may have made London a little less "quaint," but it also made her a very much healthier, happier place to live in. And it provided the overture for her present phase of . . .

LIVELY LONDON: Contemporary London really does jump—it has more rock groups than New York, more discos than Paris, more nude shows than Tokyo. Her youngsters dress more zanily than American youths, and her theater is more experimental than any on earth.

London is currently the only capital city that permits gambling clubs to flourish. And if you study the little handwritten ads you'll see in some shop windows in Soho and Notting Hill, you'll get an idea of just how permissive a society can get.

The burst of joie de vivre beginning in the late '60s was not a uniquely modern novelty for London. London was merely reverting to type.

Throughout most of her long, long history, London was a distinctly wild and wicked town. Shakespeare, Marlowe, and their roistering, hot-blooded tavern cronies personified London life during the reign of "Good Queen Bess." Seventeenth-century London shocked visiting Frenchmen. A hundred years later, it even managed to shock the visiting Casanova. One look at some of Hogarth's paintings in a museum will tell you just what a boozing, wenching, gambling place it was.

For only a very short period—from around 1830 to 1950—did Britain's capital don Mrs. Grundy's tight corsets, which she had worn briefly during Cromwell's short-lived Puritan Commonwealth. There were various reasons for this: the industrial revolution and the surge of the bourgeoisie, the task of Empire-building and defending, the personal stuffiness of Queen Victoria.

But 120 years is merely a punctuation pause in London's thousand-year chronicle.

After winning two World Wars and losing an Empire in the process, her people have rediscovered the zest for life that characterized their ancestors' "Merry England." For a little while it had been almost smothered by the cult of the "British Raj," the "stiff upper lip," the pervasive idea of "setting an example," and the activities of the most ludicrously hidebound censorship to be found outside of Russia.

Now London is almost her old self again.

LONDON FOR AMERICANS: Despite the historic fact that they fought two wars against each other, no two countries have stronger links than America and Britain. Throughout this book we'll be coming upon the mementos of a common heritage that cuts right across political and economic conflicts.

In London they virtually crowd in on you. Stand in front of the **National Gallery** and you'll find George Washington gazing at you. His bronze statue, proudly erect, looks out over Trafalgar Square.

Visit **Westminster Abbey** and you'll see a memorial tablet to President Roosevelt, a bust of Longfellow in the Poet's Corner, and the graves of Edward Hyde (Hyde Park, N.Y., was named after him) and James Oglethorpe, who founded the state of Georgia.

Grosvenor Square, in the heart of the West End, is known as "Little America." Overlooked by a statue of FDR, it contains the sumptuously modern U.S. Embassy and the home of John Adams when he was minister to Britain.

Norfolk House, St. James Square, was General Eisenhower's Allied Headquarters during World War II, the spot from which he directed the Normandy landing in 1944.

At **36 Craven Street,** just off the Strand, stands Benjamin Franklin's London residence. And in **St. Sepulchre,** at Holborn Viaduct, lies the grave of Capt. John Smith of Pocahontas fame, who had been prevented from sailing in the *Mayflower* because the other passengers considered him an "undesirable character."

96 Cheyne Walk, Chelsea, was the London home of American-born James McNeill Whistler, and at the plush **Café Royal** in Regent Street you'll find the lounge where he exchanged barbed epigrams with Oscar Wilde.

The most moving reminder of national links is the **American Memorial Chapel** at St. Paul's Cathedral. It commemorates the 28,000 U.S. servicemen who lost their lives while based in Britain during World War II. The Roll of Honor containing their names was handed over by General Eisenhower on the Fourth of July 1951, and the chapel—with the Roll encased in glass—has become an unofficial pilgrimage place for visiting Americans.

UNDERSTANDING THE ENGLISH: For an American it can be a disheartening experience to discover that the English in fact speak *English. We* speak *American.* There are just enough differences between the two lingos to result in totally crossed wires, and occasionally communication breakdowns. For although the British use words and phrases you think you understand, they often have quite different connotations from their U.S. equivalents.

When they call someone "mean" they mean stingy. "Calling" denotes a personal visit, not a phone call. To "queue up" means to form a line. A "subway" is an underground pedestrian passage. The actual subway system is "the underground." The term "theater" only refers to the live stage; a movie theater is a "cinema," and what's playing in them "the pictures."

In a grocery you don't buy canned goods but "tins" of this and that. Rutabagas are "swedes," chops are "cutlets," and both cookies and crackers are "biscuits" which can be either "dry" or "sweet." That is, except for graham crackers which—unaccountably—are "digestives."

The going gets rougher when you're dealing with motor vehicles. Gas, for a start, is "petrol," and a service station is a "petrol station." And when talking about the actual vehicle, very little means the same except the word "car." The hood is the "bonnet." The windshield is the "windscreen," bumpers are "fenders," and the dashboard is the "facia." The trunk is the "boot" and what you do on the horn is "hoot."

Luckily most of us know that an English apartment is a "flat" and that an elevator is a "lift." But are you aware that what you wash your hands in is a "bowl"? The term basin, to the English, is a utensil you mix salads in.

Please note that none of the above terms are slang. For in that particular realm madness lies, particularly if you are foolhardy enough to try and unravel Cockney. Cockneys are indigenous Londoners, although strictly speaking the label refers only to people born within the sound radius of the bells of St. Mary-le-Bow in Cheapside.

The exact derivation of the word Cockney is lost in the mist of antiquity, but it's supposed to have meant an "odd fellow." And the oddest feature about this fellow is undoubtedly the rhyming slang he concocted over the centuries, based on the rhyme—or the rhyme of a rhyme—that goes with a particular word or phrase. Listen to a group of market porters or taxi drivers or stevedores conversing and you'd swear they're speaking in any tongue but English. Which, incidentally, was partly the purpose of the exercise, since rhyming slang grew up as a kind of underworld code designed to mystify eavesdroppers.

You'll get some idea of its dazzling intricacy when you learn that a buddy is a "China" (from china plate=mate), a hat a "titfer" (from tit-for-tat), children are "Godforbids," a wife is "trouble and strife," feet are "plates o' meat," and stairs are "apples" (from apples and pears.) And these are merely a few primitive basics. So take our advice and don't try to delve further, unless you happen to be Professor Higgins—pardon us—'iggins.

... AND MEETING THE LONDONER: The first thing you notice about Londoners is their perpetual air of preoccupation. Don't be put off by this. It's merely a mask—a kind of detachable face they wear in public.

Approach them about anything and you'll find them possibly the most courteous and helpful people you're ever likely to meet. They'll go blocks out of their way to show you directions, explain where, when, and for how much you can buy whatever you need, and draw little diagrams to clarify some transportation problem. No matter how ignorant you appear of local currency, rarely will cab drivers, barmaids, or shopkeepers shortchange you. And they will patiently expound for your benefit all the immensely complicated rules that govern English drinking hours, club admissions, and telephone communications.

But . . . you have to approach them first! Londoners are not given to opening casual conversations, even when they share tables or bus seats or breast a bar alongside you. And this is not through lack of sociability but from a deeply rooted respect for privacy. All people who live on densely populated islands develop that trait, and with Londoners it's almost an unwritten law.

Their reserve vanishes the moment *you* start talking. Then follows a ritualistic exchange about the weather—how it might —or might not—stop or start raining. After that, the ice is considered broken and actual conversation begins.

All of which may strike you as rather quaint and formal. But look around you and note with what a minimum of friction the wheels of this giant city turn. How that touch of dignified politeness saves nervous tension. How few people you ever see snarling at each other.

And then you'll realize that London's formality fulfills the same purpose as the air in a motor tire—it makes for a smoother ride.

Chapter II

GETTING TO KNOW LONDON

THERE IS—FORTUNATELY—an immense difference between the sprawling vastness of Greater London and the pocket-sized chunk that might be called Tourist Territory.

For a start, all of the latter is *north* of the River Thames. Except for a couple of quick excursions, we'll never have to penetrate the southern regions at all.

Our London begins at Chelsea, on the north bank of the river, and stretches for roughly five miles up to Hampstead. Horizontally, its western boundary runs through Kensington while the eastern lies five miles away at Tower Bridge.

Within this five-by-five-mile square, you'll find all of the hotels and restaurants and nearly all of the sights that are usually of interest to visitors.

Make no mistake—this is still a hefty portion of land to cover and a really thorough exploration of it would take a couple of years. But it has the advantage of being flat and eminently walkable, besides boasting one of the best public transport systems ever devised.

The logical (although not geographical) center of this area is Trafalgar Square, which we'll therefore take as our orientation point.

The huge, thronged, fountain-splashed, pigeon-infested square was named after the battle in which Nelson destroyed the combined Franco-Spanish fleets and lost his own life. His statue tops the towering pillar in the center, and the natives maintain that the reason he's been up there all these years is that nobody has told him the lions at the base are made of stone.

If you stand facing the steps of the imposing National Gallery, you're looking northwest. That is the direction of Piccadilly Circus—the real core of tourist London—and the maze of notorious streets that make up Soho. Farther north runs Oxford Street, London's gift to moderately priced shopping, and still farther northwest lies Regents Park with the Zoo.

At your back—that is, south—runs Whitehall, which houses or skirts nearly every British government building, from the Ministry of Defence to the official residence of the prime minister in Downing Street. In the same direction, a bit farther south, stand the Houses of Parliament and Westminster Abbey.

Flowing southwest from Trafalgar Square is the table-smooth Mall, flanked by magnificent parks and mansions and leading to Buckingham Palace, residence of the Queen. Farther in the same direction lie Belgravia and Knightsbridge, the city's plushest residential areas, and south of them Chelsea, with its chic flavor plus Kings Road—the freaky shopping drag.

Due west from where you're standing stretches the superb and distinctly high-priced shopping area bordered by Regent Street and Piccadilly (the street, *not* the Circus). Farther west lie the equally elegant shops and even more elegant homes of Mayfair. Then comes Park Lane and on the other side Hyde Park—the biggest park in London and one of the largest in the world.

Running north from Trafalgar Square is Charing Cross Road, past Leicester Square and intersecting with Shaftesbury Avenue. This is London's theaterland, boasting an astonishing number of live shows as well as first-run movie houses. A bit farther along, Charing Cross Road turns into a browser's paradise, lined with new and secondhand bookshops.

Finally it funnels into St. Giles Circus. This is where you enter Bloomsbury, site of the University of London, the awesome British Museum, some of our best budget hotels, and erstwhile stamping ground of the famed "Bloomsbury Group," led by Virginia Woolf.

Northeast of your position lies Covent Garden, known for its Royal Opera House.

Follow The Strand eastward from Trafalgar Square and you'll come into Fleet Street, the most concentrated newspaper section on earth, the place every reporter in the English provinces dreams about reaching one day.

At the end of Fleet Street lies Ludgate Circus—and only there do you enter the actual City of London. This was the original walled settlement and is today what the locals mean when they refer to "The City." Its focal point and shrine is the Bank of England in Threadneedle Street, with the Stock Exchange next door and the Royal Exchange across the road.

"The City" is unique insofar as it retains its own separate police force (distinguished by a crest on their helmets) and Lord Mayor. Its 677 acres are an antheap of jammed cars and rushing clerks during the week and totally deserted on Sunday, because hardly a soul lives there. Its streets are winding, narrow, and fairly devoid of charm. But it has more bankers and stockbrokers per square inch than any other place on the globe. And in the midst of all the hustle rises St. Paul's Cathedral, a monument to beauty and tranquility.

At the far eastern fringe of the City looms the Tower of London, shrouded in legend, blood, and history, and permanently besieged by battalions of visitors.

And this, as far as we will be concerned, concludes the London circle.

A TANGLE OF STREETS: Now we'd like to be able to tell you that London's thoroughfares follow a recognizable pattern in which, with a little intelligence, even a stranger can find his or her way around. Unfortunately they don't and you can't.

London's streets follow no pattern whatsoever, and both their naming and numbering seems to have been perpetrated by a group of xenophobes with an equal grudge against postmen and foreigners.

So be warned that the use of logic and common sense will get you nowhere. Don't think, for instance, that Southampton Row is anywhere near Southampton Street and that either of these places has any connection with Southampton Road.

And this is only a mild sample. London is checkered with innumerable squares, mews, closes, and terraces, which jut into or cross or overlap or interrupt whatever street you're trying to follow, usually without the slightest warning. You may be walking along ruler-straight Albany Street and suddenly find yourself flanked by Colosseum Terrace (with a different numbering system). Just keep on walking and after a couple of blocks you're right back on Albany Street (and the original house numbers) without having encountered the faintest reason for the sudden change in labels.

House numbers run in odds, evens, clockwise or counterclockwise as the wind blows. That is, when they exist at all, and frequently they don't. And every so often you'll come upon a square which is called a square on the south side, a road on the north, a park on the east, and possibly a something-or-other close on the west side.

Your only chance is to consult a map or ask your way along. Most of the time you'll probably end up doing both.

But there are a couple of consoling factors. One is the legibility of the street signs. The other is the extraordinary helpfulness of the locals, who sometimes pass you from guide to guide like a bucket in a fire chain.

CLIMATE AND CLOTHING: Mark Twain once said that the trouble with the weather is that everybody talks about it, but nobody does anything about it. Well, Londoners talk more weather than any other breed of city dwellers, but they have also done something. It's called air pollution control and it's enforced ferociously.

The result has been the virtual disappearance of those peasoup fogs that regularly blanketed the city in Sherlock Holmes's day. Up till now, however, they haven't found a method of generating sunshine.

A typical London area weather forecast any given summer predicts "scattered clouds with sunny periods and showers, possibly heavy at times." This sums it up nicely.

London may be moist, but it's very rarely humid. Summer temperatures seldom rise above 78 degrees. Equally rarely do they drop below 35 degrees in winter, which makes for a somewhat damp but fairly stable climate, avoiding extremes at both ends.

The catch is that the British consider chilliness wholesome, and always try to keep their room temperatures about ten degrees below the American comfort level. They're also hopelessly enamored of fireplaces, which warm little except whatever portion of your anatomy you turn toward them. Hotels, of course, have central heating, but even that is usually kept just above the goosebump margin.

The most essential items of your wardrobe are, therefore, a good raincoat, a sweater or jersey, and, if possible, an umbrella.

Apart from this, it's wise to remember that Londoners tend to dress up rather than down and that they dress very well indeed. This is particularly noticeable in theaters and at concerts. Nobody will bar you for arriving in sports clothes, but you will stick out. So include at least one smart suit or dress in your luggage.

Better class restaurants usually demand that gentlemen diners wear ties and that women don't wear shorts, but those are the only clothing rules enforced. As a final thought, *do* bring along a pair of reasonably sturdy walking shoes. The most interesting areas of the city can only be properly enjoyed on foot.

MONEY: Britain's monetary system is based on the pound (£), a medium-sized greenish bill called a "quid" by the Cockneys. One pound, as of this writing, is worth approximately $1.95 in U.S. terms. It's made up of 100 new pence, written "p."

Since the rate of exchange fluctuates from day to day, the conversions that appear in the book may not be accurate by the time you reach London. We advise that you check with your banker before leaving home.

Here are some approximate conversions, based on the value of the pound in early 1982.

Pence	U.S.$	Pounds	U.S. $
1	.02	1	1.95
2	.04	2	3.90
3	.06	3	5.85
4	.08	4	7.80
5	.10	5	9.75
10	.20	7.50*	14.63
25	.49	10	19.50
50	.98	15	29.25
75	1.46	20	39.00

*Note: You read £7.50 as 7 pounds, 50 pence.

SOME TIPS ON TIPPING: Most hotels and restaurants in Britain now follow the European practice of adding a 10% to 12% service charge to their bills. If so, this will be clearly marked and saves you the trouble of working out tips. Just add a few more pence if you were happy with the service.

Otherwise, when not included, it is customary to add 10% to

15% to your bill in restaurants and nightclubs, and to leave a 5% amount in your hotel room for the room staff.

Taxi drivers expect 5 pence on top of the fare up to 20 pence, then 10 pence up to 50 pence, and after that 15% of the fare. Porters get about 5 pence per suitcase they carry for you. Barbers and hairdressers receive around 20% on top of the bill.

From all of which you can gather that tipping in London won't exactly impoverish you. What's more, you'll get a great many more "thank you's" in return than you would in the States.

GETTING AROUND LONDON: The area known as Greater London possesses one of the (if not *the*) finest transportation systems in the world.

London Transport—the outfit that operates the area's public transportation—has a large Underground and bus network, covering 630 square miles of urban territory with more than 4000 Underground cars and 5000 buses, carrying nearly 190 million passengers per year.

The service it provides is not only fast, frequent, clean, and comfortable, but also (by U.S. standards) amazingly cheap. However, London Transport suffers from one grave drawback: it keeps lamentably early hours. Nearly all buses and trains stop running around midnight (11:30 p.m. on Sunday), forcing you to take taxis after a night out.

The Underground

Known locally as "The Tube," this is the fastest and easiest (although not the most interesting) way to get from place to place. The Tube has a special spot in the hearts of Londoners— during the Blitz thousands of people used its underground platforms as air raid shelters, camping down there all night in reasonable safety from the bombs.

The Piccadilly Line, recently extended to serve Heathrow Airport, rushes passengers to or from the airport to the center of London's West End in less than 40 minutes on newly designed trains with special luggage areas and sleek comfortable styling. The Heathrow Central Station, the terminus for the extension, is right at the center of the airport, convenient to all airlines.

All underground stations are clearly marked with a red circle and blue crossbar. You descend either by stairways or escalators or huge elevators, depending on the depth.

Some subway stations have complete shopping arcades underground and several boast gadgets like push-button information machines.

Compared to, for instance, its New York counterpart, the Tube is a luxury cruiser. The stations are clean, ventilated, orderly, and fairly quiet. Above all, they're superbly signposted, and in such a well-calculated fashion that it takes a certain amount of talent to catch the wrong train.

You pick the station for which you're heading on the large diagram displayed on the wall, which has an alphabetical index to make it easy. You note the color of the line it happens to be on (Bakerloo is brown, Central is red, etc.). Then, by merely following the colored band, you can see at a glance whether and where you'll have to change and how many stops there are to your destination.

That's all there's to it. It's so simple and logical that we can't imagine why all other subway systems in the world haven't copied it.

If you have the right change, you can get your ticket at one of the vending machines. Otherwise you buy it at the ticket box. But *don't* forget to keep it, because they collect it at the other end.

Fares vary according to distance, from 20p (39¢) for short rides to a high of £1.60 ($3.12) to the outer extremities of Greater London. Fares for journeys outside the London area can be higher. The fare from Heathrow to Piccadilly Circus is £1.10 ($2.15), and the average fare in central London is 20p (39¢).

On Sunday and public holidays, there is a maximum fare to anywhere (except Heathrow) on the network of 40p (78¢) for a single journey and 60p ($1.17) for a round trip. These are not "Rover" tickets and therefore each ticket can be used only once.

A warning: If you're going out on the town and are dependent on the underground, watch your time carefully: the subways stop running just after midnight (11:30 p.m. on Sunday).

Buses

London has just two types of buses, which you can't possibly confuse—the red double-decked monsters that bully their way through the inner-city areas, and the green single-deckers which link the center with the outlying towns and villages.

The upper deck of a red bus provides wonderful sightseeing (smoking, but no standing, permitted). But if you're in a hurry, it's better to take the tube, as the buses frequently get stuck in traffic snarls.

The first thing you learn about London buses is that nobody just gets on them—you "queue up," that is, form a single file, at the bus stop. The English do it instinctively, even when there are only two of them. It's one of their eccentricities, and you get to appreciate it during rush hours.

You choose your bus by its number. A panel at every stop post tells you precisely which numbers stop there, and where they go. When the conductor (or conductress) comes around, you state your destination and pay your fare accordingly.

London Transport's Services for Visitors

Information on bus and underground services and sightseeing tours can be obtained by calling at London Transport's Travel Information Centres (tel. 222-5600) at Heathrow Central, Victoria, Piccadilly Circus, Oxford Circus, St. James's Park, Euston, and King's Cross underground stations. These offices are open every day from 8:30 a.m. to 9:30 p.m. (St. James's Park is open Monday to Friday from 8:30 a.m. to 6:30 p.m. and Heathrow Central from 7:30 a.m. to 9:30 p.m. Monday through Saturday, 8:30 a.m. to 9:30 p.m. on Sunday). They sell Go-As-You-Please tourist tickets and take bookings for London Transport's guided coach tours. They can also supply free underground and bus maps and other information and leaflets designed to help visitors.

Of special value to tourists are:

Go-As-You-Please Tourist Tickets—very useful bargains for visitors to London. They give three, four, or seven days of unlimited travel on London's red buses and most of the underground, and can be bought at underground stations of Travel Information Centres. They cost £8 ($15.60) for adults, £2.50 ($4.88) for children for three days; £10 ($19.50) for adults, £3.50 ($6.83) for children for four days; and £15 ($29.25) for adults, £5 ($9.75) for children for seven days.

Central London Rovers: These tickets are available for unlimited travel for one day on London's red buses and the underground in central London. They can be bought from any underground station or Travel Information Centre in central London and cost £1.60 ($3.12) for adults, 60p ($1.17) for children.

Red Bus Rovers: These tickets give unlimited travel on London's red buses for one day and can be bought at any Travel Information Centre, most underground stations, bus garages, and agents of National Travel. They cost £1.20 ($2.34) for adults, 30p (59¢) for children.

'Round London Sightseeing Tour

One of London's most popular tours, covering some 20 miles, passes virtually all the major places of interest in Central London in two hours. It starts from Piccadilly Circus, Victoria, and Marble Arch, and runs every day of the year except Christmas Day. Some journeys are in open-top buses. From March to October this tour operates at least every hour between 10 a.m. and 8 p.m., and from October to March between 9 a.m. and 4 p.m. There is no guide. Passengers are given an illustrated diagram of the route, showing points of interest. The fare is £2.60 ($5.07) for adults, £1.50 ($2.93) for children under 16. Seats cannot be booked in advance.

Taxis

London cabs are specially designed for their function, have a glass partition to prevent driver and passengers from bothering each other, and have the maneuverability of fighter planes. At first glance they seem oddly staid and upright, but you quickly learn to appreciate the headroom they provide and the uncanny U-turns they can execute. They are, in fact, the best designed taxis anywhere.

However, they share the drawback of their ilk the world over. Meaning that they encircle you in massed columns when you don't want them and become invisible the moment you do. And their drivers have precisely the same tendency as their Stateside brethren of going off duty when it starts to rain.

Otherwise, the drivers are immeasurably more polite, know their streets better, and thank you for tips.

Cabs are also relatively cheap. The minimum fare is 50p (98¢). On weekends and at night a surcharge of 30p (59¢) is added. You should tip about 20% of the fare, but never less than 20p (39¢).

You can either hail a taxi or order one by calling 286-6010, 286-6128, or 272-3030.

Rented Cars

Driving around London is a tricky business even for the native motorist. While London isn't quite as permanently stalled as

Rome, and traffic is much better disciplined than in Paris, it is still a warren of one-way streets, and parking spots are at premium.

In England, as you probably know, you drive on the left and overtake on the right. Roadsigns are clear and internationally unmistakable, but keep in mind that at all zebra-striped crossings the pedestrian has the right of way—and this not just in theory.

Petrol prices (gas to you) are pretty steep, due to a truly savage 25% tax on motor fuels. Incidentally, an Imperial gallon is one-fifth bigger than the U.S. measure.

Car rentals are reasonable and London offers a large array of companies to choose from. Most of them will accept your U.S. driving license, providing you're over 21 and have held it for more than a year. Don't forget, however, that the car you get will have the steering wheel on the "wrong" side.

Herewith a survey of some rental firms and rates:

Hertz, 35 Edgware Rd., Marble Arch, W.2 (tel. 542-6688), or at Heathrow Airport (same phone), plus four other major offices in London. The airport office maintains 24-hour service. Their cheapest and smallest car is the Ford Fiesta, seating four passengers. You're granted unlimited mileage for rentals lasting more than two days. On the short-term rentals in the medium-priced bracket, the super Ford Cortina is the best choice.

Avis also maintains offices at Heathrow Airport (tel. 897-9321, although its international reservation number is 848-8733). It offers nine price levels on its rental cars, a special feature being the weekly rental, for which you're granted unlimited mileage. Their cheapest car is the Ford Escort, seating four.

Motorcycles

These are real money savers in this land of steep gas prices, if you don't mind getting drenched occasionally. **Rent-A-Scooter,** 7 Broadwell Parade, Broadhurst Gardens, N.W.6 (tel. 624-8491), has Hondas and gives free unlimited mileage plus gratis safety helmets. These cycles do up to 200 miles per gallon. The one-seater Honda moped rents for £3 ($5.85) per day, or £15 ($29.25) per week. More expensive Hondas can cost from £12 ($23.40) per day upward or £60 ($117) per week. A deposit of £50 ($97.50) is required.

Bikes

This is the cheapest transportation apart from that you walk on. You can rent bikes by the day or by the week from a number of outfits, such as **Rent-a-Bike,** Kensington Student Centre, Kensington Church Street, W.8 (tel. 937-6089).

Another popular place to rent a bike is **Savile's Stores,** 97 Battersea Rise, Battersea, S.W. 11 (tel. 228-4279), which has been renting out bikes for more than 70 years. Stan Savile's father started the company back in 1912! Prices are £8 ($15.60) per week, which is about half the charge of most of its competitors. This firm is not only the cheapest but also the most reliable bike rental company we can find. A deposit of £10 ($19.50) is required with a passport, £20 ($39) without. Padlocks are provided free, and insurance costs £1 ($1.95) for any one rental period. It's closed all day Wednesday.

Your Self-Drive Itinerary Planned

If you plan to drive yourself around the countryside, you can save the cost on gas by having Peter Barnes prepare a route including road numbers, the places you want to see, and suggestions for overnight accommodations and places to eat. His vast experience, touring the country on behalf of the British Tourist Authority and leading his own tours, enables him to produce a driveable itinerary.

Just send a check for $25 (U.S.) for the first seven days and $3.75 per day thereafter. Include a brief description of what you hope to see and do. The itinerary from Mr. Barnes will be mailed to you, but you must submit your request at least eight weeks before your departure from home.

Mr. Barnes also provides a London orientation tour (with his personal commentary), a nonstop trip by car around the places of major interest. The cost is $140 (U.S.) for the seven-hour tour, and as many as four passengers can go along for the ride. Lunch in a pub or restaurant is extra. A day's guided tour through the countryside costs around $160 for up to four passengers.

For small parties, Mr. Barnes will plan an itinerary, reserve accommodations, and personally escort two or more day tours by private car or minibus throughout the island. You must make up your own group, however. The cost for six or seven passengers is around $300 per person weekly, including the services of Mr. Barnes and transport. Accommodations, meals, and admission charges are extra, but for this figure you get 1400 miles of touring.

For more information, write to Peter Barnes, Willow Point, Friary Island, Wraysbury, near Staines, Middlesex TW19 5JR, England, or call Wraysbury 2259. For long distance, simply dial 078-481-2259.

For those who need to stretch their golfing muscles, there are several courses around London, including Wentworth and Royal Ascot, Moor Park, and the less formal Datchet. Club rental and caddy can be arranged, and Mr. Barnes will collect you from your London hotel, smooth your way at the clubhouse, and return you to London after half a day's exercise. The cost is £ 30 ($58.50) plus greens fees, club, and caddy rental. For the buff, a complete tour of the courses of England and Scotland can be arranged. Mr. Barnes knows them well.

London: Average Monthly Temperatures

January	41.1	July	64.1
February	41.3	August	63.8
March	44.7	September	59.5
April	49.1	October	52.5
May	55.9	November	45.4
June	60.9	December	41.8

Bobby with tourists, and Big Ben

Chapter III

WHERE TO STAY

LONDON BOASTS some of the most famous hotels in the world. Hallowed temples of luxury like Claridge's, Grosvenor House, where top film stars like to stop off, the Ritz (which originated the slang term "ritzy" for smart), the Connaught, the Savoy, and their recent vintage rivals, the London Hilton and Sonesta.

All these establishments are superlative, but nobody would call them budget hotels. It is in that bracket that you get the most fantastic contrasts, both in terms of architecture and comfort. Most of London's hotels were built around the turn of the century, which gives the majority a rather curlicued appearance. But whereas some have gone to no ends of pain to modernize their interiors, others have remained at Boer War level, complete with built-in drafts and daisy-strewn wallpaper.

In between, however, you come across up-to-the-minute structures that seem to have been shifted bodily from Los Angeles. These aren't necessarily superior, for what the others lack in streamlining they frequently make up in personal service and spaciousness.

Our task was to pick the raisins out of the pudding, so to speak. To select those hotels that combine maximum comfort with good value, in all price categories.

In most, but not all, of the places listed, there's a service charge ranging from 10% to 15% added to the bill. Again in most, although not all, the rates include breakfast, either a full English one or else a continental one.

In the spring of 1973, however, the British government introduced a special Value Added Tax (VAT). At present 15% is added to your bill.

All hotels, motels, inns, and guest houses in Britain with four bedrooms or more (including self-catering accommodations) are required to display notices showing minimum and maximum overnight charges. The notice must be displayed in a prominent position in the reception area or at the entrance. The prices shown must include any service charge and may include VAT, and it must be made clear whether or not these items are included. If VAT is not included, then it must be shown separately. If meals are provided with the accommodation, this must be made clear, too. If prices are not standard for all rooms, then only the lowest and highest prices need be given.

And now, a brief summary of local hotel peculiarities.

Very few English hotels provide free matches for their patrons, hardly any supply a washcloth (bring your own), and most keep their soap tightly rationed—a private reserve bar is a good idea.

What is termed "continental breakfast" consists of coffee or tea and some sort of roll or pastry. An "English breakfast" is a fairly lavish spread of tea or coffee, cereal, eggs, bacon, ham or sausages, toast, and jam. Don't expect fruit juice, however. That's strictly a luxury item.

If you want to remain undisturbed, don't forget to hang the "Do Not Disturb" sign on your doorknob. English hotel maids —most of whom aren't English—have a disconcerting habit of bursting in simultaneously with their knock.

Elevators are called "lifts" and some of them predate Teddy Roosevelt's Roughriders and act it. They are, however, regularly inspected and completely safe.

And, as mentioned earlier, hotel rooms are somewhat cooler than you're accustomed to. It's supposed to be healthier that way.

For those who demand really superior accommodations, we'll lead off with a selection among deluxe and first-class hotels.

Deluxe Hotels

Facing Hyde Park, the **Dorchester,** Park Lane, W.1 (tel. 629-8888), on the fringe of Mayfair, built and opened in 1931, enjoys many of the benefits of early 20th-century design. A big refurbishing program of the public rooms on the first floor has recently been completed. The bar, decorated with mirrors and ceramics, is London's smart meeting place, particularly in the evening when guests relax to piano music. The new promenade which extends from the lobby through the old lounge to the ballroom entrance provides elegant and comfortable seating accommodation for afternoon tea or for cocktails before lunch or dining. The

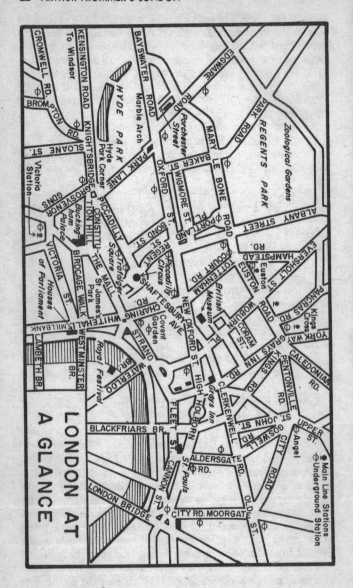

new Terrace Restaurant, with a view across Hyde Park and discreet dining alcoves on one side, is a sophisticated, beautiful room open for dinner only, with dancing on Friday and Saturday.

The Oliver Messel Suite is as popular as ever, and his penthouse and Pavilion Room for small parties have been redone exactly as he originally designed them. All rooms and suites in the hotel are tastefully decorated in different colors and styles. Singles start from £65 ($126.75) and doubles from £85 ($165.75), including tax and service. The Dorchester offers numerous services, such as valet and maid service, hairdressing salons, a florist, in-house films, and radio and television in every room.

And who hasn't heard of the **Savoy?** The address couldn't be more choice, The Strand, W.C.2 (tel. 836-4343), overlooking the Thames. The Savoy has been a London institution since Victorian times, when it was founded by Richard D'Oyly Carte, who first staged the operettas of Gilbert and Sullivan. Today many of the costly Victorian decorations remain, but all the fittings are most up-to-date. Service is as unself-consciously excellent as you could hope for anywhere. All the rooms come with private baths and cost from £85 ($165.75) in a single, from £110 ($214.50) in a double. The Savoy Grill and Savoy Restaurant, right on the premises, are *the* places to go.

Claridge's, Brook Street, W.1 (tel. 629-8860), stands in Mayfair and dates from the days of Victoria. It is a dedicatedly subdued, unostentatious hostelry. Those on official state visits who have been wined and dined at Buckingham Palace often proceed to Claridge's for a private stay in England. The rooms are deluxe in fittings, most of them styled in a turn-of-the-century idiom. The basic rate for a twin- or double-bedded room is £95 ($185.25), £70 ($136.50) in a single. However, these are only basic guidelines. The hotel contains such a variety of rooms and apartments, at such different prices, that it is best to write the general manager, Mr. B. Lund Hansen, for the tariffs if you're considering a stay. Do reserve well in advance for a room at Claridge's. A string orchestra plays at lunch and dinner, although not for tea. The hotel contains a formal restaurant and also a less formal Causerie where, if desired, guests may help themselves to smörgåsbord from a table in the center of the room.

The Ritz, Piccadilly, W.1 (tel. 493-8181), has undergone an extensive four-year renovation program, costing millions of dollars, keeping it in the ranks of London's most luxurious hotels. The original color scheme of apricot, cream, and dusty rose enhances gold-leafed molding, marble columns, and potted palms. The oval-shaped Palm Court, dominated by a gold-leafed statue, *La Source,* adorning the fountain, is still the most fashionable place in London to meet for afternoon tea, enjoying a selection of finger sandwiches including cucumber and smoked salmon and specially made French pastries, scones, and cake.

The bedrooms and suites, each with its own character, are spacious and comfortable, all with modern private bathrooms, color television, Ceefax, radio, in-house films, and 24-hour room service. Prices are £58.85 ($114.76) for a single room, from £83.95 ($163.70) to £101.20 ($197.34) for twins and doubles. VAT and service are included.

The Louis XVI Restaurant, one of the loveliest dining rooms in London, has also been faithfully restored to its original splendor. Service is efficient yet unobtrusive, and the tables are spaced to allow the most private of conversations, perhaps the reason Edward and Mrs. Simpson dined so frequently at the Ritz.

Ranking with Claridge's in prestige, style, and amenities is the **Connaught Hotel,** Carlos Place, W.1 (tel. 499-7070), right in the center of Mayfair. It appeals to those nostalgic for the days of the 19th century, and is considered, in fact, an architectural landmark of that time. Service is extremely attentive in the lounge, the paneled bar, the dining room, the tea room, and the rooms, all of which are decorated with antiques and reproductions thereof. Here at the Connaught, single rooms cost from £50 ($97.50) to £65 ($126.75), doubles from £80 ($156) to £105 ($204.75), if you can get them—reservations are hard to come by, so try to book as early as possible. Service adds another 15%.

The Connaught is constantly taking top awards for its restaurant. A semi table d'hôte lunch is priced by the cost of the main course, averaging between £20 ($39) and £25 ($48.75) per person, including wine.

First-Class Hotels

Duke's Hotel, 35 St. James's Pl., S.W.1 (tel. 491-4840), provides elegance without ostentation. A hotel since 1908, it stands in a quiet courtyard, off St. James's Street with its romantic, turn-of-the-century gas lamps. From the hotel it's possible to walk to Buckingham Palace, St. James's Palace, and the Houses of Parliament. Shoppers will be near Bond Street and Piccadilly.

At St. James's Place, Oscar Wilde lived and wrote for a period. Each of the well-furnished bedrooms, 46 in all, is named after a historic duke and decorated in the style of a particular period. In a single, the charge is from £49 ($95.55); in a double or twin, from £78 ($152.10), including service charge and VAT. There is a 25% discount on Friday and Saturday nights for rooms. The St. James's Restaurant serves main meals, and room service is available 24 hours a day. The hotel, in a word, is dignified.

Hilton International Kensington, 179 Holland Park Ave., W.11 (tel. 603-3355), is a superb example of skillful space distribution. Although with 611 bedrooms it actually houses more guests than its Park Lane relative, it manages to look smaller. That's because the beautiful white structure lies horizontally rather than towering vertically, thus blending nicely with the Kensington skyline. Yet, the interior is spacious, with a lobby that never seems crowded and rooms offering all the elbow space you may crave.

The Kensington is one of the most finely designed and equipped Hiltons anywhere. Happily it is also considerably cheaper than its West End counterpart. The reason for the price difference has nothing to do with comfort: simply, it boasts fewer restaurants, bars, lounges, and other peripherals.

The hotel restaurant, the Hiroko of Kensington, features authentic Japanese cuisine and handsome decor. The Tudor Grill dispenses English meals and international potations, and on Sunday the hotel offers the best value brunch in town. You will find a magnificent buffet laid out with a full selection of breakfast and luncheon dishes: cereals, fruit, pastries, a variety of hors d'oeuvres, a superb selection of salads; chafing dishes of sausages, mushrooms, tomatoes, hash-brown potatoes; bacon and eggs cooked to order on the open grill; a special hot dish, such as Hungarian goulash; and, of course, the famous roast beef with all the trimmings. Apart from that, there are special dishes such as hamburgers and soft frozen yogurts to tempt even the youngest appetites.

The hotel's bedrooms strike a balance between eye-pleasing decor and practical gadgetry. The color schemes—beige, cream, and russet—are blended for soothing restfulness. The lighting is both discreet and effective, the carpeting rich, the beds wide, soft, and slumbersome. Apart from bath and shower, dial telephone, color TV, radio, and fingertip-control air conditioning, the rooms also come with one of the handiest hotel installations ever invented. This is a self-service combination of bar and refrigerator plus breakfast dispenser. On insertion of the appropriate key, this contraption disgorges 12 different alcoholic drinks as well as soft beverages, coffee, tea, AND a continental breakfast! You just pick your fancy, press a button and *voila!* Instant room service. Free in-house movies are shown daily through a TV system. The "Uniqey" electronic door-lock system has replaced the conventional key-lock system, affording guests greater security. The Crescent Lounge, just off the lobby, serves beverages and light snacks 24 hours a day.

Single rooms start at £31.90 ($62.21); twins range from £40 ($78).

London Hilton, Park Lane, W.1 (tel. 493-8000). Reportedly, hundreds of traditionalists swooned at the idea of a 30-story American skyscraper right in the heart of the West End, so close to Hyde Park. Well, since 1963 the Hilton has proved itself a superb hostelry, with not only high-level comfort and standards, but style as well. As important as its slick bathrooms and bedrooms with every convenience is the quick and efficient service tailored to the needs of today's traveler. Each of the 509 bedrooms is air-conditioned, with a multichannel radio and television. Each floor has its own color theme; and a tasteful level has been maintained in the decorations, the best of today combined with reproductions of antiques. Single rooms range in price from £72 ($140.40) to £83 ($161.85), doubles from £85 ($165.75) to £96 ($187.20), breakfast extra.

You may never get out of the Hilton: it's its own "city." Seemingly, there are restaurants for every occasion: the Roof Restaurant, the Wellington Restaurant, the London Tavern, Trader Vic's, even the Scandinavian Sandwich Shop, in the International Shopping Arcade. For drinks, there are the Roof Bar, St. George's Bar, and the Patio, the last in a setting of ornamental miniature gardens. For late-night entertainment, 22 Park Lane presents a rock group and dancing.

The **Drury Lane Hotel,** 10 Drury Lane, High Holborn, W.C.2 (tel. 836-6666), is a Grand Metropolitan hotel set in Covent Garden, with its memories of Nell Gwynne, Sarah Siddons, and David Garrick. A steel and glass structure, with terraced gardens and its own plaza, the hotel is elegantly decorated in greens and beiges, its extensive planting evoking a garden effect. The bedrooms are well furnished, each containing a tiled bath. Inclusive tariffs, except for VAT, are as follows: from £40 ($78) in a single, from £56 ($109.20) in a double. Maudie's Bar makes a good post-theater rendezvous, and Maudie's Restaurant is open for lunch and dinner seven days a week. Who was Maudie? She's named after Sir Osbert Lancaster's famous arbiter-of-chic cartoon character Maudie Littlehampton. Tube: High Holborn.

Brown's Hotel, Dover Street and Albemarle Street, W.1 (tel. 493-6020), is highly recommended for those who want a fine hotel among the first-class traditional choices. This upper-crust prestigious establishment was created by Lord Byron's valet, George Brown, who knew the tastes of gentlemen of breeding and wanted to open a dignified, clublike place for them. All this took place in 1837, the year Queen Victoria ascended to the throne of England.

To this day, old-fashioned comfort is dispensed with courtesy. A liveried doorman ushers you to an antique reception desk where you check in. The rate for a single room with private bath is £59 ($115.05), from £75 ($146.25) for a twin-bedded room with bath. A suite of rooms, including a sitting room, twin-bedded room, single room, and private bath is from £130 ($253.50) daily. Family rooms—that is, two rooms with one private bath for three persons—costs from £98 ($191.10). Two rooms with one private bath, accommodating four persons, costs from £120 ($234).

Most of the bedrooms at Brown's have been redecorated and furnished in a fine traditional manner. Most offer a good amount of room; few, however, are quite small.

Brown's position is ideal for many: a minute or two from Berkeley Square, a block from Piccadilly and Green Park, within walking distance of many theaters and museums, and just minutes from the Burlington Arcade, Savile Row, and Regent Street. Two of the fine old dining rooms have been named after guests who frequented Brown's: Theodore Roosevelt and Rudyard Kipling. The Byron Lounge honors the connection between the poet and the hotel's founder. It's richly, yet tastefully, paneled and furnished with either antiques or reproductions—a fine selection for drinks or afternoon tea, the latter in front of a crackling fire in cooler months, a fast-disappearing ritual in London.

Kensington Palace Hotel, De Vere Gardens, W.8 (tel. 937-8121), is so totally revamped we didn't recognize the place at first, having slumbered there many seasons ago. Its position was always choice, on the periphery of Kensington Gardens (with its celebrated statue of Peter Pan), and at Hyde Park. The modern treatment is professional and tasteful, aimed at good, solid comfort, rather than high-fashion style.

The 300 bedrooms, with private bath and television, have been well conceived and combine contemporary furnishings and provincial pieces. One room might contain a wall of natural pine, while another relies on primary colors. There is a great deal of built-in luggage space, plus wardrobes. A single rents from £40 ($78), twins from £54 ($105.30), including service, VAT, and a continental breakfast. If you prefer an English breakfast, it's available for £4.50 ($8.78) in the Pavillion Coffee House.

In the Kensington Restaurant, you can enjoy both luncheons and dinners.

The **Royal Garden Hotel,** Kensington High Street, W.8 (tel. 937-8000), is another of Kensington's deluxe hostelries, equally famous for its stylish accommodations and superlative supper club, the Royal Roof (see our nightlife chapter). An immense cubist structure, seeming to float on its concrete pillars, the Royal Garden towers on the fringe of Kensington Gardens and fronts one of London's most fashionable shopping streets.

It's a big place in every respect, from the lofty glittering foyer to the green-hued Garden Café, whose floor-to-ceiling picture windows offer an uninterrupted view of the groomed greenery outside. The hotel, in fact, has 434 bedrooms and suites, three restaurants, three bars, and a row of conference and exhibition chambers. The Bulldog Bar is dark paneled and intimately pub-like. The Garden Bar, by contrast, is modernistic and pastel colored with a sunken bar area and settees specially designed for lounging and sipping. On the roof the cuisine is international, but in the Bulldog Chophouse, at ground level, it's traditional British fare, offering an inclusively priced menu for food and wine at about £11 ($21.45).

The bedrooms are modern, but in a wonderfully warm and cozy way, with discreet lighting, brightly colored decor, and some of the softest carpeting in town. All rooms have radios, dial telephones, air conditioning, electronic message systems, color TV sets, and, of course, private baths and showers. Singles start at around £40 ($78), increasing to £65 ($126.75) and £75 ($146.25) for a twin. These rates include tax. Breakfast, English or continental, costs extra.

The **Westbury,** New Bond Street, W.1 (tel. 629-7755), offers all the ingredients for a prestigious London address. It certainly is smartly located, within the heart of the West End (the "better end" off fashionable Grosvenor and Berkeley Squares), nestled in the midst of some of London's choicest boutiques and shops. It's part of the Trust Houses Forte Ltd. chain.

The efforts of the management have been directed toward

making a homelike, traditional atmosphere, a "country home" decor that brings to the Westbury a sense of peace and richness. Built in 1955, the hotel offers 254 bedrooms and 14 suites, spread across seven floors. All the modern facilities have been installed as well, and every room has its own bath with shower, plus a radio, telephone, and color TV. A single is from £57 ($111.15), a double from £78 ($152.10), inclusive of service and tax. Suites, of course, are more expensive.

In the afternoon, guests are attracted to the wood-paneled Tenison Room, with its fireplace, for cocktails or tea. There's a Polo Bar as well. The black, green, and white main dining room features dishes prepared by a French-trained chef. The smoothly operating hotel offers such conveniences as 24-hour service, instant laundry and dry cleaning, shoe-shining, a barbershop, a theater-booking office, and parking for your car.

Cavendish Hotel, Jermyn Street, S.W.1 (tel. 930-2111), became a legend under Rosa Lewis (the "Duchess of Jermyn Street"), who acquired the hotel at the turn of the century. As an Edwardian favorite, it became the "in" place of London, drawing both royalty and theatrical personalities. However, Rosa's fabled hotel was torn down and rebuilt in 1966.

The newer Cavendish is quite a contrast to the old. Administered by the London Division of Trust Houses, all of its 255 bedrooms contain private tiled baths and showers, as well as minibars, radios, and color televisions. The bedrooms are traditionally furnished, and they have a modern freshness to them. In a single, the tariff starts at £55 ($107.25) a day, increasing to £73 ($142.35) for a double room.

The Sub Rosa, honoring the memory of the former owner, is dark and intimate; and the Cavendish Restaurant, open 24 hours a day, offers an extensive international à la carte menu, as well as an alternative of *cuisine minceur*, (cooking without fats). It also is open 24 hours a day, features a special supper menu from 11 p.m. till 7 a.m., and is ideal for after-theater meals.

The **Churchill,** Portman Square, W.1 (tel. 486-5800), manages to combine Regency grace and modern facilities under one luxurious roof. A stately mansion-like building in a sedately elegant West End Square, the hotel receives you via a superb lobby—all marble floors, crystal chandeliers, and milky-white light. Somehow, despite the active crowds, the atmosphere is quiet, almost reserved.

The same subtle touch has been applied to the "No. 10," the hotel's dining room, which resembles a scarlet tent; the beige and white snackbar; the vast Regents Ballroom; and the private banqueting chamber called "The Library," with walls covered in deep green leather.

The 500 rooms (all doubles) are air-conditioned, and decorated with period pieces conveying the mood of another century. Only the gadgetry is up-to-the-minute: color TV and radio, a telephone on which you can dial overseas directly, with a bathroom extension for those calls that always come when you're in the shower. There's a glowing message light, individually controlled temperature, and outstanding room service, facilitated by a huge staff of 550, many of them multi-lingual. They will book theater tickets for you, arrange for a babysitter, and pamper you as much as you wish. Singles at the Churchill cost £54 ($105.30); doubles, £60 ($117). There's a 15% service charge, plus VAT.

Additional First-Class Choices

The **Europa Hotel**, Grosvenor Square, W.1 (tel. 493-1232). With justified pride, you can tell your friends back home to write you at your hotel on Grosvenor Square. On one of the poshest squares in London, it is an incongruous place for a hotel, with the U.S. Embassy on one corner, a statue of Franklin Roosevelt in the park. But London municipal authorities allowed it, insisting that there be no offensive outside advertising on its essentially Georgian-style facade.

The elegantly appointed rooms contain private baths, and cost £46 ($89.70) in a single, £60 ($117) in a double with bath, plus VAT. A continental breakfast is £2.80 ($5.46). All rooms have color TV. Many of the hotel's 276 accommodations overlook the square or else the courtyard, with its beds of seasonal flowers.

The Europa is the home of the well-known Diplomat Restaurant and the Coffee Exchange.

Cumberland Hotel, Marble Arch, W.1 (tel. 262-1234), is a virtual city, one of the largest hotels in Europe, boasting 900 rooms. It's also one of the most successful and up-to-date business persons' hotels, doing a thriving tourist business in summer as well. The position is remarkably convenient: right at the nerve center Marble Arch and across the way from Speakers Corner, where you're likely to hear everything debated.

There is a redecorated but subdued residents' lounge. The emphasis is focused on the bedrooms. Singles rent for from £46 ($89.70), twin-bedded rooms for £60 ($117) and up. All tariffs include VAT and service.

Each bedroom contains a bathroom with shower, plus radio and TV, telephone, a good-size wardrobe, bedside tables with built-in lamps and minibars, as well as a small lounge area and a desk-dressing table. In addition, all rooms contain color television sets, plus pressers for trousers.

Downstairs is one of the super-bargain restaurants of London, the Carvery, where you can help yourself to all you want from the roast lamb, pork, and beef, at a set price of £7.50 ($14.63). In addition, there is the Wyvern, dispensing more elaborate and elegant repasts; plus a coffeeshop, offering quick meals and light snacks till 1:30 a.m. All the big hotel facilities are offered, such as a valet service and a theater booking agent.

The **De Vere,** Hyde Park Gate, W.8 (tel. 584-0051), was built during the Victorian era for "the landed gentry," who stayed there for the season. Its position is ideal for many: overlooking Kensington Gardens, within walking distance of the Victoria and Albert Museum, the Albert Memorial, and the South Kensington museums. Over the years, extensive modernization of the ornate red-brick hotel has kept the basics up-to-date and serviceable.

The bedrooms are mostly spacious, with a boudoir look enhanced by slipper chairs, dressing tables, and rather lushly upholstered pieces. The tariffs are £28 ($54.60) in a single, from £38 ($74.10) in a double. All rooms have private baths. Rates include service, VAT, and a continental breakfast.

The dining room, opening toward the view of the park, is dignified, providing suitably English meals. Afternoon tea is still a ritual at the De Vere.

The **Imperial,** Russell Square, W.C.1 (tel. 837-3655), replaces the aging grande dame that stood for decades as a virtual landmark on Russell Square. Its replacement is a 720-room, gleaming modern structure, offering in each accommodation a private bath and shower, television, radio, razor sockets, and central heating. However, sentimental guests of yesteryear haven't been overlooked entirely. For example, what has traditionally been considered "London's ugliest clock," the ship off the old Imperial's tower, coats-of-arms, oak paneling, and clusters of Renaissance figures have been saved for the dining room.

The queen mother of the Imperial group of hotels (which includes the New Royal, the National, the President, the Bedford, and Tavistock) has long been an important gathering point in the Bloomsbury district, and life is gracious in this quiet intellectual center, with its many tree-shaded squares, the University of London and the British Museum nearby.

For a single room, the daily rate is £25 ($48.75), £35 ($68.25) for a twin. A full English breakfast is included, but not the service charge. Incidentally, the eggs for your morning meal, as well as the butter for the toast—in fact, much of the produce—was grown on the chain's own farm in Hertfordshire. Even the flowers for the lounges are home grown.

In addition, the hotel boasts an underground garage, plus a courtyard entrance allowing for a traffic-free arrival. On the ground floor, the Emperor Bar draws the gentleman drinker, but more popular is the Panoramic Cocktail Lounge, high enough up so that you can see the twinkling lights of London. Even if the Imperial can't accommodate you, chances are that one of its sister hotels can in one of their 3500 bedrooms.

Strand Palace Hotel, The Strand, W.C.2 (tel. 836-8080), accomplished the seemingly impossible, emerging victorious after an extensive reconstruction and restyling. Its position combines glamor and convenience: right on the Strand, within walking distance of many theaters, the pubs of Fleet Street, the Thames Embankment, and Trafalgar Square and Piccadilly.

The total overhaul has brought a sumptuous clarity to the reception lounge on the street floor, as well as a streamlined modernity to the freshly appointed bedrooms. Strong colors on the beds and chairs, as well as at the windows, contrast with the bonewhite walls. Built-in headboards contain master dialing for lights, radio, and telephones, plus a valet service, and same-day laundry. Each of the mammoth number (nearly 800) of bedrooms contains its own bath and shower. The rates are £33 ($64.35) in a single and £42 ($81.90) in a twin or double-bedded room, and £48 ($93.60) in a triple. All rates are inclusive of VAT and service.

For that price, you get superb service, as the staff numbers about 700 persons. Although the famous Simpson's-on-the-Strand is across the way, don't ignore the restaurants on the premises of the hotel. At the Carvery, you can eat all you want of tasty roasts of beef, lamb, and pork. The 369 Strand coffeeshop attracts show people. The bar of the hotel, the Mask, is named after a collection of Saul Steinberg cartoons adorning the walls. To complete the dining possibilities, La Pizzerie serves what its name promises.

The tone of the Strand Palace is set as you enter by the semiluxurious lobby of gleaming marble.

Luxurious Living

Lamb's Service Flats, 21 Egerton Gardens, S.W.3 (tel. 589-6297), is an address to remember for those planning a longer stay and preferring to live in style as well as privacy. These are furnished luxury apartments par excellence, located in one of the most opulent patches of the city, yet well below the price range of equivalent hotel accommodations.

Egerton Gardens forms part of a tiny enclave of Knightsbridge known collectively as "The Egertons." The building is an imposing Victorian red-brick structure, just off busy Brompton Road, yet basking in an aura of tree-shaded seclusion suggesting a suburban retreat. The 24 flats vary from self-contained one-roomers with concealed twin beds to those with separate bed and living rooms. But all of them come with genuine antique furniture, such as 19th-century writing desks, as well as up-to-the-minute kitchen and bathroom fittings.

You get your own private dial telephone (your calls are metered), plus a house phone. Each flat has a TV set, a radio, a fan heater on top of central heating (which is often too cool for American skins), and even a selection of books on your mantelpiece. The big, sparkling, all-electric kitchens are stocked with a full range of cooking utensils (including an American coffee percolator—a true rarity in these parts) and an ironing board. The management also provides a continental breakfast, left outside your door, plus the use of a sauna and patio garden. In addition, you get daily maid service.

Prices start at £25 ($48.75) for one to two guests, ranging up to £53 ($103.35) for as many as four overnighters. The different tariffs depend on the location of the rooms and include service, tax, and a continental breakfast.

Piccadilly Hotel, Piccadilly, W.1 (tel. 734-8000). Many prefer a hotel close enough to places they want to visit, allowing them to break up their day of sightseeing and shopping with short rests. This heartbeat hotel is only a few minutes from Piccadilly Circus, the theaters of Shaftesbury Avenue, within walking distance of Trafalgar Square, the Thames, the Mall, and Buckingham Palace. Built in the glory of the Edwardian age, the Piccadilly retains much of its original art nouveau architecture and decoration, including an impressive grand hall with a colored stained-glass ceiling.

The 290 bedrooms have been modestly modernized, singles with bath costing from £46 ($89.70), a twin with bath from £58

($113.10). You can help yourself to succulent roasts from the Carver's Table Restaurant.

The **Post House**, 104 Bayswater Rd., W.2 (tel. 262-4461), is one of the new breed of hotels sprouting up in London, this one operated by the Trust Houses, which includes such other prestigious selections as Brown's and the Cavendish, as well as the Hyde Park and the Meurice. Across from Kensington Gardens, it lies in an area of London unofficially designated as "Bayswater," one of those residential districts that grew to prominence during the rise of the upper middle class in the 19th century.

Privacy Plus

Bailey's Hotel, Gloucester Road, S.W.7 (tel. 373-8131), has been around since 1880, but it isn't on the usual tourist list. This six-story, handsome, red-brick structure, with white stone trim and a mansard roof, was in its day a pacesetter (the first hotel, for example, to install an "ascending room"—that is, an iron cage elevator). To this day, it harbors those who admire an aura of Victoriana. Social memories recall a great ball attended by 700 members of the nobility, including the Prince of Wales. It has recently been taken over by the Taj International Group of Hotels of India.

The hotel's 157 bedrooms have private bath/shower, remote-control color TV, radio, direct-dial telephones, and facilities which include wake-up calls and messages. An extensive upgrading program has been carried out, resulting in many new amenities, such as automatic elevators, a daily in-house movie facility, a good coffeeshop, and a hotel bar and wine bar with a first-class restaurant specializing in foreign food. There's also a fully computerized reservation and billing system.

Single rooms are £28 ($54.60), and twin rooms are £34 ($66.30) per night. All prices are inclusive of VAT and service.

Although the streamlined architecture is severe, much thought has gone into the comfort of the rooms—and that view of the park across the way. The hotel has 175 bedrooms, each with its own bath, razor sockets, telephone, radio, and color TV, plus facilities for making coffee and tea. The front rooms are fully air-conditioned (centrally heated in winter), and the windows are double glazed. Cots and highchairs are available. Services provide for laundry and ironing, even babysitting. There are also facilities for the disabled. The hotel has its own free parking for 80 cars.

The bedrooms are well conceived, becoming studio living rooms during the day. In high season, from May to October 31, you pay £32 ($62.40) in a single, £42 ($81.90) for a double. The decor is functional, neat, with a good use of strong colors.

In an airy dining room with picture windows, you're served modest meals, and there's a small pine-paneled bar for drinks.

The **Goring Hotel,** Beeston Place, Grosvenor Gardens, S.W.1 (tel. 834-8211), was built in 1910 by Mr. O. R. Goring. It was the first hotel in the world to be equipped with a private bathroom in every bedroom. It was also the world's first hotel to be centrally heated. The hotel was erected just behind Buckingham Palace, and it lies within easy reach of the royal parks, Victoria Station, the West London air terminals, Westminster Abbey, and the Houses of Parliament.

Today top-quality service is still provided, this time by the founding father's grandson, George Goring. Rooms here are called apartments. Singles rent for £45 ($87.75), doubles or twins for £58 ($113.10). Color television sets are included in the tariffs, as are service and VAT. The best arrangement for staying here is the half-board plan at a cost of £55 ($107.25) per person. Some of the chef's specialties include a fine duckling pâté, calf's liver (with bacon and onions), venison, and roast boned best end of lamb. The charm of a traditional English country hotel is reflected in the paneled drawing room, where fires burn in the ornate fireplaces on nippy evenings. Nearby is a sunroom with a view of the gardens in the rear and a new bar situated by the window.

The **Sherlock Holmes Hotel,** 83 Chiltern St., W.1 (tel. 486-6161), is an establishment evoking the aura of the immortal sleuth, although it's doubtful whether Sherlock's furnished quarters at Mrs. Hudson's were anywhere near as comfortable. One entrance, naturally, is on Baker Street, but the main one is on Chiltern Street. The Sherlock Holmes has a knack of combining period flavor with contemporary trimmings.

The 149 bedrooms come in a warm decor, all with private baths or showers, radio, telephone, color TV, and bedside panels from which to operate light switches and radio dials. They have writing cum makeup tables with three-panel mirrors, soft wall-to-wall carpeting and built-in wardrobes. In the bathrooms you'll find a handy folding clothes-line arrangement on which to hang wash-and-wears.

The public rooms downstairs are pillared, with lights from chandeliers reflecting on ivory-hued walls and ceilings. Leather couches and wing chairs give them a club-like atmosphere that seems far removed from the standardized hotel lounges. The coffeeshop is fast-moving, even by American standards. The bar, on the other hand, has a dreamy leisure air, as befits a nook dedicated to Dr. Watson. (The good doctor frequently prescribed himself a B and S—brandy and soda—for "remedial purposes.") At the Baker Street entrance stands a glass showcase filled with Holmesiana in book form.

Singles rent from £27 ($52.65), twins from £36.50 ($71.18), including VAT, service, and a continental breakfast. Tube: Baker Street.

The **Charles Dickens Hotel** (tel. 262-5090) is a handsome white-fronted building in quiet Lancaster Gate, W.2, one street away from Hyde Park. The interior is more modern than Dickensian, which certainly benefits transatlantic visitors who appreciate contemporary comforts more than Victorian quaintness.

The lobby is elegant, the lounge resplendent with scarlet settees, and the Oliver Twist Coffee Shop handsome and equipped for fast service to boot. In Mr. Pickwick's Bar, which has a distinctive rustic flavor, the barman will serve you an ancient concoction called Moonbeams, which was one of Dickens's favorite tipples.

The six-story hotel has two lifts and 200 bedrooms, connected by impeccably kept corridors with unusual torch-bracket light fixtures that give them a baronial air. The rooms are bright, although not very large, all with private bathrooms equipped with showers and tubs. The decor is a bright blend of red and black bedspreads and carpeting, combined with orange draperies. Lights and radio can be worked from a handy bedside panel, and every room has a telephone.

Rates for singles are from £23 ($44.85), from £29 ($56.55) for doubles, including service, VAT, and a continental breakfast. Some triples are also available at £38 ($74.10) nightly.

The **Londoner** and **Clifton Ford,** Welbeck Street, W.1 (tel. 935-4442), stand next to each other and share a joint reservation service. They are members of the Great Metropolitan chain, dedicated to rejuvenating aging London hotels. Tucked away in Mayfair, off Wigmore Street (near Cavendish Square and Wigmore Hall), the hotels are excellent remakes of older buildings. Spaciousness is the mood, especially in the clean-cut and uncluttered reception areas. The bedrooms have been furnished in shipshape Nordic fashion, each having its own shower bath. Singles rent for £30 ($58.50), doubles for £40 ($78), including

VAT, service, and a continental breakfast. All units have TV, radio, and 24-hour room service. At the Londoner, Oliver's Tavern serves traditional English dishes, and in the Chesterfield Room the martinis are dry.

The Best of the Rest

All of the following hotels offer rooms with full private baths; but, with one or two exceptions, many of them also contain many rooms with hot and cold running water only, which the British themselves are fond of booking. If you find that a medium-priced room with private bath is more than you can afford—and you want something fancier than a "bed-and-breakfast" house—then consider asking for one of the bathless rooms. You'll enjoy the same facilities, the same central location, the same hotel services, but you'll be paying far less.

OFF PICCADILLY: The following hotel is on Half Moon Street, a small, svelte thoroughfare connecting Piccadilly with Curzon Street. It's smack in the heart of the West End, right among the theaters and nightspots, yet fringed with greenery and removed from din. It's in what the British would call a "favored position."

Flemings Hotel, Half Moon Street, W.1 (tel. 499-2964), is in the heart of fashionable Mayfair, close to Green Park and within easy walking distance of the major shopping centers, nightlife, and sights.

The hotel has been recently renovated. All of its 120 bedrooms have central heating, digital clock, radio, color TV, refrigerator, 24-hour room service, and private bath or shower with toilet. The room rate is inclusive of service charge, VAT, and a continental breakfast in summer. A single room costs from £31.50 ($61.43) and a twin room from £42 ($81.90) in summer season. An extra bed is £10 ($19.50). An English breakfast supplement costs £2 ($3.90).

NEAR OXFORD STREET: The next three hotels are as choicely located as the previous—close to London's main shopping drag, but tucked away from the traffic noise amid serene Georgian terraces on the fringes of Regents Park.

The **Londoner,** Welbeck Street, W.1 (tel. 935-4442), has retained its traditional facade, but completely modernized the interior. The contrast, the moment you walk in, is delightful. Awaiting you are a spacious and comfortable lobby, small speedy elevators, and corridors heavily carpeted and soothingly decorated.

All of the 120 rooms come with private bath. They also boast full-length dressing mirrors, bedside telephones, radios, and televisions. Bedrooms and bathrooms have closets with space-saving sliding doors, the tubs have hand-shower attachments, and the towels are of American dimensions.

Downstairs, you'll find the Olivers Tavern, which has a homey atmosphere and offers a choice of good country fare. On the ground floor is the Chesterfield Cocktail Bar.

Single rooms are from £33 ($64.35) and doubles from £45 ($87.75). These tariffs include VAT, service, and a continental breakfast.

The **New Mandeville Hotel**, Mandeville Place, W.1 (tel. 935-5599), has been rebuilt and upgraded until it now offers 165 bedrooms, a total of 74 singles and 91 twins. These comfortably furnished rooms, each with a bath or shower, plus color TV, phone, radio, and background music, rent for £39 ($76.05) daily in a single, from £55 ($107.25) in a twin. Service is included in the tariffs but breakfast is extra. The location is only a few minutes' walk from the large department stores and shops of Oxford Street, Regent Street, and Bond Street. The wardrobes are pleasantly roomy, and the carpeting is excellent. The à la carte restaurant, La Cocotte, evokes the salon of a Mediterranean villa, although if you're rushed you may prefer the Orangery Coffee Shop. Traditional beer and ale, along with "pub food," are served in Boswell's Pub, and you'll find the Studio Lounge, serving sandwiches, cold dishes, and drinks, open 24 hours a day.

The **Central Park Hotel**, Queensborough Terrace, W.2 (tel. 229-2424), was so named because: as Oxford Street passes Marble Arch, it becomes Bayswater Road, and just off Bayswater is Queensborough Terrace. It may interest you to know that Bayswater Road runs along the perimeter of Hyde Park . . . and now you know why this hotel is called the Central Park. It is a pleasant-looking, seven-story hotel, where all is furnished in a streamlined contemporary idiom. Every colorful room here comes equipped with private bath (showers in singles), television, radio, message lights, and automatic alarm clock. Amenities of the hotel include a coffeeshop, cocktail bar, coffee lounge, garage, bookshop—even a sauna. The hotel charges these rates: £30 ($58.50) in a single, £42 ($81.90) in a double, including VAT, service, and a continental breakfast.

IN BLOOMSBURY: This is one of the best hotel areas in London, adjoining Soho, yet worlds removed from it. It contains beautiful squares and old houses, the British Museum, the University of London, fascinating bookshops, and hordes of unattached college students of both sexes.

The **Tavistock Hotel,** Tavistock Square, W.C.1 (tel. 636-8383), is a massively modernistic corner block, overlooking a delightful park, which goes in heavily for up-to-date creature comfort. All of the 301 rooms have baths as well as showers, plus large-screen television sets, radios, universal shaver sockets, and telephones. The rooms are of medium size, well furnished, and come with little entrance halls; bathrooms are large as well as air-conditioned.

Lounge and bar are equally and stylishly modern, the latter decorated with pop murals. There's also a handy city map near the front door, with a moving indicator to help you locate places.

Including a full English breakfast, rates for a single with bath are £21 ($40.95); doubles with bath are £27 ($52.65).

The **Bloomsbury Centre Hotel,** Coram Street, W.C.1 (tel. 837-1200), is a five-story cube which seems to consist mainly of windows. Its main feature is that it manages to offer every Atomic Age convenience without pricing itself into the luxury class. All is streamlined, except for the showcases with antique prints downstairs and pictures of vintage fighter planes on the corridor walls.

The lobby is large and severely functional, the corridors remind you of an ocean liner interior, bars and restaurant are studies in leather and chrome. The corridors offer electric shoeshine machines and, rare for London, free ice cube dispensers.

All of the 250 rooms have private baths as well as ample elbow space, pastel-colored draperies, wall-to-wall carpeting and a special air ventilation system. Comfort upon comfort is provided—radios, color TVs, and telephones, built-in electric alarm clocks, fluorescent lighting, and in the small, compact bathrooms, showers as well as tubs. The television lounge boasts a large color set.

A single with bath rents for £30 ($58.50), increasing to £40.50 ($78.98) in a double, also with bath, these tariffs including VAT and service. Breakfast is extra. However, on weekends, prices are lowered to £26 ($50.70) in a single, from £38 ($74.10) in a double, including VAT, service, plus a continental breakfast.

AROUND VICTORIA STATION: Bustling, crowded, and color-ful, the region adjoining the giant railroad station is traditional travelers' territory, marked by rows of hotels and rooming houses in assorted shapes, sizes, and price brackets.

The **Rubens Hotel,** Buckingham Palace Road, S.W.1 (tel. 834-6600), is a large reddish-brown, five-story corner building which appears to contain many more than its 145 rooms, an impression brought about by the whopping dimensions of those rooms. The lobby is relatively small, but the lounges open up huge, and the restaurant, lit by chandeliers, resembles a lavishly styled ballroom.

The elevator shifts impressive loads fairly fast. The 172 rooms (147 with private bath) range from big to very big, some hand-somely decorated in browns. As a concession to American blood temperatures, the rooms come with electric heaters on top of the central heating. All rooms have color TV sets, radios, and phones. Wardrobes run from modern to mid-Victorian, but are universally spacious. Bathrooms (likewise big enough to raise an echo) have heated towel racks and gleam with loving mainte-nance.

Singles with bath rent for £30 ($58.50); doubles with bath, £40 ($78). A continental breakfast is included, as are service and VAT. Tube: Victoria.

The **St. James Hotel,** Buckingham Gate, S.W.1 (tel. 834-2360), is not one building but several, all surrounding a court-yard. But inside is a world of contemporary furnishings, stream-lined bedrooms (520 of them), coffeeshop, bars, and restaurants. Most of the rooms have private baths and TVs, and all have telephones, radios, and piped-in music. Rooms vary consider-ably in size, and rates, depending on the plumbing, and range from £18 ($35.10) in a bathless single to £26 ($50.70) in a single with bath, from £31.50 ($61.43) in a double or twin, also with bath. Tariffs include VAT, service, and a continental breakfast.

IN PADDINGTON: The area separated from Hyde Park by pul-sating Bayswater Road is pleasantly residential, yet lively enough to be interesting, equally close to sweeping parklands and to some of the best shopping centers.

Norfolk Towers, Norfolk Place, W.2 (tel. 402-5311), stands just off Bayswater Road and almost within sight of Hyde Park. This small, cream-colored hostelry combines the intimacy of a private home with some of the facilities of a much larger hotel.

In 1974 the Norfolk Towers became a link in the rapidly growing chain of C.G. hotels. The place now has a modern lobby; a cozy little drinking nook, the Cavalry Bar, decorated in scarlet; and a well-appointed dining room serving meals until 10 p.m. Most, but not all, of the bedrooms have their own baths. Every one, however, comes with telephone and radio. The furnishings are comfortable, although not luxurious, and some of the rooms are much larger than you would expect in a hotel this size. They have been redecorated in bright pastel hues, and the beds are ideal resting places for footsore sightseers.

Singles with bath go for £14.50 ($28.28), doubles with bath for £21 ($40.95). For a bargain, ask for a bathless single at £12.50 ($24.38), a bathless double at £16 ($31.20). These rates include a continental breakfast. Children's beds come to another £3 ($5.85) per night. Tube: Paddington.

The **Park Plaza Hotel**, Lancaster Gate, W.2 (tel. 262-5022), not only has a beautiful facade, but an ornate period lobby to match. This entryway is lit by chandeliers, gleaming with dark polished wood, and is usually as busy as a miniature air terminal. The Park Plaza is one of the handsomest establishments in its particular price range and has an air of immaculate grooming that extends through the corridors into every nook and cranny of the building.

The coffeeshop is open all day and the Medusa Restaurant for dinner, featuring Greek-style food and entertainment.

The 370 bedrooms, while not large, are charming. Armchairs and bedspreads are in deep scarlet. All of the rooms have laminated hand basin corners apart from the bathroom facilities— great if one of you wants to clean up while the other is using the bath. The beds are springy, and the radio and lighting are controlled from bedside panels. Every room comes with private bath plus shower, as well as telephone, color TV, and radio.

Singles rent from £24 ($46.80), twins from £33 ($64.35), including a continental breakfast and VAT.

A white building with contrasting black entrance, **Hyde Park Towers,** Inverness Terrace, W.2 (tel. 229-9461), lies close to Hyde Park and just around the corner from two tube stations and the cosmopolitan shop and restaurant row of Queensway. The hotel is excellently maintained and offers a great many facilities for its size. A sunny and spacious coffeeshop is available for inexpensive meals or snacks until 10 p.m., and you can enjoy drinks in the Tropical Bar.

The 110 bedrooms are cozy and compact, each with either

bath or shower. They also have wall telephones, radios, color TVs, and bedside panels from which to work the buttons the lazy way. The decor is modern, and the fitted wardrobes contain a surprising amount of hanging space.

Single rooms cost from £20 ($39), doubles from £24.50 ($47.78). These rates include the service charge, VAT, and a continental breakfast.

Mornington Lancaster Hotel, 12 Lancaster Gate, W.2 (tel. 262-7361), brings a touch of Swedish hospitality to the center of London. Just north of Hyde Park and Kensington Gardens, the hotel has been completely redecorated with a Scandinavian-designed interior. The bedrooms, 65 in all, are not only tastefully conceived and most comfortable, but each unit is complete with private bath and shower, a color TV, plus a phone and radio. Rates are £28 ($54.60) in a single, rising to anywhere from £35 ($68.25) to £41 ($79.95) in a double or twin. If you're traveling with a child, the Swedish-speaking staff will place an extra bed in your room for an additional charge of £5 ($9.75). Tariffs include a continental breakfast, service, and VAT. Naturally, there's a genuine Finnish sauna, but you'll also find a well-stocked bar where you can order snacks and, if you're back in time, afternoon tea. In the library, visitors wind down, entertaining their friends or making new ones. Considering what you get, especially the comfort and service, the price is most competitive for London. Tube: Lancaster Gate.

The **Viceroy Hotel,** Lancaster Gate, W.2 (tel. 723-1144), is a small white corner building, neatly maintained, well fitted, and in an economical price range. Another plus is the location—in the center of what constitutes one of London's chief hotel territories. The region probably has more tourists per square yard than any other portion of the metropolis.

The reception hall is tiny but quite elegant. The establishment only has 51 bedrooms, all with private bath or shower. Although fairly small, the rooms are comfortably furnished and kept in attractive matching colors. All are soft carpeted and equipped with wall telephones and color TVs. And the beds feel good to tired sightseers. Singles rent for £20.50 ($39.98), doubles for £26.50 ($51.68), including a continental breakfast and VAT.

All hotel facilities of the adjoining Park Plaza Hotel are available to Viceroy guests.

The **Royal Norfolk Hotel,** 25 London St., W.2 (tel. 402-5221), is a small economy establishment offering a combination of packaged comforts. Run American motel-style, with a minimum of personal service, it's a find for anyone who likes streamlined living and doesn't care for atmosphere.

The 56 rooms are modern and pastel shaded, with wall-to-wall carpets, private showers, central heating, and radios. Wardrobe space is reasonable, and there's a built-in "vanitory unit" with specially lit mirror. Tea- or coffee-making facilities are available in all rooms.

The hotel charges no service tax (there is no service, except for room cleaning), and every meal is additional at the brightly colored, picture-windowed restaurant on the premises.

Singles with shower rent for £16 ($31.20), a double with shower for £25 ($48.75). Tube: Paddington.

One street away you'll find the **Hotel Edward,** Spring Street, W.2 (tel. 262-2671). A study in contrast, this quietly charming white corner building exudes an aura of good living, Edwardian style.

The lobby is surprisingly modern, separated by a grill from a smartly intimate bar. Corridors are silent, tastefully carpeted, and carefully groomed, decorated by framed oil paintings several cuts above the usual hotel art.

Most of the 58 rooms have private showers, but no toilets, which are out in the hall. The rooms are not large, but well fitted and carpeted, with bedside radios, telephones, and streamlined sinks, all in cheerful matching colors. The staff is friendly and helpful, even by English standards, and there's the added advantage of a Spanish restaurant under the same roof.

The rates are pleasantly moderate. Singles with showers cost from £14 ($27.30), doubles from £24 ($46.80), and triples from £28 ($54.60).

The **Royal Bayswater Hotel,** 122 Bayswater Rd., W.2. (tel. 229-8887), is a charming economy hotel overlooking Hyde Park. The friendly atmosphere, comfortable rooms, and reasonable prices attract the visitor looking for high standards at reasonable prices.

The 36 rooms are modern, tastefully furnished, and have wall-to-wall carpeting, private bath/showers, central heating, and radios. Wardrobe space is reasonable, and there is a built-in "vanitory unit" with specially lit mirror. Tea- or coffee-making facilities are available in all rooms.

The hotel does not charge for service as there is none, except for room cleaning. Every meal is additional at the contemporary restaurant on the premises.

Singles with bath rent for £18.50 ($36.08), doubles with bath for £28.50 ($55.58). Tube: Queensway.

IN KENSINGTON: This is the region south of Kensington Gardens containing, among other landmarks, the Albert Hall and the West London Air Terminal. Mostly residential and characterized by tree-lined streets and pillared rows of terraces, it boasts a score of Middle Eastern embassies, the Commonwealth Institute, and a vast number of hotels in every price bracket.

Originally four Edwardian homes, **Embassy House Hotel,** 31 Queen's Gate, S.W. 7 (tel. 584-7222), retains the quiet charm of that period while featuring modern hotel facilities. The double row of trees gives Queen's Gate a Parisian look, and there is an air of tranquility about these pillared Edwardian facades that few contemporary buildings can match.

This hotel, recently refurbished, offers 70 bedrooms all with private bath or shower, color television, newly decorated public areas which retain original 19th-century features, and personal attention from the manager and his staff.

Rates include full English breakfast, service, and tax. Singles cost £29 ($56.55); doubles are £36 ($70.20) per night. Nine self-catering, fully serviced apartments are available adjacent to the hotel.

The **Clearlake Hotel,** 19 Prince of Wales Terrace, W.8 (tel. 937-3274), is a real find for travelers with families—one of the few establishments that enable you to set up housekeeping while abroad. For apart from the usual hotel facilities and bedrooms, the Clearlake has an adjoining wing with two- and three-room apartments, easily accommodating five or more persons. And that isn't all. The management also provides highchairs, strollers, diaper (nappy) and laundry service, plus child-minding service day and night at £1 ($1.95) an hour.

Originally a row of handsome private homes in a serene residential street facing Kensington Gardens, the hotel now incorporates a lounge-bar, TV and radio in all units, as well as an unusually house-proud and attentive owner-manager in the person of Ms. Herskovits.

Most, although not all, of the 20 single or double rooms come with private baths. But the two- to five-person apartment units have every facility you need for a home away from home. The bedrooms and kitchens vary in size from quite small to very spacious, and the bathrooms are uniformly excellent. Furnishings, while not luxurious, are ample, and this includes wardrobe space for any number of occupants. Kitchens are all-electric, equipped with cooking utensils and including refrigerators. The outstanding feature throughout the establishment is the care lavished on the fittings—nothing slapdash and no skimping on creature comforts.

Rates cover a wide range, from £9 ($17.55) for a bathless single to £37 ($72.15) for a large apartment suitable for four.

SOUTH KENSINGTON: South of Kensington Gardens and Hyde Park, South Kensington is essentially a residential area, not as elegant as bordering Belgravia and Knightsbridge. However, the section is rich in museums, and it has a number of colleges.

Number Sixteen, 16 Sumner Pl., S.W.7 (tel. 589-5232), is considered a luxury "pension" in central London. Just off Old Brompton Road, it's a three-minute walk to the South Kensington underground station. Michael Watson is the creator of this offbeat hotel which is much patronized by people in the performing arts. It is made up of three adjoining properties of classical Victorian style, with high-ceilinged period rooms converted to self-contained bed-sitting accommodations, with private shower/bathrooms (some of them have tubs as well). Rooms are decorated with antiques and Victorian pieces, along with pictures, Hans Holbein prints, and lithographs. Mr. Watson prefers guests who will stay at least three nights or more. Singles range from £21 ($40.95) to £26 ($50.70); doubles and twins from £35 ($68.25) to £48 ($93.60).

The **Regency Hotel,** 100–105 Queen's Gate, S.W.7 (tel. 370-4595), is a skillful conversion of six lovely old houses which now provide 200 simply furnished but comfortable rooms with private bath or shower, color TV, radio, and phone. Elevators service all floors, and there is porter service 24 hours a day. The hotel offers good value, charging £20 ($39) in a single, from £26 ($50.70) in a double, and from £32 ($62.40) in a triple, including a continental breakfast, service, and VAT. The high-ceilinged, warm red-walled dining room serves a set lunch or dinner, three courses for around £6 ($11.70). Or, if you prefer, you can order from a limited à la carte menu, costing around £12 ($23.40) per person. The bar is large and cheerfully decorated with green walls, dark wood and button chairs, serving coffee, tea, and sandwiches as well as drinks. The South Kensington museums are near at hand, as are the South Kensington and

Gloucester Road underground stations to either the West End or Heathrow Airport.

The **Alexander,** 9 Sumner Pl., S.W.7 (tel. 581-1591), is between Brompton and Fulham Roads, on the borderline of Kensington and Chelsea. This small attractive hotel looks like a private residence and has a pleasantly relaxed, almost private, atmosphere. One of its most attractive features is a secluded little garden, well kept and entirely reserved for hotel guests. Behind a white-pillared 19th-century facade, the hotel is surprisingly modern. The dining room decor is natural pine, and the small television lounge looks like a living room and boasts color TV. However, private rooms also contain their own television sets. The licensed hotel has an attractively designed private bar in the lounge.

The bedrooms are fairly spacious, with nicely matched ivory and green color schemes, soft russet carpeting, and built-in cupboards and dressing tables. Except for two singles, each centrally heated unit has a private bath. Every room also comes equipped with telephone, radio, and dual-voltage shaver points. The reception desk downstairs will not only organize theater tickets for you, but also looks after car rentals and tour bookings.

Singles with private shower cost £23.50 ($45.83), doubles with bath go from £34 ($66.30), and triple rooms with baths and toilets cost £38 ($74.10). Rates include a full English breakfast, although VAT is extra.

Eden Plaza Hotel, 68–69 Queensgate, S.W.7 (tel. 370-6111), completed in 1972, is an attractive, white-painted corner building, offering bedrooms furnished in the modern style and tastefully decorated. An elevator carries guests to all floors, where bedrooms with double-glazed windows await them. Other amenities include color TV sets, along with private baths and showers. The cost in a single is £24 ($46.80), rising to £34 ($66.30) in a twin or double. These tariffs include a full English breakfast, service, and VAT. Families might like to inquire about one of the three-bedded rooms, also with private baths, costing from £40 ($78) nightly. Both business people and vacationers meet in the cocktail lounge and bar, and later go to the restaurant, offering continental and English cuisine. On the ground level are such additional facilities as a sauna, massage, and solarium. The location is near Hyde Park, close to the London Air Terminal, and convenient for shoppers heading for such emporiums as Harrods and Selfridges.

AT WESTMINSTER: In proper Westminster, the seat of the British government since the time of Edward the Confessor, you can have your own well-equipped flat at the following location.

Dolphin Square, Dolphin Square, S.W.1 (tel. 834-9136), is one of the largest apartment blocks in Europe. Many residents make it their permanent home, but it's also open to transients as well. On the Thames, between Chelsea and Westminster, it lies near the Tate Gallery. Each of the apartments is fully furnished, containing the necessary supply of china, kitchen equipment, and cutlery. Apartments, all with color TV, come in a wide range of sizes. A one-room apartment with a double bed goes for £40 ($78) nightly. For a twin-bedded-room flat, the charge is £45 ($87.75) a day. Larger apartments at more expensive tariffs are also available. The longer you stay, the better the rate you'll be quoted. The Dolphin Square Restaurant overlooks the heated swimming pool, which is kept at a constant temperature of 75 degrees Fahrenheit. In addition, there are eight squash courts and a sauna, and there are gardens outside the building.

IN BAYSWATER: North of Kensington Gardens is an unofficial section of London known as Bayswater. Most of it lies north of Bayswater Road and west of Hyde Park. This section contains a number of inexpensive B & B hotels, but also the following unique accommodation.

Portobello, 22 Stanley Gardens, W.11 (tel. 727-2777), lies in what might be called an unfashionable area, but it's very fashionable. The hotel forms part of an elegant Victorian terrace, overlooking a private garden. It stands near the Portobello antique market. Julie Hodgess designed the reception lounge and dining areas, making use of muted color tones and mirrors. The scarlet curtains were made of livery cloth, the same used to make the full-dress uniform worn by the Life Guards of the Household Cavalry. Recently added are some beautiful, specially decorated rooms—such as the "Bath Room" with antique mirrors, the "Four-poster Room" (18th-century mahogany), and the "Brass Room" with brass bedstead—individually done by Ms. Hodgess.

Other bedrooms are handsomely furnished as well. They combine something of the era of brass-cornered military chests with many 20th-century conveniences, including private showers, color television, and a small refrigerator stocked with cool drinks. In addition, each room has its own facilities for making tea or coffee. A single room, quite small, goes for £22 ($42.90), although a regular single rents for £26 ($50.70). Doubles begin at £32 ($62.40), going up to £40 ($78). On a luxury note, some suites are also available, costing from £60 ($117) to £70 ($136.50), all tariffs including a continental breakfast and VAT. There is no service charge, and guests reward special services by individual tipping. There is no room service, but at a 24-hour bar and restaurant you can get what you want if they have it.

AT EUSTON STATION AND KING'S CROSS: In a somewhat nondescript section a few blocks north of Bloomsbury a group of hotels caters mainly to three large railway stations, St. Pancras, Euston, and King's Cross. A modern hotel in this section follows.

Kennedy, Cardington Street, N.W.1 (tel. 387-4400), is one of the most Stateside-type hotels in London. Near Euston Station, the hotel is a grayish building with a drive-in entrance for private motorists and taxis. The Kennedy is just five stops by tube from Piccadilly. The hotel contains rooms with comfortable beds, plus full air conditioning and a private bath with shower for each accommodation. Of course, there are direct-dial extensions, televisions, and radios as well.

A member of the Grand Metropolitan hotel chain, the Kennedy charges £29 ($56.55) in a single with bath, £38 ($74.10) in a double. These tariffs include a continental breakfast and VAT. In the Kennedy Bar, you can relax with a drink before dining in the Planters Restaurant. Its skillful use of plants, full air conditioning, and intriguing decor give the restaurant a relaxed atmosphere to enjoy anything from a cup of coffee to a full three-course meal with wine.

EARL'S COURT: Below Kensington and bordering the western half of Chelsea, Earl's Court is one of the most popular middle-class hotel and rooming-house districts. A 15-minute ride on the underground from Earl's Court station will take you into the heart of Piccadilly, via either the District or Piccadilly lines.

The **Town House,** 44–48 West Cromwell Rd., S.W.5 (tel. 568-1361), is a small, privately owned place made over from three Victorian houses. Friendly and informal, it is well suited to younger visitors. All rooms have hot and cold running water, radio, and phone, and most are also equipped with shower and toilet. Color TV is standard in most units or else available at a small extra charge in others. There is a cozy, comfortable bar lounge and a larger games bar with dartboard, pool table, slot machines, dominos, backgammon, and bridge.

Singles range in price from £20 ($39) to £25 ($48.75) a night, and doubles or twins run from £28 ($54.60) to £34 ($66.30), these tariffs including service, although VAT is extra. The staff also offers some family rooms which work out at about £42 ($81.90) per night for four persons. Laundry and dry cleaning can be taken care of.

Breakfast can be served in your room or else in the main dining room. Snacks are available throughout the day, and in the evenings a three-course dinner is offered, costing from £7.50 ($14.63). The fare is simple, traditional English cookery.

ELEPHANT & CASTLE: In Southeast London, Elephant & Castle was once a decidedly unchic address. To some extent it still is, but many changes are taking place, as reflected by:

London Park, Brook Drive, S.E. 11 (tel. 735-9191), was once an enormous warehouse on the south bank of the Thames. But now it's been completely renovated and converted into a moderately priced hotel of some 380 bedrooms. Many of these are equipped with private baths. The decor is functional, streamlined, and efficient. In a bathless single, the tariff is £12.50 ($24.38), going up to £14.50 ($28.28) with a private shower. In a twin- or double-bedded room, the cost ranges from £21.50 ($41.93) to £24.50 ($47.78), depending on the plumbing. These tariffs include a full English breakfast, as well as service and VAT. At the hotel's restaurant you can order a set luncheon at £6 ($11.70) or a table d'hôte dinner at £7 ($13.65). The nearest tube is, of course, Elephant & Castle.

Accommodation Agencies

Hotel & Personal Accommodation Ltd., 10 Lower Belgrave St., S.W.1 (tel. 730-6181), is a company operated by trained hotel people, and it performs a service that can, on occasion, be invaluable. They arrange your hotel accommodation according to your specifications (within realistic limits) and without charging you a fee. They operate not only in London but throughout the United Kingdom and cover the entire range from tourist to luxury hotels.

The agency is not connected with any hotel, but has a large number of them on its books. It offers furnished apartments (from one day to three months) as well as the usual hotel accommodations. The service is especially useful for parties planning a stay of several weeks or more.

Keep in mind that the more time you give them, the greater the chance of getting exactly what you want, particularly in peak summer season. The best thing is to write them from home, specifying your exact requirements including dates, type of accommodation, standard, and area required, and your maximum budget. As stated above, there's no agents' fee.

The **South London Accommodation,** 428 Southcroft Rd., Streatham, S.W.16 (tel. 769-2117), is a family-run business, serving some 5000 visitors to London yearly who are looking for nice and inexpensive "self-catering" accommodations for seven days or more. Michael or John Slade will try to provide you with a fully equipped, private, clean, cozy, modern flatlet, flat, or house, depending on the number in your party or your needs. Mini-flatlet prices start at £70 ($136.50) a week. Family mini-flatlets are from £92 ($179.40) a week. Discounts are available if you mention you obtained the address from *Arthur Frommer's Guide to London.* Accommodations are in quiet pleasant suburbs only about five miles from the center of London, reached by excellent public transport services.

Upon arrival, you will be presented with a free Welcome Pack containing bus and train maps, and advice on things to do, places to see, and how to get there. A free service is also offered by the Slades from their local station to the accommodation.

The offices are open Monday through Friday from 9 a.m. to 4:30 p.m., and Saturday from 9 a.m. to noon. It's closed Sunday and bank holidays. If you don't have time to prebook, which is advised, simply telephone the office when you arrive, and they will do their best to accommodate you. Rentals are for a minimum of seven days, plus any number of additional days or weeks you require, and start on any day and end on any day. No lease is required, no extra fees, no fuss—in fact, it's as simple as booking into a hotel, but it only costs about half the price of comparable accommodations.

GB Hotel Reserves Ltd., 79 Buckingham Palace Rd., S.W.1 (tel. 581-0161), operates a hotel-booking service for individuals and groups in hotels of all categories. Additionally, during the summer months of June through September it controls exclusive renting of 250 studio bedrooms in two modern residential complexes in north-central London. Each "study" room has its own wash basin with hot and cold water. Fresh bed linen, soap, and towels are provided. Adequate baths, showers, and toilets are available on each corridor. Guests have the use of game rooms, bar, and coin-operated laundry. Two types of accommodations offered are: bed and full English breakfast costing £10 ($19.50) daily, with lunch and an evening meal optional at £2.50 ($4.88) per person; and a self-catering, fully equipped kitchen per 11 rooms, with your own food locker. A refrigerator is provided. The cost is £40 ($78) per week per person. London's West End is 15 minutes away by London Transport. All reservations are made free.

Bed and Breakfast

London's numerous budget hotels are uniquely English. Throughout every major district of the city, these so-called bed-and-breakfast houses are clustered around gracious old squares, with leafy trees and occasional flower gardens. Most are former Victorian town houses which have been converted into **B&B** hotels. Once they were occupied by one family; nowadays, virtually every broom closet has been fitted with a bed to receive budget-minded travelers from all parts of the world.

Usually, the front parlor has been turned into a residents' lounge, the basement into a breakfast room (and the morning meal—"a proper English breakfast" or else a skimpy continental one—is the only one served). Hot and cold running water has been installed in nearly all of the bedrooms, but generally there are few private baths (rather, a bath and toilet for each floor). Most of these houses are owner operated and are decidedly informal, providing a cheap, home-like base for your London stay. Rarely will you find an elevator, so be prepared in some cases to scale three or four flights, often carrying your own luggage. Service is at a minimum.

We've selected only a few typical bed-and-breakfast houses to recommend because of space limitations. Enough, however, to get you started, as all of them are in districts filled with low-cost accommodations. If you should arrive in London without reservations (risky indeed in summer), then, if possible, try to begin your search for a room in the morning. Areas of London where B&B houses predominate are Bloomsbury, King's Cross Station, Bayswater, Sussex Gardens, and the area around Paddington Station.

The **Leicester Hotel Group,** 18-24 Belgrave Rd. (Eccleston Square), S.W.1 (tel. 834-4296), is one address, but its door opens up the possibility of a room in six additional hotels. Business has been that good, in large part from "repeat travelers." Mrs. Russell-Duffy, who offers good value for the money she charges, asks from £8.50 ($16.58) for single rooms, from £12.50 ($24.38) to £13.50 ($26.33) for doubles, including an English breakfast.

Camellia Hotel, 16 Longridge Rd., S.W.5 (tel. 373-3848), lies in an unspoiled section of Kensington, on the better side of Earl's Court Road. The exterior is graced with an abundance of flowers in boxes and urns and baskets hanging from the windows. The lounge and breakfast room are made more inviting with Austrian pine furnishings. Central heating and color television add to the amenities. Singles cost £9 ($17.55). Doubles with private bath cost £17 ($33.15), although a few with hot and cold running water are priced at only £15 ($29.25). A continental breakfast, VAT, and service are included. A full English breakfast is available at an extra charge. Tube: Earl's Court.

Hotel 167, 167 Old Brompton Rd., S.W.5 (tel. 373-0672), is a converted corner town house, maintaining its Victorian architectural features, although the decor has been considerably updated by Christina Rasmus, a Finnish designer. In clean, comfortable rooms, the hotel charges £12.50 ($24.38) for a bathless single, £18.50 ($36.08) for a bathless double, and £21 ($40.95) for a double or twin with private shower. Rates include a continental breakfast, service, and VAT. A short walk from the hotel will take you to boutique-strewn King's Road. Tube: Gloucester Road.

Vicarage Private Hotel, 10 Vicarage Gate, W.8 (tel. 229-4030), is a simple and unpretentious B&B hotel, just a short walk from Kensington Gardens and some of the major shopping areas of London. Rates are uncomplicated here: £10 ($19.50) in a single, £9 ($17.55) per person in a double room. The rooms have hot and cold running water, modest furniture, and are thoroughly clean, with comfortable beds. Mr. and Mrs. Diviney are friendly hosts, Mrs. Diviney not only producing an English breakfast, but acting as an amateur social director as well by introducing fellow guests. The nearest tube stops are Kensington High or Notting Hill Gate.

The **Hotel Lindsay,** 12 Ashburn Gardens, S.W.7 (tel. 370-5294), enjoys a particularly handy location, almost opposite the West London Air Terminal, just off busy Cromwell Road, but sheltered from the traffic din. A plain frontage decorated with a blue awning leads into a simple, neat, well-kept establishment boasting highly competitive rates. The five-story hotel has no elevator, but an attractive TV lounge equipped with comfortable armchairs. Breakfast is served in the basement dining room, a friendly spot with international souvenirs and Delft china plates decorating the walls. None of the 20 bedrooms has a private bath, although there is either a shower or a bathroom (spotless) on each floor. All the rooms have hot and cold water, dual-voltage razor plugs, wall-to-wall carpeting. The furniture is plain but adequate, the beds springy, and there's ample space for your clothes in the wardrobes and chest of drawers. Electric heaters are in the rooms in case the weather turns chilly (it frequently does). Singles pay from £14 ($27.30), twin rooms cost from £20 ($39). These rates include a full English breakfast as well as tax. There is no service charge. Take the tube to Gloucester Road, which is now directly linked to Heathrow Airport on the Piccadilly line.

The **Easton Hotel,** 36–40 Belgrave Rd., S.W.1 (tel. 834-5938), was named after its former owner, Dorothy Easton, one of the original Cockran beauties. The rate is £11.50 ($22.43) for singles, £9 ($17.55) per person in doubles. All the rooms have hot and cold running water, central heating, and are neatly decorated and spotlessly clean. To take care of their repeat clients and increasing new friends, the owners have acquired two more town houses nearby: **Arden House,** 12 St. Georges Dr., S.W.1 (tel. 834-2988) (double rooms only), and **Holly House,** 20 Hugh St., S.W.1 (tel. 834-5671). Victoria tube.

Culford Hall, 7 Culford Gardens, S.W.3 (tel. 581-2211), offers a bonanza of inexpensive accommodations. Proprietor A. R. Kleiner has four other similar small hotels, all just off Sloane Square in Chelsea. In most of them, B&B goes from £12 ($23.40) in a single, from £17 ($33.15) in a double- or twin-bedded room. With a private bath or shower, a double- or twin-bedded room rents from £19 ($37.05). These prices include breakfast and service charge, although VAT is extra. The hotel is comfortable, central, and close to transport.

Morgan Hotel, 24 Bloomsbury St., W.1 (tel. 636-3735), is one of a long row of similar buildings, but distinguished by its gold-tipped iron fence railings. Several of its 18 rooms overlook the British Museum, and the whole establishment is very much part of the international scholastic scene of Bloomsbury. The lobby is a bit cramped, the stairs rather steep, but the rooms are pleasant, the atmosphere congenial, and the hotel consequently is unusually heavily booked. The standard rate of £12 ($23.40) per person per night includes a full English breakfast. The hotel is centrally heated. The bedrooms vary in size; some are rather large, but all come well carpeted, equipped with big beds (by British standards), hot and cold water, dressing tables with mirrors, and ample wardrobe space. Showers and toilets have been installed on each floor. The nearest tubes are Russell Square and Tottenham Court Road.

Waldor Hotel, 38 Craven St., W.C.2 (tel. 930-0609). This is the most centrally located B&B haven on our list, and it's not to be confused with the more expensive Waldorf. Craven Street runs off the Strand, almost within shouting distance of Trafalgar Square, smack in the geographical heart of London. The street, while rather gray, is not noisy, and you have every facility the city offers right at your doorstep. The Waldor is a cheerful place, run by a helpful and very knowledgeable London-born manager, Joseph Kew. The hall, small and a bit cluttered, has a bulletin board featuring tourist tidbits in the shape of restaurant menus, car rentals, handy pubs, and hairdressers. The 31 rooms rent from £8 ($15.60) to £10 ($19.50) per night per person inclusive of a continental breakfast and VAT. All rooms have wall-to-wall carpets, hot and cold water, and dressing tables. There are four impeccable bathrooms and a shower room. Tube: Trafalgar Square.

Mr. and Mrs. A. Demetriou, 9 Strathmore Gardens, W.8 (tel. 229-6709), run a nice, homey pension close to Hyde Park and Kensington Gardens. The place is kept immaculately, and the hosts are most gracious, especially considerate to first-time visitors to London. Their attractively decorated rooms rent for £9 ($17.55) per person nightly for a bed and a full English breakfast.

Hotel One Two Eight, 128 Holland Rd., W.14 (tel. 602-3395), lies in Holland Park, a section of Kensington within reach of the Exhibition Halls at Olympia and Earl's Court. Wrought-iron balconies and summer flowers greet you in high season, when you're charged the most expensive tariffs. Off-season, there is a reduction of about 15% in the rates. Of the 36 bedrooms, 13 contain private showers and another 16 have not only showers but toilets as well. All have bed lights, radio, television, and electric razor points. Singles range in price from £15 ($29.25) to £19 ($37.05), doubles from £20 ($39) to £26 ($50.70), these tariffs including a full English breakfast. The owners, Mr. and Mrs. Novakovic, can be requested to rent you a room facing the garden in the rear, with its big lawn, stone walls, and trees. Tube: Shepherd's Bush.

The Ys

Y Hotel, 112 Great Russell St., W.C.1 (tel. 637-1333), may shatter your expectations of a YMCA. This Bloomsbury version is a modern hotel built by the London Central YMCA for men and women of all ages. At the Oxford Street end of Tottenham Court Road, its prices reflect its standard of comfort: £19 ($37.05) in a single room, and £28 ($54.60) in a double- or twin-bedded room, including VAT and service. Every bedroom has an outside window, central heating, color TV, radio, and private bath with shower, and is comfortably furnished complete with wall-to-wall carpeting. On the premises are squash courts, a gymnasium, a swimming pool, shops, and underground car parking. In fact, the recreational facilities cover three entire floors and include a billiards room, a sauna, and a solarium. But there are no telephones in the bedrooms.

The **YWCA Central Club,** Great Russell Street, W.C.1 (tel. 636-7512), is large and attractive, a fine neo-Georgian building. All of its rooms contain hot and cold running water, and accommodations are offered to women and girls and married persons (for stays not exceeding four weeks). All of the bedrooms are on the fifth, sixth, and seventh floors. Singles rent for £12 ($23.40) nightly, two-bedded rooms for £11 ($21.45) per person, triples for £7.50 ($14.63) per bed, and five-bedded rooms for £6.50 ($12.68) per bed. An extra 50p (98¢) per person is assessed for stays of only one night; VAT is added to the bill. Reservations can seldom be made over the telephone, but should be by mail, enclosing an international money order in the amount of the first night's rent. Included in the rate is breakfast and use of the bathrooms, showers, central heating, and the public address system. The cafeteria is open to the public for all meals. The facilities are spacious and dignified, with lounges and writing room, hairdresser, as well as a car park, launderette, TV room, library, and swimming pool. Tube: Tottenham Court Road Station.

Youth Hostels

Although hostels were created primarily for rural living, they do, nevertheless, exist in London. For overseas visitors, there is often a limit of only four nights at many of them. And there are hostel rules that you must live by, as well as having a low-cost membership card. But if you can work within the frame, you'll find the all-time bargain of London living by staying at one of the hostels. The survey below is merely a sampling of the hostels available. The criterion used was not quality but locality; we tried to give a selection of as many areas as possible.

The **Kensington Students Centre,** The Barracks, Kensington Church Street, W.8 (tel. 937-5701), is a vast establishment with a travel bureau for students on the premises. Guests are accommodated in double, triple, and four-bedded rooms at a flat rate of £5 ($9.75) per person, which takes care of the VAT surcharge as well. A continental breakfast is included. Tube to High Street Kensington.

Baden-Powell House, 65 Queen's Gate, S.W.7 (tel. 584-7030), is the bright, spacious, and immensely busy base that caters only to Cubs and Scouts of both sexes, their leaders, and families of both. Dormitories run to £5 ($9.75) per person, and in a multibedded room (that is, three to four persons), the charge is £7.50 ($14.73) per person. Twin and single rooms are £12 ($23.40) to £14.50 ($28.28) per person per night (tube to Gloucester Road).

Gayfere Hostel, 8 Gayfere St., S.W.1 (tel. 222-6894), lies in the center of London, near the Houses of Parliament and Westminster Abbey. It bills itself as a center for "young holiday makers," and the age limit is 25 years (ID required). The standard rate is from £4.50 ($8.78) per person nightly or from £27 ($52.65) weekly. The establishment provides no breakfast, but cooking facilities are available. The accommodation is in small dormitories only, with about five to seven bunk beds per. Tube: Westminster.

Fieldcourt House, 32 Courtfield Gardens, S.W.5 (tel. 373-0152), keeps the student market firmly in mind and is a hostel immaculately kept by its manager, Harry Day, along with his wife and staff. It is a favorite among many of the better economy tour operators. The residential hostel lies in a pleasant garden square near the now disused West London Air Terminal on Cromwell Road. The house is midway between Gloucester Road and Earl's Court underground stations (Piccadilly and District lines).

Fieldcourt was formed by combining two large Victorian mansions which were adapted to provide comfortable accommodations. There are wash basins, central heating, constant hot water, ample showers, baths, and toilets (the latter three facilities off the public hallways). Other amenities include a quiet room for writing or study, plus a TV lounge with a color set. To keep the hostel charges low, general cleaning is carried out by the staff, but residents are expected to make their own beds. Accommodation charges are payable weekly, in advance. A dormitory costs £4.50 ($8.78) per person nightly, and in a three- or four-bedded room the charge ranges from £5 ($9.75) to £5.50 ($10.73) per person. More expensive are the double rooms, going for £6 ($11.70) per person, and the singles at £7.50 ($14.63), these tariffs including VAT and a continental breakfast.

J.D. Student House, 285 Pentonville Rd., King's Cross, N.1 (tel. 278-5375), is a hostel for young students and vistors, male and female, between the ages of 17 and 28. The dormitories have up to four beds in a room. The charges range from £4.50 ($8.78) per person nightly, or else £27 ($52.65) weekly. You cook your own breakfast. That tariff includes bed linen, cooking, washing and ironing facilities, hot showers, television, and central heating. New arrivals must check in by midnight. The nearest underground station is King's Cross.

Country Homes and Castles

At 138a Piccadilly, London, W.1 (tel. 491-2584), **Country Homes and Castles** is a program offering overseas visitors the chance to stay in private homes as guests of the owners. There are some 250 houses in all parts of Britain, ranging from small cottages, historic manor houses, ancient Scottish castles to large mansions in their own parkland. The owners vary in their interests, ages, and professions, and every effort is made to send visitors to families it is thought they will particularly enjoy. As it is such a personal service, there are no set tours, but the agency will arrange just one or two nights in a house to fit in with your own travel plans or a complete tour using hotels and country homes and bearing in mind your interests. Prices range from about £85 ($165.75) to £155 ($302.25) per couple per night, including drinks, dinner with wine, accommodations with private baths, and breakfast. All payments are made through the agent to avoid the embarrassment of hosts and guests having to discuss money. The U.S. representative is Sue Duncan, 6265 Courtside Dr. NW, Norcross, GA 30092 (tel. 404/448-2185).

A GUIDE TO INFORMATION: This concludes our hotel survey. But we can't close this chapter without telling you about a pretty wonderful institution called the **London Tourist Board.** Headquartered at 26 Grosvenor Gardens, S.W.1, with branches in Victoria Station and Selfridges and Harrods stores, the board can and most certainly will help you with almost anything of interest to a tourist in London.

Staffed by the most courteous, tactful, sympathetic, patient, and understanding men and women this side of Utopia, the board deals chiefly with accommodations in all size and price categories, from single travelers, family groups, and students to large-scale conventions. The staff also arranges for tour ticket sales and theater bookings, and has a bookshop as well. Hours are daily (except Christmas) from 8 a.m. to 10:30 p.m. in summer (from 9 a.m. to 8:30 p.m. in winter). The main information center is at Victoria Station near Platform 15, although there are branch offices at Selfridges and Harrods which operate during store hours. For general tourist information phone 730-0791 from 9 a.m. to 5:30 p.m., Monday to Friday.

Westminster Abbey

*Bella
Pasta*

Chapter IV

EATING AND DRINKING

GEORGE MIKES, Britain's famous Hungarian-born humorist, once wrote about the culinary prowess of his adopted country: "The Continentals have good food. The English have good table manners."

Quite a lot has happened since.

Basically, of course, the English are still woeful cooks, and their table etiquette is as impressive as ever. But with the pressure of tourism and the influx of foreign chefs, the local cuisine picture has brightened considerably.

In the snackeries of suburbia the vegetables may still taste as if they had a grudge against you, and the soup remains reminiscent of flavored tapwater. But in the central sections of London —where you'll do your eating—the fare has improved immeasurably. This is largely due to intense competition from foreign establishments, plus the introduction of espresso machines, which made English coffee resemble—well, coffee.

In the upper brackets, London has always boasted magnificent restaurants, several of which have achieved world renown. But these were the preserve of the middling wealthy, who'd had their palates polished by travel abroad. The lower orders enjoyed a diet akin to parboiled blotting paper. For about a century, the staple meal of the working class consisted of "Fish 'n' Chips"— and they still haven't learned how to properly fry either the fish *or* the chips (potatoes).

There are some dishes—mostly connected with breakfast—at which the English have always excelled. The traditional morning repast of eggs and bacon (imported from Denmark) or kippers (smoked herring, of Scottish origin) is a tasty starter, and the locally brewed tea beats any American bag concoction.

It's with the other meals that you have to use a little caution. If you want to splurge in a big way, you have the London "greats" at your disposal: gourmet havens such as the Savoy

Grill, Parkes & Mr. Benson's Bar, Carrier's in Islington, À l'Ecu de France in Jermyn Street, or half a dozen others.

If these star eateries are too expensive for you, you'll find more moderately priced restaurants such as Flanagans or the Baker & Oven. And then we'll turn to the budget establishments that charge even less for a three-courser.

The prevailing mealtimes are much the same as in the U.S. You can get lunch from about midday onward and dinner until about 11 p.m.—until midnight in the Soho area. The difference is that fewer Londoners go in for the "businessman's lunch." They'll either make do with sandwiches or take a snack in a pub (see the last part of this chapter). The once-hallowed custom of taking afternoon tea is now the preserve of matrons unworried about their waistlines.

What may astonish you is the profusion of international restaurants. London offers a fantastic array of Italian, Indian, Chinese, French, German, Swiss, Greek, Russian, Jewish, and Mid-Eastern dineries, which probably outnumber the native establishments. You'll find them heavily represented in our list.

Most of the restaurants we mention serve the same meals for lunch and dinner, so they're easily interchangeable. And most—but not all—add a 10% service charge to your bill. You'll have to look at your check to make sure of that. If nothing has been added, leave a 12% to 15% tip.

All restaurants and cafés in Britain are required to display the prices of the food and drink they offer, in a place where the customer can see them before entering the eating area. If an establishment has an extensive à la carte menu, the prices of a representative selection of food and drink currently available must be displayed as well as the table d'hôte menu, if one is offered. Charges for service and any minimum charge or cover charge must also be made clear. The prices shown must be inclusive of VAT.

Finally, there's the matter of location. Once upon a time, London had two traditional dining areas: Soho for Italian and Chinese fare, Mayfair and Belgravia for French cuisine.

Today, the gastronomical legions have conquered the entire heart of the metropolis—you're liable to find any type of eatery anywhere from Chelsea to Hampstead. The majority of our selections are in the West End region, but only because this happens to be the handiest for tourists.

And that's enough of the preliminaries. Let's go and dine.

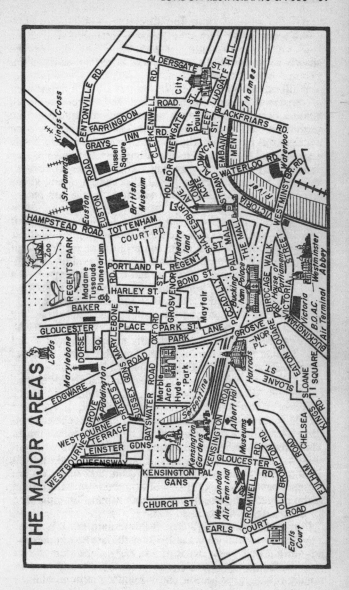

The Top Choices

We begin, as we warned before, with restaurant visits in the "splurge" or "near-splurge" category. While these charge prices slightly above our ideal allotment, they might still be visited for that very special occasion.

Waltons, 121 Walton St., S.W.3 (tel. 584-0204), is a restaurant of considerable merit, beginning first with its creative chef, Shamus Barrett, a Scotsman of tremendous culinary talent who turns out a subtle and delicate cuisine. The setting helps, too; on a quiet street in Chelsea, the restaurant offers a leisurely dining experience. The decor is in an intimate modern style, using Trianon gray with buttercup yellow and mauve tiles. The cutlery is Georg Jensen, the china Royal Copenhagen. Many guests arriving early make their menu selections in the bar on the second floor.

At prices ranging from £20 ($39), a four-course dinner is offered. It might begin with the chef's specialty, green vegetable pâté, and follow with a main course such as rainbow trout poached in a whisky sauce, saffron chicken (based on an 18th-century recipe), chicken suprême, and collops in the pan. The wine list includes many selections from aristocratic vintages but also a modestly priced Chablis. It is essential to reserve.

In addition, you can visit for a light lunch called "simply Waltons," costing £7.50 ($14.63). It is not served on Sunday. A three-course luncheon is offered daily except Sunday for £13 ($25.35). On Sunday the traditional English weekend lunch of roast meats is offered for £7 ($13.65) and a three-course dinner for £12 ($23.40). In addition to the regular dinner, a late supper, costing £7 ($13.65), is presented after the theater, including a selection of principal dishes along with petit-fours. VAT and service are extra. The extensive wine list offers 90 château-bottled clarets from a wide range of vintages at reasonable prices. Thirty red burgundies are listed and champagne featured extensively, with 35 labels always available. Warre's 1963 port is decanted daily, and a full list of liqueurs and single vintage cognac from the House of Hine is always obtainable. The restaurant is open for luncheon from 12:30 to 2:30 p.m. (last order) and for dinner from 7:30 to 11:30 p.m.

Parkes & Mr. Benson's Bar, 5 Beauchamp Pl., S.W.3 (tel. 589-1390), was founded in the 1950s by the late Ray Parkes and got off to a slow start. But it was an early pioneer among the creative cookery restaurants, and gradually it's improved its standards until it has become one of London's most imaginative gourmet restaurants. Tom Benson now carries on in the fine tradition of the founding father.

The cuisine is both distinctive and inventive. The setting is sophisticated, but the entrance on boutique alley is deceivingly small. The menu depends on the fresh produce available in London on any particular day. The host will seat you in one of three intimate rooms. Menu selections are made at leisure while enjoying a drink.

A set dinner goes for £17 ($33.15); however, if you order à la carte, expect to pay about £22 ($42.90) per person with a simple wine. A recent meal began with figs and smoked salmon as an appetizer (although many prefer mussels in Pernod sauce, if featured or perhaps asparagus and nut soup). Main dishes are likely to include boned chicken Florentine or roast partridge, depending on the season. Perhaps sole and crab en croûte or duckling breasts will be featured. For dessert, the sorbets are always delicious. Dinner is from 7:30 to 11 p.m. Lunch, when a shorter menu is offered, is from 12:15 to 2:45 p.m. At that time, the cost will likely average £15 ($29.25) per person, plus service. The restaurant is closed on Saturday and Sunday.

Savoy Grill, The Strand, W.C.2 (tel. 836-4343), basks in its own glory. "Let's dine at the Grillroom" is an invitation oft repeated since the days of Edward VII and Lily Langtry. Unlike many other dining legends, the modestly named Grill continues to maintain unimpeachable quality when dispensing the haute cuisine of France. It's been especially popular with a theatrical clientele since its patronage by Sarah Bernhardt, and to accommodate them it remains open until late, last orders being taken up to 11:30 p.m. Reservations are necessary, even after final curtain time at West End productions.

The chef's specialties include filet de boeuf en croûte François Villon (beef wrapped in puff paste and garnished with artichokes, celery heart, and foie gras) and omelette Arnold Bennett. Excellent hors d'oeuvres include smoked trout and lobster mousse. For dessert, try a selection from the extensive and colorful "sweet trolley." There's a distinguished collection of vintage wines, although you can order a large carafe of hock. Expect to pay around £25 ($48.75) per person, including tax and service, for a complete meal and a reasonable bottle of wine.

Carrier's, 2–4 Camden Passage, The Angel, N.1 (tel. 226-5353), is one of London's best gastronomical centers even though the location is offbeat. The restaurant is run with loving dedication by Robert Carrier, one of Great Britain's leading cookbook writers. After years of telling others how to cook, he could only do his finest in his London showcase. The clientele and the decor are most sophisticated. Carrier's is found in a tiny antique row district of Islington where inveterate shoppers go for that special bric-a-brac.

Mr. Carrier offers a set luncheon and a set dinner, at prices going from £13.75 ($26.81) to £16 ($31.20). A three-course supper menu is available after 10:30 p.m. at a cost of £9 ($17.55). For service, VAT, and your choice of wine, you pay extra. The food is not only appetizingly served and presented, it is cooked with flair, skill, and imagination, using fresh produce whenever possible. It's impossible to recommend any specific dish, as the menu changes daily and with the seasons. But we've particularly enjoyed brandade of smoked trout as an appetizer. One autumn day we liked an excellent leek and pumpkin soup, just perfect for the season. Main-dish selections are made from "the open fire" or else from "the great dish of the day." To go with the main course, a green salad with a well-seasoned and perfectly balanced herbal dressing is served. If featured, we'd most heartily suggest the cold chocolate soufflé. Much of the wine is personally selected in France by Mr. Carrier himself.

The restaurant is open Monday through Saturday from 12:30 to 2:30 p.m. and from 7:30 to 11:30 p.m. Tube to the Angel stop.

Å l'Ecu de France, 111 Jermyn St., S.W.1 (tel. 930-2837), is classically French and most stylish, with pillars and mirrors reflecting the dark walls in discreet lighting. It has a relaxing atmosphere, with a touch of elegance. Just off Piccadilly Circus, it has been known by gastronomes for years. The service is impeccable—no one rushes you, no one hovers over you, but the staff is ready to wait on you when needed. The menu is long and hand-scrawled in the Gallic tradition. A prix-fixe luncheon goes for £10.25 ($19.99), which is reasonable in price considering the quality. A set dinner is offered on Saturday and Sunday only; otherwise, expect to spend about £20 ($39) and up for an à la carte meal. On our latest rounds, the coquilles St-Jacques (scallops baked in their shells) was done to perfection. Also pleasing is veal served in a delicate wine sauce. Always our choice, if featured, is boeuf en croûte (filet of beef cooked in a pastry shell and served with truffle sauce). The restaurant is open from 12:30 to 2:30 p.m. and from 6:30 to 11:15 p.m.; however, it is closed on Saturday and Sunday at lunchtime. On Sunday evenings, hours are from 7 to 10:30 p.m.

Savoy Restaurant, The Strand, W.C.2 (tel. 836-4343), in the

Savoy Hotel, has a prime position—its tables open toward the river and as you have breakfast or lunch you can watch the boats passing by on the Thames.

Lucius Beebe, in his history of the hotel, wrote: "Supper at the Savoy became legendary. It remains to this day a formidable tradition of London night life."

At the apex of its fame, Auguste Escoffier was the director of the cuisine, earning for himself the title of "the king of chefs and the chef of kings." It is said that Escoffier invented peach Melba, one of the world's most imitated desserts, and named it after Nellie Melba.

The River Restaurant has an intimate dance floor, surrounded by tables, where a four-person band plays for dinner. (The great Russian dancer, Anna Pavlova, once appeared at the Savoy.)

Dinner starts at 7:15 p.m. and is served until 2 a.m. Music for dancing begins around 9 p.m. Monday through Saturday.

The à la carte menu is most ambitious. Nearly every dish is prepared to perfection and only the most exacting gastronome will find fault. Specialties include caneton (duckling) du Norfolk poéle à l'orange and grilled chateaubriand with pommes soufflées for two persons. Crêpes suzette make a lavish dessert, although the peach Melba is more classic. Under "les savouries," perhaps you'll try "devil on horseback." On weekdays, a set dinner is offered for £13.50 ($26.33). Lunch is £10.75 ($20.96) per person. Otherwise, expect to pay from up to £50 ($97.50) for two persons for a complete à la carte meal, and make an evening of it.

The newly created Thames Foyer makes an ideal meeting place where coffee, pre-lunch and dinner drinks, afternoon tea, and light refreshments are served.

Lacy's, 26 Whitfield St., W.1 (tel. 636-2323), is run by a perfect culinary duo, William Lacy and his wife, Margaret Costa. She is one of the leading food authorities in the British Isles—in fact, the author of *Four Seasons Cookery Book* and *London at Table.* Mr. Lacy is the chef, an award-winning one at that. He was the chef des cuisines at the Empress in Berkely Street, and he trained under the last living disciple of Escoffier.

The ceilings are vaulted, and the art on the walls is modern. On the ground level is a small cocktail bar and a reception area. The dining room, in the Moorish style, is reached after going down a flight of stairs. The food is mainly French and most inventive, with several (to us, at least) original dishes. The ingredients are very fresh, a rarity these days.

For hors d'oeuvres, we'd recommend, if featured, the fish pâté with a yogurt sauce at £3.20 ($6.24). A truly heavenly soup is the watercress, lettuce, and almond at £1.75 ($3.41). Main dishes begin at £6.50 ($12.68). We particularly enjoy the seafood pancakes and the lamb kidneys flambéed with Dutch gin in a juniper-berry-flavored sauce. Desserts begin at £1.90 ($3.71). Reservations are essential. Meals are served from 12:30 to 2:30 p.m. and from 7:30 to 11 p.m. The luncheon menu is still fine value for present-day London. It starts at about £11.50 ($22.43) for a three-course meal, including tax, cover charge, and coffee, but not service. The price of the main course is the price of the full meal. VAT is extra.

The Beefeater

According to a great number of its patrons, this is one of the best entertainment spots in London. Some of its special charm undoubtedly comes from the location. The **Beefeater Ivory House,** St. Katharine's Dock, East Smithfield, E.1, functions in a former warehouse by the Tower of London in a riverside complex called St. Katharine's Dock. High arching walls, flagstone floors, and heavy oak furniture establish the setting. From the central hall a series of meticulously arranged niches illustrates historical English scenes, ranging from the glittering pomp of the Court of St. James's to the eerily torch-lit dungeons of Traitor's Gate and Newgate Prison.

The welcoming reception begins with huge goblets of wine and a fanfare of trumpets. The assembled guests take their seats in period vaults, each decorated in the manner of its time. Then the feasting begins: six courses (sorry, removes), presented by costumed players amid flaring torchlight.

The players then present a cavalcade of tableaux, each reenacting some grim, comic, or deeply moving scene from England's past—triumphant, tragic, or farcical.

There is Henry VIII, hearty and deadly, welcoming you to the revelry of his court, with warring knights, court jesters, serving wenches, and the "Royal Entertainers."

The grand finale is a tribute to the immortal spirit of London, with the sound of Bow Bells and the old, eternally young street songs.

The whole evening will stay with you long after you leave this town. Arrive at 8 p.m. The Beefeater is open daily during the season; otherwise, it receives guests from Wednesday to Saturday. The cost is £17.95 ($35) from Wednesday to Friday, rising to £19.95 ($38.90) on Saturday. For reservations, telephone 408-1001. Tube: Tower.

Verrey's is one of those restaurants where it's difficult to decide which is more impressive—the decor or the cuisine. At 233 Regent St., W.1 (tel. 734-4495), this is not only one of London's oldest and finest eating houses, but one of the handsomest as well. It has the kind of quiet elite elegance that doesn't dazzle, but rather enfolds and caresses you like a pine-scented bath. The sort of sumptuousness that goes naturally with unobtrusively perfect service, sterling silver tableware, and the brandy of Napoleon. It comes as no great surprise to learn that Charles Dickens, Prime Minister Disraeli, and Edward VII—the gourmet king—used to eat there. You half expect to spot them at the next table.

The walls are paneled, thick rich carpets muffle unseemly noises, and there's an intimate little bar where you sip your apéritif until a discreet voice announces that your table is waiting.

As in most of London's top-drawer traditional dineries, the fare is overwhelmingly French but with English touches to preserve a national flavor. Appetizers, for instance, range from an aromatic pâté maison to Scottish smoked salmon, from frog legs poached in white wine to the very British potted shrimp.

On the luncheon menu you'll find such daily specials as escargots bourguignons at £4.50 ($8.78) and lamb kidneys served with a blend of three mustards and honey, £6 ($11.70). In the evenings, a set dinner, costing from £15 ($29.25), is featured to the tune of a resident pianist and is likely to include smoked Scottish salmon with a trout pâté, beef Wellington, plus a syllabub for dessert, followed by coffee. Flambés are a feature.

Verrey's, by the way, lies close to the theater district and serves a pretheater supper. It is open from 12:30 to 3 p.m. and from 6 to 11:30 p.m. every day but Sunday. Tube: Oxford Circus.

Trader Vic's, at the Hilton Hotel, Park Lane, W.1 (tel. 493-7586), is a dream fulfilled for its founder, who set for himself a high culinary level. The restaurant specializes in "fantasy dishes" that satisfy one's romantic conception of what South Seas island food tastes like. Trader Vic once said that if travelers were to sample the truly native food, nine times out of ten they would reject it as unpalatable to the Western taste. His dishes, therefore, reflect the cuisine of the Pacific area, including China, but are original creations.

The atmosphere matches the culinary offerings, relying on a forest of bamboo, coconuts, native drums, masks, spears, cork floats, nets, exotic shells—a successful melange. The menu is divided into parts, including "at the beginning" Trader Vic's "tidbits": fried prawns, spare ribs, crab Rangoon, and sliced pork, £3.40 ($6.63). One of Trader Vic's specialties (the same dish that is served at its Beverly Hills counterpart) is paper-thin filets of beef flambé, £7.80 ($15.21). From the "lakes, rivers, and sea" come such selections as filet of Dover sole Trader Vic, also £7.80. The curry dishes are, by now, world famous, including such susu (cream) specialties as lobster curry, £8 ($15.60). A personal favorite is the pressed duck, steamed with delicate spices, then boned and shaped into cakes with water-chestnut flour, fried, and served with a spicy plum sauce and sprinkled with crushed almonds, £6 ($11.70). "At the end," you're faced with such a bewildering choice that you may remain the rest of the evening, or else settle for coconut honey ice cream.

Lunch is served from noon to 3 p.m.; dinner, 5:30 p.m. till midnight (the restaurant is closed for lunch on Saturday). A postscript: Try one of the exotic drinks, but be forewarned—their potency is hard to determine, as the wallop is hidden by the beguiling fruit juices.

Tiddy Dols Eating House, 2 Hertford St. (tel. 499-2357), in the heart of Mayfair's Shepherd Market and on the actual site of the original May Fair of the 16th and 17th centuries, is one of the most original *English* restaurants in London.

Built in 1785 and now listed by the government as a building of historical and architectural interest, the Eating House is named after an eccentric English gingerbread salesman nicknamed Tiddy Dol, who sold his wares at the May Fair and at the public hangings at Tyburn, where he is captured by Hogarth's immortal brush in a picture entitled *The Hanging of the Idle Apprentice.*

Today, the Eating House is owned by ex-Tank Corps officer John Campbell, who started in 1959 with one small shop and now owns the entire block which Tiddy Dols comprises. At least, he owns the 999-year lease, signed in 1740 at a ground rent of six shillings and eight pence a year.

A strange old house full of twisting staircases, secluded, tucked-away alcoves, low ceilings, beams, and low, flickering lights, Tiddy Dols is a virtual museum of old English knick-knacks from the collection of old prints and books in the foyer to the huge, button-upholstered red leather chairs and genuine Victorian polyphon—a kind of 19th-century jukebox.

The food keeps to the same authentic and excellent standard, the recipes being taken from old English cookbooks. How about kipper mousse with hot oat cakes or Isabelle's emerald soup to start with? And then perhaps beef Wellington, prime steak wrapped in a light, fluffy pastry; or fisherman's pie, Dublin Bay prawns, shellfish, and seafood in a white wine and lobster cream sauce in a shell of duchess potato and cheese grilled to a golden finish? As for desserts, try real gingerbread—honey, nuts, and stem ginger—with whipped cream or butter, or perhaps black currant fool (black currants crushed with fresh cream and sugar).

As to wine, Tiddy Dols has a superb list at some of Europe's lowest prices: eight house wines starting at £3.95 ($7.70), Mouton Cadet Rouge at £6.65 ($12.97), Chablis ler cru (1979) at £8.90 ($17.36), Dom Perignon vintage champagne (1973) at £25.70 ($50.12), and the excellent 1976 Marquês de Riscal Rioja Alavesa at only £5.95 ($11.60).

But that isn't all. From 7 to 11 p.m. nightly there's entertainment: the Mayfair Syncopators, Lord Julian Shepherd, the village town crier, the Food of Love playing madrigal to modern music on their extraordinary range of instruments, and Instant Sunshine, the trio of singing doctors who've starred on television, made several records, and scored international successes. Then from 11 p.m. to 2 a.m., there's a sophisticated disco to suit everybody.

A new budget menu at £1.60 ($3.12) offers all you can eat. For example, you might choose quiche Lorraine with a mixed salad on the side. There are also light suppers at £5.75 ($11.21) and £7.25 ($14.14) for before- or after-theater diners, or indeed at any time of the evening. For those celebrating something special, the management will be happy to arrange for an inscribed birthday cake, a rose, or an exclusive perfume to arrive unexpectedly at the table.

The final pleasant surprise Tiddy Dols has in store is the bill—only about £12.50 ($24.38) to £16.50 ($32.16) per person, including the wine, drinks, entertainment, cover, dancing, service, and VAT. It's open from 6 p.m. to 2 a.m. daily for dinner.

Moderately Priced Restaurants

At 100 The Strand, W.C.2, **Simpson's-in-the-Strand** (tel. 836-9112) carries on as though the sun had never set on the British Empire. It is an elegant cavern, replete with gleaming woodwork and pewter, staffed by a corps of walrus-mustachioed waiters who are as starched and proper as their long white aprons would

The London Room

A unique theater restaurant in a unique setting, that's the London Room. The setting is the New London Centre, an entertainment complex at Parker Street, off Drury Lane, W.1, the heart and soul of the city's theaterland. The restaurant is ingeniously designed so that every guest gets "the best seat in the house." By using a circular layout and varying floor levels, everyone in the place has an uninterrupted view of everywhere. There's no "seat behind a pillar" debacle to sour your evening.

It's hard to decide whether to call this a theatrical dinery or a restaurant with theater attached. But either way it adds up to an evening's total entertainment, because you can dance as well. Admission here is a package deal, including everything. The set four-course dinner is a banquet with seasonal trimmings and comes accompanied by all the wine you can drink during dinner. A typical repast starts with fresh pineapple laced with kirsch, continues with mushroom pancakes and spring chicken, and ends with a flourish of charlotte russe.

There's a fully automated stage equipped with dazzling sound and visual effects. A recent revue consisted of elaborately beautiful highlights from the musicals that have echoed through Drury Lane, complete with gorgeous costumes, spectacular sets, well-drilled choruses, and leading ladies. After that there's a cabaret at 10:30 p.m. The package price is £20.95 ($40.85) on five nights, plus a £2 ($3.90) supplement on Saturday. For bookings (essential), phone 831-8863. Tube: Holborn.

indicate. Whoever said English cooking is *all* bad had obviously never eaten here. Large slices of roast sirloin of beef, carved on a silvery trolley at your table and accompanied by Yorkshire pudding, costs £5.95 ($11.60); saddle of lamb with red currant jelly goes for £5.60 ($10.92); and roast Aylesbury duck with apple sauce, £4.50 ($8.78). Vegetables are extra. Further charges include a 75p ($1.46) cover charge. In addition, you should give the expected 25p (49¢) or more to the man who carves your meat. With the addition of an appetizer, dessert, and tea, the bill should amount to around £11 ($21.45) per person. This is one of the most satisfying restaurants in Europe; reservations are recommended. Closed Sunday.

Au Jardin des Gourmets is an "île de France." Off Soho Square, at 5 Greek St., W.1 (tel. 437-1816), this French "garden of gourmets" is where devotees of the Gallic cuisine gather for their pâté maison. There is an à la carte menu, with a comprehensive selection offered. As an appetizer, try the pâté maison for £1.95 ($3.80). The soups are exceptionally good: vichyssoise for £1.45 ($2.83); soupe à l'oignon gratinée, the same. House specialties include carré d'agneau at £4.95 ($9.65); red snapper with fennel sauce, £3.95 ($7.70); and a hot seafood dish in wine sauce at £3.95 also. Vintage wines are available, but you can also order by the glass. The restaurant is open from 12:30 to 2:15 p.m. and from 6:30 to 11:30 p.m. It's closed on Sunday. Tube: Tottenham Court Road.

Manzi's, 1–2 Leicester St., off Leicester Square, W.C.2 (tel. 734-0224), is London's oldest seafood restaurant. Famous for fish, Whitstable and Colchester oysters, and other seafood specialties, Manzi's has a loyal patronage, drawn to its moderately priced fare and fresh ingredients. In season, you can order half a dozen of the legendary Whitstable oysters for £4 ($7.80). If you'd like something less expensive, we'd suggest a prawn cocktail at £1.50 ($2.93), even fresh sardines at £2.20 ($4.29). If it's a luncheon stopover, you might happily settle for the crab salad at £4.20 ($8.19). Main-course specialties include Dover sole at £6 ($11.70) and grilled turbot at £6 also. The house also has a good selection of wines and sherries. You can dine either in the simply decorated ground-floor restaurant or else in the Cabin Room upstairs, any time from noon to 2:40 p.m. and from 5:30 to 11:45 p.m. Tube: Leicester Square.

Restaurant Café Jardin, 10 Lancashire Court, 122 New Bond St., W.1 (tel. 493-2896). In a tiny passageway between two shops on fashionable Bond Street, a small courtyard with bay trees leads to the unobtrusive door of this charming basement restaurant. On the ground floor is a bar with mirrors and plush stools, then a winding stairway to the cellar where tables crowd the walls, and the decor is graced with potted plants, bamboo screens, mirrors, and lights.

The manager, Jean-Louis Commeureuc, is forever in attendance, and the cuisine is essentially French, although the chef is an Englishman, Alan Bird. They have two daily menus at £5.95 ($11.61) and £7.95 ($15.50) for three courses. Appetizers include very good soup, smoked salmon, boiled clams, or melon. The main dish of either menu is likely to be sautéed beef with onions and mushrooms or else braised beef with green peppers. Fresh vegetables are included, and the meal finishes with a dessert from the tray.

Specialties include eggs Benedict or an omelet stuffed with mushrooms. The à la carte selection includes crayfish tails cooked in cream and served in a pastry case, chopped lobster with poached egg, and a cheese soufflé. Main emphasis is laid on fresh fish dishes, including mousseline of sole with lobster sauce, fresh brill, and the day's fish from the market cooked in whatever way you ask.

There are also grills and steaks—try the tournedos with beef marrow and red wine sauce. A three-course meal finishing with dessert or cheese will cost about £11 ($21.45), with the house wine priced at about £4.50 ($8.78) per bottle. There's a 12½% service charge added to the bill, plus a cover charge of 50p (98¢). This is a very busy place, and service tends to be slow, but your meal is worth waiting for.

Joe Allen's, 13 Exeter St., W.C.2 (tel. 836-0651), is a fashionable restaurant attracting theater people. It lies north of the Strand in the vicinity of the Savoy Hotel. The restaurant, serving an American and international cuisine, is a sister to other branches in Paris, Los Angeles, and New York. The decor is inspired by the New York branch, with theater posters, gingham tablecloths in red and white check, and a blackboard menu offering such specialties as black bean soup, barbecued spare ribs, a regular spinach salad, a bowl of chili, calf liver and onions, and carrot cake. A simple meal will begin at £6 ($11.70), although you can spend far more, of course, depending on how much you order to drink. Joe Allen's is open until 1 a.m. Monday through Saturday, till midnight on Sunday. The bar closes from 3 to 5:30 p.m., from 2 to 7 p.m. on Sunday.

Time has been kind to **The Ivy,** a revered French restaurant at 1 West St., W.C.2 (tel. 836-4751). In days of yore, it was the preferred dining haunt of such luminaries as Sir Winston and Lloyd George. Established theatrical personalities—Noël Coward, Sir Cedric Hardwicke, Rex Harrison—met here to discuss play contracts.

The Ivy had been getting a bit désuet, but with the arrival of Lord Lew Grade's wife Kathleen, who now owns the Ivy, the old tradition of theatrical star-spotting is coming back. The paintings, paneling, and luxurious furnishings remain, and the menu tends to be a little old-fashioned in its length and detail.

Sole is available with 13 different sauces and garnishes, but the table d'hôte luncheon or dinner is what you'll probably go for at £12 ($23.40). If you don't see anything you like, then go for the lunchtime plats du jour, including a gigot of lamb or roast beef with the trimmings.

In the evening you can try a chateaubriand steak for two persons or duck in orange sauce among an array of dishes. Meals begin at £15 ($29.25) per person, but this is quite amusing for a night out among the celebrities.

The Ivy is open between 12:30 and 2:15 p.m. for lunch and from 6 to 11:15 p.m. for dinner. Closed Sunday and for Saturday lunch. Tube: Covent Garden or Leicester Square.

Langan's Brasserie, Stratton Street, W.1 (tel. 493-6437), is a relaxed, café-style restaurant modeled after a Parisian brasserie. Although the chef is English, the food and atmosphere are very French. Langan's is the brainchild of restaurateur Peter Langan, in partnership with actor Michael Caine and the chef de cuisine, Richard Shepherd, and has become a chic spot since it opened in 1976. The potted palms and overhead fans created a faded '30s atmosphere; you expect the evening instrumentalists to break into "As Time Goes By" at any moment. Langan's is open for lunch Monday to Friday from 12:30 to 3 p.m. and for dinner from 7 p.m. to midnight, Monday through Friday. On Saturday, hours are from 8 p.m. to 1 a.m., and the restaurant is shut all day on Sunday. Complete dinners, including wine, VAT, and service, come to about £17 ($33.15) per person. Upstairs is a more intimate dining room with silver service, although the same prices are charged. The Venetian decor was the work of Patrick Proctor, the artist.

There are 16 **London Steak Houses** in the metropolitan area, differing in decor but in the same price bracket and of equal excellence. The one we'll describe is at 116 Baker St., W.1 (tel. 935-1932), in a long, narrow room housing a single row of dainty little tables set in a very chic color scheme. The walls are decorated with framed pages of the French periodical *Gil Blas,* the ceiling inlaid with oak beams, the whole scene illuminated by gas lamps or what looks very like them.

But while the design is subtly delicate, the fare is hearty. The accent, as indicated by the establishment's name, is on beef, although you can also choose from a goodly array of pork and seafood dishes. The house specialties, however, are items like steak Diane with shallots and parsley and the rump, sirloin, and filet steaks, which come in three sizes each: standard, medium, and large. Vegetables cost extra. For an appetizer, we recently ordered the tangily piquant avocado with prawns, and for a finale the excellent bananas au kirsch. Coffee is extra, but the

Restaurants Afloat

Perhaps the most charming oddities on the London dining scene are the nautical eateries that have sprung up. They range from converted barges to craft the size of Mississippi steamers and may either be permanently docked or mobile, but invariably offer good cuisine in intriguingly different surroundings. Since they stick to the placid Thames or the canal system there is no chance of your appetite's being disturbed by seasickness.

R.S. (for restaurant ship) **Hispaniola.** Moored on the Thames at Victoria Embankment, Charing Cross, this large and luxurious air-conditioned ship offers a splendid view of the heart of London from Big Ben to St. Paul's, armchair comfort at the tables, and two cocktail bars for other brands of comfort. Meals are served on both upper and lower decks, and at night the sparkling lights along the banks turn the entire area into a romantic setting. The cuisine is Spanish and will cost you around £14 ($27.30) to £20 ($39) per person. Lunch and dinner are served seven days a week, except on Saturday at noon. For reservations, telephone 839-3011.

The **Fair Lady,** a cruise-while-you-dine establishment, anchors at 250 Camden High St., N.W.1, about two miles from central London. Traditionally decked out, this motor-driven barge noses through the Regents Canal for three hours, crossing the zoo, Regents Park, passing through subterranean tunnels until it reaches Robert Browning's Island at Little Venice, where a popular singer-guitarist joins you for the return journey.

While cruising you eat an excellent three-course meal for £15 ($29.25) and enjoy the passing scene along the banks. Lunch is served on Sunday only, for £7 ($13.65), with the cruise starting at 1 p.m. The dinner trip departs at 8 p.m. For reservations and information, telephone 485-4433 or 485-6210.

little plate of sugar-powered Turkish delights that appears with your cup is on the house. Expect to spend from £10 ($19.50) for a complete meal. There's a 60p ($1.17) cover charge, which, however, does not include the tip. The restaurants are open for lunch and dinner seven days a week. Other locations: 10 Broadway, Westminster; 29 Ebury St.; 17-20 Kendal St.—plus others all over town.

Coconut Grove, 3–5 Barrett St., W.1 (tel. 486-5269), lies in Mayfair, at the end of St. Christopher's Street, just off Oxford Street. Bright and shiny, it invites with brown wood, pink napery, green frondy plants upstairs. More seats are found downstairs, and in summer tables tumble onto the pavement to accommodate tired and thirsty shoppers. Find a table or a seat at the bar and relax with a margarita or a Mississippi mule. For £2.40 ($4.68) you get a long, frosty glass.

Then select a meal from the bewildering list of dishes with an international flavor. Guacamole, eggs Benedict, and chili vie with deep-fried potato skins with sour cream and chives and brie cheese baked in almonds with hot garlic bread at around £2.25 ($4.39). A soup of the day is always featured, and there are a dozen or so salads, including Waldorf and Caesar. A 16-ounce T-bone is served with fries, and beefburgers are on the menu, as well as deep-fried chicken with corn. Meals begin at £8 ($15.60). It's open seven days a week from noon to 1 a.m.

Shezan, 16 Cheval Pl., off Montpelier Street, S.W. 7 (tel. 589-7918), is one of the most sophisticated Pakistani restaurants we've ever dined in, and one of the best. In a cul-de-sac behind Harrods, Shezan is a brick and tile establishment, where the preparation, cookery, and presentation is excellent. Although the setting is deceivingly modern, the cookery is based on recipes known for generations. Meals here are a pleasurable, pampered experience. Order, if possible, one of the exquisite dishes from the tandoor ovens, such as murgh tikka lahori (marinated chicken) at £2.85 ($5.56). We also like the diced lamb cooked in butter with tomatoes and spices. It's called bhuna gosht and costs £3 ($5.85). Most kebabs begin at £2.85 ($5.56), and tandoori charcoal barbecues and grills are usually priced at £2.85 also. The tandoori breads are a special treat, especially the nan-e-babri, a white-flour bread. Lunch is served daily except Sunday from noon to 3 p.m., and dinner is from 7 to midnight. Tube: Knightsbridge.

Keats, Downshire Hill, Hampstead, N.W.3 (tel. 435-1499), is called "a small serious restaurant for committed gourmets." Not more than a stone's throw from Keats's house, it's out in Hampstead and is the finest dining choice you can uncover in that residential suburb. Proprietor Aron Misan takes pride that only the finest ingredients go into his dishes. Some items are actually flown in. The large and varied menu lists the finest classic French cuisine. But Mr. Misan has even more pride in his wine cellar, where the best choice is among the clarets. Expect to pay about £14 ($27.30) for the average dinner, and that figure doesn't include your selection of wine. Definitely reserve your table before heading out to Hampstead, since the restaurant accommodates only about 50 people. Closed Sunday.

Mexico was rather late in arriving at the London banquet, but has now made up for it with the opening of **La Cucaracha.** This Soho hostelry, at 12-13 Greek St., W.1 (tel. 734-2253), is eye-pleasing and palate-caressing. It passes muster with even the fussiest aficionado of South-of-the-Border cooking. Inside (meaning downstairs) the restaurant consists of a series of inter-connected small rooms that create the impression of privacy while dining. Tables and chairs are authentically Mexican, the whitewashed adobe walls, wooden screens, and heavy wrought-iron lanterns create an enchanting hacienda atmosphere, which is further enhanced by the bowls of salsa Mexicana—the characteristic Mexican tortilla dip—standing on the tables.

The fare is not quite as mouth-scorchingly hot as you might have experienced in sombrero land, but biting enough to please the fans. You can start with a vast variety of enchiladas, although they tend to be filling. The cost: £2.40 ($4.68). Alternatively, as an appetizer you might prefer the classic gazpacho at £1.05 ($2.05) or an enormous avocado stuffed with crabmeat and a touch of chili, £1.95 ($3.80). As a main course we'd recommend either the roast turkey covered with a crazy blend of chocolate and chile sauce, £2.50 ($4.88), or the pollo en mole verde, a superbly spicy chicken dish, also £2.50. The desserts are equally appealing. If the traditional tequila is too aggressive with your dinner, La Cucaracha has an excellent and gentle house wine, a Rioja at £7 ($13.65) a bottle. As an additional touch, there are big glowing braziers. The owner is James Denny, and he's wisely selected Vincent Sevilla as his manager. La Cucaracha is open for lunch and dinner Monday to Friday until 11:30 p.m., for dinner only on Saturday. Closed Sunday. Tube: Tottenham Court Road.

In the center of Mayfair, opposite Brown's Hotel, you'll find the **Gaylord,** an elite Indian restaurant at 16 Albemarle St., W.1 (tel. 629-9802). Actually there are two Gaylords in London, but this is the newer one, having opened in 1974. It has established an enviable reputation among local connoisseurs of Indian cuisine. Some, in fact, consider it the finest of its breed by a long shot. One reason for this is that the Gaylord offers samplings of several regional cooking styles, so that you can feast on Kashmiri and Mughlai as well as on the usual Tandoori delicacies. The decor is on a par with the fare. The entire restaurant blazes in purple and gold from the ornate Oriental lamps hanging over each table to the gold-studded door and glass ceiling (specially imported from India). The pervasive palatial air was designed to put patrons in the proper banqueting mood.

The menu is downright dazzling in its variety. The few items we were able to sample can convey only a feeble idea of the culinary encyclopedia available. The best idea here is to follow our example and order as many of the smaller dishes as you can, so that you can taste a variety.

Try the keema nan (leavened bread stuffed with delicately flavored minced meat) and certainly the little spiced meat pasties known as samosas. For a main course, you might choose gosh-taba (lamb "treated and beaten beyond recognition"), or the murg musallam (diced chicken sauteed with onions and tomatoes). If you don't happen to like curry, the staff will help you select a meal of any size totally devoid of that spice, although flavored with a great many others. You'll find the manager help-ful in guiding you through the less familiar Kashmiri dishes. Just follow his tips and you're headed for a culinary adventure. Non-vegetarian dinners begin at £6.65 ($12.97), although vegetarians can dine here for £5.25 ($10.24), plus service. Gaylord is open for lunch and dinner seven days a week.

Good Friends, 139 Salmon Lane, E.14 (tel. 987-5498). Re-member "Limehouse Blues"? These lime kilns, from which this East End parish is named, were done away with after the war. But their reputation lives on. The district lies on the north bank of the Thames and often attracts retired seamen. But fashionable West Enders visit to sample the wares of this small restaurant, which is open from noon to midnight. Some of the finest Can-tonese food in England is served at this family-owned, interna-tionally known establishment. Knowing diners call up way in advance to have their favorite dishes especially prepared. But you may want to settle happily for what's on the regular menu. Featured are beef and peppers at £2.25 ($4.39); sweet-and-sour pork, £2.10 ($4.10); and spare ribs for £2.25 ($4.39). Other specialties include prawns Chinese style and Cantonese roast duck. Mrs. Lynne Wickers, the manager, will help you in making your menu selections. Salmon Lane is off Commercial Road before it forks at the West and East India Dock Roads. Call ahead for a reservation.

London's Chinese accent has long passed from the Limehouse in the East End. It moved first to Soho and now has invaded Covent Garden in the shape of **Poons,** 41 King St., W.C.2 (tel. 240-1743). The restaurant is run by Wai-Lim (Bill) and his wife,

Cecilia Poon. Mr. Poon's great-great-grandfather cooked for the Chinese emperors, and succeeding generations of the family have all interested themselves in traditional Chinese cookery. The decor is an island see-through kitchen which has been the subject of some controversy. We personally like it, as it's fascinating to stand and watch the chefs go through their intricate steps. The house specializes in wind-dried meat and sausage, which is quite different in flavor from smoked. Two of the most recommendable courses include Poons special crispy duck, costing from £9 ($17.55), and Poons special wind-dried meat with seasonal greens, £4.80 ($9.36). For a beginning, you might select the sharkfin broth, £2.80 ($5.46), or the bird's-nest soup, £2.80 also. Other preferred specialties include Poons sweet-and-sour pork based on an original recipe, £3.80 ($7.41) and the special crispy chicken (one half), £6 ($11.70).

If you're a dedicated gourmet of the Chinese cuisine, as are many people these days, you'll find Poons willing to prepare for you some rare and delectable specialties, providing you give them 24 hours' notice. Ever had stewed duck's feet with fish lips? Cecilia Poon is usually on hand to explain the niceties of the menu and to discuss the ingredients of any particular dish. They also do a set lunch at £11 ($21.45) for two persons, £16.50 ($32.16) for three persons, or £22 ($52.90) for four diners. The restaurant is open from noon to midnight daily except Sunday.

A steak house with an ambience and flavor all its own is **Star's.** At 11 Soho Square, W.1 (tel. 437-6525), Star's gets many of its steady patrons from the movie companies in nearby Wardour Street, and they have left a decided imprint on the place. On the elegantly oak-paneled walls you'll see a gallery of show biz celebrity photos, signed and dedicated by the stars to Star's.

Otherwise the establishment has an air of quiet repose and subdued stylishness, including candles in glass bowls flickering gently on the tables, soft, select music in the background, operatic arias and light classics. For openers we can recommend the smoked mackerel at £1.50 ($2.93), followed by either a variety of steak—up to £7 ($13.65), depending on the size and the cut—or the delectable braised chicken Gorgio. With it you can choose from eight kinds of salads and extra vegetables, ranging from £1.25 ($2.44). You can conclude with either a dessert of sherry trifle for £1 ($1.95) or the biting British Stilton cheese and celery. The best buy is the three-course table d'hôte luncheon or dinner, costing from £5 ($9.75) and including coffee.

But the coffees here deserve special mention and can rate as desserts as well. Ten national varieties of them, all very alcoholic and costing £1.75 ($3.41)—from Van der Hum (South African with brandy and cream) to Muscovite (with vodka), Napoleon (with brandy), Scottish (with Drambuie), and Left Bank (with Cointreau), and, of course, Irish. Turkish delights come along gratis. The Star is open seven days a week for lunch and dinner.

Flanagans

At 11 Kensington High St., W.8 (tel. 937-2519), is an Edwardian fish parlor, recreating the madness, the gaiety of the turn of the century. It's a trip back through the years to a world of handlebar mustaches, cut-velvet walls, honky-tonk piano, gaslights, sawdust on the floor—and the inevitable singalongs. All the Florrie Forde favorites are aired here, everything from "Has Anybody Here Seen Kelly?" to "Flanagan" itself.

The pièce de résistance is lobster Lily Langtry, Edward VII's favorite. The shelled lobster is sautéed in chablis with tarragon and thyme and covered with a piquant cream sauce, then sprinkled with parmesan cheese and grilled. The Dover sole is so huge it extends over the edges of your plate. It is accompanied by a large helping of french fries. For an adventure in old English fare, order the homemade game pie with mashed potatoes, and perhaps a side dish of pease pudding, for those who want to go Cockney all the way. A large dish of Irish stew, big enough for two, is a hearty dish. For an appetizer, there's an order of cockles, and for dessert there's the original "golden spong" pudding. A simple meal of three courses, with a half liter of wine, will cost from £8.50 ($16.58); however, you'll spend far more by ordering either the Dover sole or Edward's Lily Langtry.

Flanagans is open daily from noon to 3 p.m. and from 6 p.m. to midnight. Just mind your manners and obey the sign, "Please Do Not Expectorate."

In past centuries, **Cheshire Cheese,** a venerable alehouse at 145 Fleet St. (tel. 353-6170), was the hangout of Samuel Johnson —his favorite table is still on the first floor—where he dined with his friends and entertained them. Today, it's as popular as ever, offering solid English fare of high quality. The atmosphere is thoroughly enchanting: shining mahogany walls, sawdust on the floor, Wedgwood china on the tables.

A favorite plate is the steak, kidney, mushroom, and game pie, quite filling and priced at £3.75 ($7.31). Equally popular is the

Scottish roast beef, with Yorkshire pudding, at the same price. Also the noble mutton chop is preferred by many. For dessert, "ye famous pancake" goes for £1 ($1.95). Closed Saturday and Sunday.

A quartet of sister restaurants, each named the **Carvery,** found only in Strand hotels, answers the ridiculous accusation that "the English have no cuisine." They're found at the **Regent Palace Hotel,** Glasshouse Street, W.1; the **Cumberland Hotel,** Marble Arch, W.1; the **Strand Palace Hotel,** The Strand, W.C.2; and the **Tower Hotel** by Tower Bridge, E.1. At any one of the Carvery showcases, you can enjoy all you want of some of the most tempting roasts in the Commonwealth.

For example, you can select (rare, medium, or well done) from standing ribs of prime beef with Yorkshire pudding, horseradish sauce, and the juice; or from tender roast pork with crackling, accompanied by a spiced bread dressing and apple sauce; or perhaps the roast spring Southdown lamb with mint sauce. Then you help yourself to the roast potatoes, the green peas, the baby carrots. Perhaps you'll prefer a selection of cold meats and salads from the buffet table. No one counts—even if you go back for seconds or thirds.

Before going to the carving table, you'll be served either a shrimp cocktail, a bowl of soup, or a cold slice of melon. Afterward, you can end the meal with a selection from the dessert trolley (especially recommended is the fresh fruit salad, ladled out with thick country cream poured over). You also receive a large cup of American-style coffee. The cost is £8 ($15.60) for "the works," and the price is the same at both lunch and dinner. At the Tower Hotel, you pay £9.50 ($18.53). No telephone reservations are accepted.

Pomegranates, 94 Grosvenor Rd., S.W.1 (tel. 828-6560), is a basement restaurant with amber lighting. The owner, Patrick Gwynn-Jones, has traveled far and collected recipes for dishes throughout the world. Asian and Indonesian delicacies vie for space on the menu along with European dishes. Likely to be featured are spiced pickled salmon with a sweet mustard sauce, leg of lamb flavored with herbs, veal kidneys deviled lightly, along with freshly cooked vegetables and bread which is baked twice daily. The decor is purely European, with mirrors and well-laid tables. A set lunch or dinner is offered for £7.50 ($14.63), although the à la carte average, including wine, is likely to be from about £18 ($35.10) up. House wines are reasonable in price, and there is in addition a good wine list. The establishment is open for lunch from 12:30 to 2:15 p.m. Monday to Friday, and for dinner from 7:30 to 11:15 p.m. Monday to Saturday.

Jonathan's Restaurant, 71 Blythe Rd., W.14 (tel. 602-2758 or 603-0070), is a special place, found in an almost suburban street, well away from the normal tourist haunts, behind Olympia Exhibition Hall. Once you have parked your car, paid off your taxi, or walked from the exhibition, ring the bell at number 71, and you'll be ushered into a small (but very well-stocked) picture-strewn bar. Raymond Clegg will pour your drinks or mix you one of his cocktails, while his Danish wife, Hanne, will discuss the merits of various dishes on the extensive French menu. Downstairs, the restaurant is cozy, with candles and fresh flowers on the linen table cloths.

A hot avocat Jonathan, filled with seafood in a béchamel sauce, is £2.25 ($4.39). Or perhaps you'll prefer escargots (snails) à la bourguignonne at £2 ($3.90), or frog legs sautéed in tomato and onion sauce with garlic and herbs. A filet with Stilton cheese and a port wine sauce goes for £5.50 ($10.73). Venison, sautéed and served with red currant sauce, is £5 ($9.75). Roast duckling, flamed with brandy and offered in a cream and green peppercorn sauce, goes for £4.75 ($9.26). Most items on the menu can also be served plain grilled. There is an interesting selection of desserts, including crêpes suzette and cherries jubilee, cooked and flamed at your table. There is an excellent wine list to accompany your meal, and a bottle of the house wine is priced at £3.75 ($7.31) per bottle.

VAT is included, but not the 10% service charge. In addition to an extensive à la carte menu, there are most attractively priced set luncheon and dinner menus from £4.95 ($9.65), including three courses, coffee, and VAT.

The restaurant is open for lunch Monday through Friday from noon to 2:30 p.m. and for dinner Monday through Saturday from 7 to 11:30 p.m. It is also open for Sunday luncheon from noon to 3 p.m. at a set price of £5.95 ($11.60).

Le Steak Nicole, 72 Wilton Rd., S.W.1 (tel. 834-7301), is a bistro run on French lines, with tables placed on the pavement in summer. There's a tiny dining room on the ground floor and more room in the basement. You can have your usual "tipple" at the bar while deliberating about your meal. Try a Kir, white wine and cassis, or one of the essentially French apéritifs, St-Raphael or Suze, so as not to destroy your tastebuds.

The owners, Graham Collard and Tony Clane, offer entrecôte

any way you wish. Desserts might include caramelized oranges, or you may prefer just cheese and coffee. VAT and service are extra. The average price for two courses is £8 ($15.60), including a half bottle of wine. The restaurant serves from noon to 2:30 p.m. Monday to Friday, and from 6:30 to 11 p.m. Monday to Saturday.

The Baker & Oven

This "Simon the Pieman" setting is not only unusual, but superb in its actual food offerings. The Baker & Oven, 10 Paddington St., W.1 (tel. 935-5072), is appropriately named: it was, around the turn of the century, a real bakery. Nowadays, the dining room has been installed in the basement, and narrow tables have been set inside the brick-lined ovens.

To commence your meal, try the country-style pâté at £1.25 ($2.44) or a good savory bowl of onion soup, 95p ($1.85). Among the house specialities are the jugged hare at £4.75 ($9.26) and the roast Aylesbury duckling with stuffing and apple sauce at £4.25 ($8.29). Desserts are in the classic English tradition, especially the hot apple pie with thick country cream at £1.25 ($2.44). Closed Saturday for lunch, Sunday, and bank holidays. Tube: Baker Street.

The Budget Restaurants

Now we turn to the budget-priced restaurants, grouped geographically—as follows:

IN SOHO: The jumble of streets and alleys known as Soho lies slightly northeast of the theater district, and is packed with cabarets, bars, and a fantastic assortment of foreign restaurants. An analogy might be drawn between Soho and New York's Greenwich Village, or San Francisco's Fisherman's Wharf. It's a place for special meals, mostly medium- to budget-priced.

Chuen Cheng Ku, 17 Wardour St., W.1 (tel. 437-1398), is one of the finest eateries in Soho's "New China." A large restaurant, Chuen Cheng Ku is noted for its Singapore noodles. Specialties are paper-wrapped prawns, rice in lotus leaves, steamed spare ribs in black bean sauce, shredded pork with cashew nuts, all served in generous portions. Dim sum (dumplings) are served from 11 a.m. to 6 p.m. The Singapore noodles, reflecting one of

the Chinese-Malaysian inspirations, are thin rice noodles, sometimes mixed with curry and pork or shrimp with red and green
peppers. A set dinner costs £6 ($11.70) per person. Featured à
la carte dishes include fried oysters with ginger and scallions,
sliced duck with chili and black bean sauce, and steamed pork
with plum sauce. An average à la carte dinner goes for £8
($15.60). A service charge of 10% is added to all accounts. The
restaurant is open daily until midnight.

The **Dumpling Inn,** 15a Gerrard St., W.1 (tel. 437-2567), despite its incongruous name and even more incongruous decor
(Venetian murals, apparently left behind by its predecessor), is
a cool and rather elegant hostelry, serving a totally delectable
brand of Peking cuisine. Also known as Mandarin cooking, this
is haute cuisine à là Chinoise, as distinct from the much more
common and familiar Cantonese kitchen. A Chinese proverb,
attesting to the food's subtle intricacy says: "It takes three generations to learn how to eat." Mandarin cuisine dates back almost
3000 years and owes some of its special piquancy to the inclusion
of various Mongolian ingredients, such as Hot Pot.

The inn boasts a legion of near-fanatical regulars, who
wouldn't dream of touching any other brand of celestial fare.
They come for the shark's fin soup, for the beef in oyster sauce,
the sliced duck with mushrooms, the grilled pork or beef dumplings, and the pancakes stuffed with a most delicately flavored
minced meat. Chinese tea is extra. The average meal goes for
£8 ($15.60), although a large plate of grilled pork and dumplings
will cost only £2.50 ($4.88). The portions are not large, so you
can order a good variety without fear of leftovers. And service
is leisurely, so don't dine there before a theater date. It's advisable to reserve a table.

A patch of Left Bank Paris transplanted to 57 Old Compton
St., Soho, W.1, **Le Bistingo** (tel. 437-0784) is a bistro which is
the nearest thing to a Latin Quarter student haunt you'll find this
side of the Channel. A mad melange of booths and tables, iron
bedrails on the walls, strings of onions in the window, Victorian
advertising posters for dog biscuits, and menus hand-scrawled
on a blackboard, the bistro is thronged morning, noon, and night
with a multilingual crowd of young people, who come to meet
each other just as much as to eat.

Yet the food is by no means a sidelight. In fact, it's excellent
and authentically French. Try the artichoke hearts salad for an
appetizer. Then, perhaps, the beef in red wine or, in season, the
meltingly tender grouse St. Hubert. Along with the courses come

heaped baskets of bread, as fresh and crackly as from a Parisian bakery. For a grand finale we'd suggest the oranges au Grand Marnier, which comes drenched in liqueur as genuine as the fruit. Expect to spend from £6 ($11.70), plus the cost of your drink. Eat here at night and you'll see a constant parade of Soho types (few of whom live in Soho—or even in England) both inside and through the windows and get an earful of as many languages as are spoken in a United Nations canteen.

COVENT GARDEN: London's former flower, fruit, and vegetable market dates from the time when the monks of Westminster Abbey dumped their surplus home-grown vegetables there. In 1670 Charles II granted the Earl of Bedford the right to "sell roots and herbs, whatsoever" in the district. Although long gone to a new location, the old veg market still makes a good choice for dining.

Boulestin, 25 Southampton St., W.C.2 (tel. 836-7061). This famous old restaurant founded more than half a century ago by Marcel Boulestin, the first Fleet Street restaurant critic, has had a facelift. It's reached by a side door which goes down into the basement beneath a bank. The decor is warmly gold and tortoise shell. Sober pictures of cattle and deer adorn the walls in a very British manner, but the menu is entirely French.

Appetizers include soups and pâtés, although you'll have to pay around £4 ($7.80) for the more elaborate "starters." For a main course, we'd recommend such dishes as filets de sole à la vapeur de Vermouth at £7.50 ($14.63) and noix de carré d'agneau (lamb) sur lit d'oignons blanc at £6.50 ($12.68). Desserts include mousses and sorbets, and there is a wide choice of house wines (half bottles available as well). VAT is included in the prices quoted, although a 15% service charge is added. The restaurant serves Monday to Friday from noon to 2:30 p.m. and from 7 to 11:15 p.m. (from 7 to 11:30 p.m. only on Saturday).

IN KENSINGTON: Chances are you'll find yourself in this popular district for lunch. If so, **Fu Tong,** 29 Kensington High St., W.8 (tel. 937-1293), is Shin Sun Chin's delightful Chinese restaurant. In our opinion, it's one of the best in town. The comfortable booths offer a great deal of privacy, although the bell button on your table will bring the waiter in a moment. Hot towels come between courses, and when you become a regular (two or three visits make you so), you'll be presented with your own chopsticks engraved with your name.

The cuisine is Cantonese/Peking style, and all the usual dishes of that kitchen are available here. If you want Peking duck or another complicated dish, order it when you reserve your table or you'll have to wait when you arrive. The average meal here costs £7 ($13.65). There's a minimum charge of £4.50 ($8.78) per person, plus a 50p (98¢) cover charge. A 15% service charge is added to all accounts, and the restaurant is open seven days a week from noon to 11:30 p.m.

KNIGHTSBRIDGE: A top residential and shopping area of London, Knightsbridge lies just south of Hyde Park. Several of the major department stores, including Harrods, are here. Take the Piccadilly underground line to Knightsbridge.

In a small street, just off Knightsbridge, the **Upper Crust**, 9 William St., S.W.1 (tel. 235-8444), is a modest, simply decorated country sort of place with bare brick walls, wheel-back chairs, and warm lights. Pies, rather obviously, are the house specialty, and they are served filled with steak and giblets, savory chicken, curried fish, and a magnificent steak and pickled walnut, an ample portion going for about £3.60 ($7.02). Main dishes, which average around £3.50 ($6.83) in price, are accompanied, for the cover charge of 80p ($1.56), by fresh country bread and herb butter, plus a selection of fresh seasonal vegetables. Cold dishes with salads are also available, beginning at £3.50 ($6.83). Puddings have a definitely "olde worlde" air, including traditional plum with custard or Yorkshire pudding with mincemeat, costing from £1.75 ($3.41). The Franks family, who own and run the place, have a secret in that Mr. Franks also owns the superbly titled butcher's shop, Wainwright and Daughter. Naturally, they select meat of prime quality for their restaurant showcase. Hours are 11:30 a.m. to 3 p.m. and 6 to 11 p.m. daily.

IN BEAUCHAMP PLACE: Tucked away in fashionable Knightsbridge, Beauchamp—you pronounce it "Beecham"—Place is a surprising fun thoroughfare set amid staid residential surroundings. It's fairly small, but packed with funky antique stores, plush boutiques, private clubs, and more than a dozen restaurants ranging from budget to ultrachic. The line-up of parked cars is indicative—minute Austins sniffing the exhausts of Rolls and Daimler limousines, interspersed with motor scooters. Here are a few selections in this area of town:

Our first choice, **Borshtch 'n' Tears**, 46 Beauchamp Pl., S.W.3 (tel. 589-5003), is a unique establishment calling itself "not so much a bistrovich, more of a way of life."

The place has two levels, the entertainment upstairs being provided by a group known collectively as Rasputniki. They play a balalaika, as well as guitars. A Ukrainian girl (who could double for the late Piaf) sings gypsy songs. Downstairs, in the salt mine, Big Al and Fat Tom are one of many English duos who play on different nights. There is a change of musicians on both floors during the evening. To call the place uninhibited would be an understatement. It's like a year-round party. To make sure you have a table, you either have to arrive very early or very late. Even then you might be asked to squeeze up and share.

The menu presents a wild melange of Russian, Italian, and French dishes, with a few English ones sneaking in here and there. Helpings are huge in any language, and we'd wager you won't get beyond two courses.

Try the Russian blinis as a comparatively light appetizer, £1.35 ($2.63); then the mighty Georgian chicken casserole at £3.10 ($6.05) or the more expensive, but outstanding, chicken Kiev, £3.60 ($7.02). "Onions for crying" are advertised as free.

It is open every day from 6:30 p.m. to 1:30 a.m.

Just in case you've been told that you can't eat well and economically in noble Knightsbridge, here's another tip. At 6 Yeoman's Row, S.W.3, off Brompton Road, stands **Luba's Bistro** (tel. 589-2950), a lovely cluttered dining room, open to the street with tables outside, dripping candles everywhere and colored lights overhead. The restaurant looks like a cross between a French auberge and a Viennese Heurigen. A firm favorite among the younger set who use it as a rendezvous spot as much as a dinery, Luba's acts simultaneously as flirtation corner, debating club, and bistro. It has no license, but you can bring your own potables, and Luba charges no corkage.

The cuisine is pretty ethnic, meaning rich. On our last visit, we had Luba's Russian borscht, followed by chicken Kiev and hot cheese cakes (two rounds of fried cream cheese cake served with jam and cream). Russian tea was served in the correct manner—in a glass with a slice of lemon. If you want to make it really Slavic, put a lump of sugar in your mouth and suck your tea through it. Expect to spend from £7 ($13.65) per person. A

10% service charge is added to your bill, but VAT is included. Luba's is closed on Sunday.

ON CARNABY STREET: While shopping for those designer jeans on Carnaby Street, you can drop in at the following selection for lunch. It's especially recommended if you didn't fit into those slim-waisted pants. **Crank's in London,** Marshall Street, W.1, makes dining on vegetarian-health food a pleasure. In fact, it's the leader in London restaurants dedicated to natural foods, prepared ingeniously so that every bite is not only brim full of vitamins, but is a "culinary voyage to give you vim and vigor." The location is unusual, just off Carnaby Street.

The decoration is reassuring—natural wood, wicker basket lamps, bare pine tables, and handmade ceramic bowls and plates. It's self-service: you carry your own tray to one of the tables on the stepped-up level. Crank's is a "temple" of stone-ground flour used for the making of bread and rolls. It's especially noted for its uncooked vegetable salad, although there's always a hot stew pot of savory vegetables (and secret seasonings), served in a hand-thrown stoneware pot with a salad. You can have two sizes of salads, paying £1.50 (2.93) for the small one, £2 ($3.90) for the large. For that, you select from any of the contents of five huge salad bowls, each an original production.

Homemade cakes, such as honey cake, gingerbread, and cheese cake, are featured, from 55p ($1.07) a portion. Tiger's milk? Of course. In an adjoining shop, bakery goods, nuts, and general health food supplies are sold. The restaurant is open Monday to Saturday from 10 a.m. to 11 p.m. It's a popular place, as much with vegetarians as with non-vegetarians, and is well worth a visit.

AT ST. KATHARINE YACHT HAVEN: A good way to spend a Sunday, when most of the restaurants in the West End shut down, is to take the tube to the Tower of London and from there walk to St. Katharine's Dock, a development created out of the old London dock area where the "bacon and egg ships" from Holland used to tie up.

We've already recommended the **Beefeater** for a dining/entertainment adventure. However, you may prefer to visit the **Dickens Inn by the Tower,** St. Katharine's Way, E.1 (tel. 488-9932), a reconstructed 19th-century warehouse that incorporates the original redwood beams and ironwork to form a balconied pub/

Frigate

You climb aboard this recreation of a clipper, turned into a pub-restaurant at 1 Upper St. Martin's Lane, W.C.2 (tel. 836-3603). The entire three floors of an old building were gutted to simulate the hull of a romantic ship. Up and down, the multilevel decks are filled with tables at which you can enjoy full meals. Of course, there's a bar with every kind of "liquid refreshment," including grog and sherries "from the wood."

Seaworthy is the seafood platter at £3.60 ($7.02). Wines are brought in from Germany, Portugal, France, and Italy. A full bottle of burgundy costs from £5 ($9.75). The Frigate sails during pub hours from noon, closing at 11 p.m. Down in the hold is a snackbar. Tube: Leicester Square.

---

restaurant on three levels. At this top-floor fish restaurant, you can order an unusual range of fish, making your selections from a slab at one end of the restaurant. For a traditional Cockney dish, try the jellied eel or perhaps the cockles and mussels. Main-dish specialties include mixed fish kebab with rice pilaf and barbecue sauce, baked river trout stuffed with spinach, and filet of plaice (deep fried). The average cost of a three-course meal, including coffee and wine, is £10 ($19.50). The restaurant is open daily except Sunday evening from noon to 3 p.m. and from 5 to 10 p.m.

For even more elegant dining, you can patronize the **Pickwick Room** (tel. 488-2208). Here a well-prepared English and continental cuisine is served. You can select from such succulent main dishes as escallopines of veal pan-fried with Marsala wine, half a roast duckling in Bigarde sauce, or a grilled pork chop stuffed with Stilton cheese. A three-course meal, along with coffee and wine, carries an average price tag of £12 ($23.40). The restaurant is open Monday to Friday from noon to 2:30 p.m. and from 7 to 10 p.m., on Saturday night from 7 to 10 p.m., but closed on Sunday evening. However, on Saturday and Sunday the chef offers a family lunch, table d'hôte style, costing £8.50 ($16.58) for adults and £5 ($9.75) for children.

Keeping regular pub hours on the ground level is the Tavern Room Bar, where you can order cockles at 70p ($1.37), mussels at 70p also, or perhaps smoked mackerel or a ploughman's lunch, each of the latter dishes going for £1.05 ($2.05).

Another dining choice here is the **Captain's Cabin,** St. Katharine Yacht Haven, East Smithfield, E.1 (tel. 480-5907). This is a waterside restaurant in a restored 1820 building, offering home-style English cooking. The restaurant is housed in the Ivory House, where ivory was once stored upstairs, slaves downstairs. Featured items on the menu include game soup, venison, or Captain Cook's Easter Island chicken. The cost of an average meal is about £8 ($15.60). The cabin is open daily from 11 a.m. to 11 p.m., including public holidays.

The Chains

Chain restaurants were born in Great Britain, and London boasts some good ones. They're ideal for quick meals at low prices, and what follows is a selection of some of the best, arranged in no particular geographical order.

An immense restaurant chain—this one an invader from the provinces—is **Kardomah.** Founded in Liverpool back in 1844, the Kardomah houses have conquered by their sheer adaptability: they blend in with whatever neighborhood they open up in. Most of them serve plain English food at nonfancy prices, but the one we have in mind—at 81 Gloucester Rd., S.W.7, (tel. 373-6900), across from the tube station—is most cosmopolitan. It offers soup of the day for 40p (78¢), spaghetti Bolognese at £2 ($3.90), and a large salad of prawns on a bed of lettuce with hard-boiled eggs, tomatoes, cucumber, radish, and coleslaw, £2.60 ($5.07). Coffee costs 30p (59¢)—and, incidentally, this particular branch sells possibly the best coffee in London, aromatically fresh and ground before your eyes.

For those not in the S.W.7 area, addresses of other Kardomahs are: 2 Kingsway, W.C.2; 10 Poultry, E.C.2; 27 Eastcheap, E.C. 3; 9 Byward St., E.C.3; 17 Cheapside, E.C.2; and 307 High Holborn, W.C.1.

You'll come across a number of **Quality Inn** restaurants which are part of a chain of popular eating houses that have been providing inexpensive meals since 1936. Many of these restaurants are in fashionable areas, such as Oxford Street, and they all serve a variety of continental and English dishes, in a warm, friendly atmosphere. The most central one is at 20–22 Leicester Square, W.C.2 (tel. 930-6823). There you can order fried plaice and chips for £2 ($3.90), or, even cheaper and more filling, spaghetti bolognaise, £1.80 ($3.51). For dessert, a big ice cream coupe goes for £1.05 ($2.05).

Richoux of London, 172 Piccadilly, W.1 (tel. 493-2204), is open from 9 a.m. to 1 a.m. seven days a week, and can be a handy address. Breakfast can be simple fare, just a juice and scrambled eggs at £2.90 ($5.66), or the Richoux brunch of juice, bacon, fried eggs, sausages, tomato, fried bread, mushrooms, toast, marmalade, and tea or coffee at £4.50 ($8.78). House specialties include steak-and-kidney pie or chicken-and-shepherd's pie, with most of these main courses costing from £3.75 ($7.31).

There's also a wide variety of well-stuffed sandwiches—club, smoked salmon, ham and lettuce, tuna fish—from £1.95 ($2.75) to £2.50 ($4.88). Many patrons drop in for afternoon tea, enjoying hot scones, strawberry jam, and fresh whipped cream, along with tea for £1.85 ($3.61). The decor is fresh and clean, with attractive waitresses in starched aprons and caps. Comfortable, well-arranged tables give a degree of privacy.

Other branches are at 41A South Audley St., W.1 (open from 9 a.m. to 11 p.m.; closed Sunday); 360 Oxford St., W.1 (open from 9 a.m. to 6 p.m.; closed Sunday); and at 86 Brompton Rd., S.W.3 (open from 9 a.m. to 7 p.m.; closed Sunday). There is a £1.50 ($2.93) minimum charge at lunchtime and from 7 p.m. (all day on Saturday and Sunday).

Lyons Corner House, 450 The Strand, W.C.2 (tel. 930-9381), is included mostly because it's a whisper from the past, a clean white-fronted place with gold trimmings. It offers a wide variety of fast food and traditional English dishes at reasonable prices, served by a new generation of waitresses known, as their predecessors were, as "Nippies," for the way they get around between the tables. Dressed in black frocks with natty white aprons, they serve hamburgers, eggs on toast, toasted cheese, Welsh rarebit, all the familiar snacks, in the coffeeshop on the ground floor.

The Garden Restaurant serves more substantial meals, including steak with french fries, roast chicken and vegetables, fried fish and chips, and scampi and chips. In the evening, they offer a set dine-and-wine menu when £5.75 ($11.22) gets you a cocktail and a bottle of wine as well as dinner. On Sunday the brunch and wine menu at £5 ($9.75) includes wine and a cocktail. Children can attend too, although they're served soft drinks with their dinner at a cost of £3.85 ($7.51). Alcoholic drinks can only be served during licensing hours, although the restaurant remains open from 10 a.m. to 11 p.m. daily.

And Others

The establishments that follow fall into no particular category, but all are well worth recommending.

Bloom's, 90 Whitechapel St., E.1 (tel. 247-6835), is London's most famous Jewish restaurant. But to reach it, you have to take the tube to Aldgate East, a station in the unfashionable East End. This large, bustling restaurant is in back of a delicatessen. The cooking is strictly kosher. Sunday lunchtime is too crowded, so we'd suggest that you try it out on some other occasion.

The cabbage borscht is the traditional opening course, although you may prefer a chicken blintz. Main-dish specialties run to sauerbraten and salt beef (corned). For dessert, the apple strudel is a favorite. Expect to spend from £6 ($11.70) for a meal. The restaurant is closed Saturday, but open on other days from 11:30 a.m. to 10 p.m.

Bloom's has a second restaurant at 130 Golders Green Rd., N.W.11 (tel. 455-1338). The Whitechapel facility has a license to serve drinks and specializes in Israeli wines.

The **Old Kentucky,** 54 Haymarket, S.W.1 (tel. 839-1956), almost opposite the Design Centre, is a fast-foods emporium. On the right is a Baskin-Robbins 31 Flavors Ice Cream Shop. On the left is a regular restaurant, and one flight of stairs down a spaghetti and pizza place. There's something to cater to most tastes and tailored to tight travel budgets. The windows, however, look decidedly Italian, loaded with decorative spaghetti, bread loaves, and pastries. There's nothing remotely "Kentucky" about them.

The whole place, however, is run on speedy U.S. lines. The premises are awash with Stateside accents and subdued mumbles translating pence into cents. Frankfurters, eggs, and chips cost £1.80 ($3.51), and a passable portion of southern fried chicken comes to £1.80 also. Pancakes come in seven varieties, from plain to "special crunch" (with caramel crunchnut), costing 70p ($1.37) to £1 ($1.95). Also—somewhat surprisingly—pretty good wine is available by the glass at 70p ($1.37). It's open seven days a week until 11:30 p.m.

Although Middle Eastern establishments of every breed have been flourishing in London for years, the **Persepolis,** 39 Kensington High St., W.8 (tel. 937-3509), is the only Persian restaurant we've encountered to date. And if this is a representative sample of Iranian cooking, let's have more of it.

The Persepolis is surprisingly sleek and modern, minus even the slightest touch of Oriental "kitsch." A small, subtly lit place, it features dark-wood tables and chairs and picture windows viewing the street. The only distinctive Persian features are beautifully wrought friezes on the walls showing winged lions and spade-bearded ancient kings illuminated by colored lanterns. You get two menus: one in flowery Persian script, the other in English.

Our three-course repast began with a spicy bowl of mixed pickles that put an edge on your palate. Following this came a course of bamyeh, which consisted of chopped lamb and okra cooked with tomatoes and a portion of rice, and finally, the more familiar halva shekari as a dessert. Most specials cost from £6 ($11.70) to £10 ($19.50), including VAT and service. The restaurant is open every day from 11:45 a.m. to 3:45 p.m. and from 6:45 to 9:45 p.m., except Sunday evening. Tube: Kensington High Street.

The Moravia, 62 Queensway, W.2 (tel. 229-4199), just opposite the Bayswater tube station, offers you a chance of sampling Czech cuisine, which is nowhere near as widespread as it deserves to be. The fare is an intriguing blend of Slavonic and Teutonic kitchen styles, with a few unique touches of its own. It's slightly on the heavy side—with a diet-wrecking tendency toward dumplings—but savory enough to make you forget about counting calories, particularly when washed down with the superb Czech Pilsener beer. You can also order good Czech wines beginning at a reasonable £ 4 ($7.80) a carafe.

The restaurant has a cheerful, pleasant air: paneled walls, wooden tables, artistically dripping candles. One wall is decorated with Czech travel posters, and the piped-in music provides the proper background with a cavalcade of taped polkas.

The Moravia's menu offers most of the better known Czech delicacies with a few Viennese ones thrown in for good measure. We can recommend either the roast duck and cabbage for £3.80 ($7.41) or the delicately smoked pork with sauerkraut and dumplings, also £3.80, accompanied by that famous Pilsener, of course, and followed by apple strudel for £1.10 ($2.15). We guarantee that you won't get hungry. You may, in fact, have difficulty getting up at all. Never mind, just forego that English breakfast next morning. The restaurant is open seven days a week till midnight.

At the corner of Queensway and Bayswater Road you'll find a little slice of Hungary, complete with paprika flavors and gypsy music. In fact, it is the only Hungarian restaurant in Europe offering gypsy music. The **Mignon,** 2 Queensway, W.2 (tel. 229-0093), is one of the oldest Magyar hostelries in London and has retained undiminished popularity in the face of considerable younger competition. It occupies an ideal corner position, the dining room windows offering simultaneous views of Hyde Park and Queensway.

The interior has pleasantly rustic touches: the cooking corner, where you can watch the chef toiling, is roofed like a peasant hut and hung with Hungarian wine flasks and kitchen utensils. Wrought-iron lanterns illuminate the scene. At night, a Danubian four-piece combo provides the right air of nostalgia by means of a bass, an accordion, a Hungarian violin, and a cimbalom, which looks like a zither and sounds like a harpsichord, specializing in the characteristic—slightly triste, frequently fiery—strains that stamp the Magyar brand of rhythm.

The food has the correct degree of palate-tingling spice that demands wine or beer accompaniment. We had a meltingly tender veal goulash with dumplings, cucumber salad, a glass of imported lager, and black coffee, and the check came to £9 ($17.55), including the cover charge. Alternatively we can highly recommend the paprika schnitzel (a spicier derivation of the Viennese product), followed by the rich chocolate mousse.

The Mignon is open daily from midday to 3 p.m. then from 6 p.m. to midnight. Closed on Monday.

As a study in contrast, there's the **Farmbar Restaurant,** 110 Baker St., W.1 (tel. 935-3924). The restaurant forms part of an entire complex called Wholefood, dedicated to the selling, preparation, and propagation of pure, unadulterated, mostly organic comestibles, including naturally fermented cider and wine. The complex embraces a food store, a bookshop, and a butchery, all devoted to the same cause. The Farmbar looks like an idyllically rustic cafeteria, redolent with peasant-style tables and chairs, its windows piled high with crackling loaves of fresh brown bread. The entire establishment, in fact, looks edible. We had some of the finest vegetable soup extant, followed by steak pie with vegetables, concluding with fresh custard. The whole meal tasted like the kind of fare your country aunt might prepare in her kitchen —if you *had* a country aunt. The average cost for a soup course and a main dish is only £2.25 ($4.39). Expect to spend another 65p ($1.27) for coffee, plus 50p (98¢) for a fruit tart. It's open from 8 a.m. to 8 p.m. on weekdays and from 8 a.m. to 3 p.m. on Saturday. Closed Sunday.

A Country Dinner

The **Bell Inn**, Aston Clinton, Buckinghamshire (tel. Aylesbury 630-252), is an 18th-century coaching inn that enjoys one of the finest culinary reputations in England. The Harris family have been much honored for their fine and elegantly presented cuisine. The inn—characterized by a large bell in lieu of the usual inn sign—lies about 40 miles from London and four miles from Aylesbury. It's best reached by private car.

Inside, much use is made of antiques. The atmosphere is mellow. The glasses sparkle and the silver shines against a cool color scheme of olive green. Menu selections are made at leisure in a bar paved with stone.

We're especially fond of the chef's pâté maison, although you may want to launch your repast with his "smokies" or the cold avocado soup. Among the main courses offered, we'd recommend roast duck with apple sauce. Try also the tournedos Rossini, the sea bass Provençale, and the saddle of hare. On Sunday at lunch tender English roast beef is a special feature. If you like fish, we'd endorse the poached salmon in season only. Meal prices begin at £8 ($15.60) per person, including half a bottle of the house wine.

Should you be too exhausted to return to London, the Bell Inn offers six bedrooms in the original building. All contain private baths and are nicely furnished. Fifteen more rooms have been installed in what was a stable block. Units, luxuriously appointed, are equipped with refrigerators and minibars, as well as bathrobes, bubble bath, and shampoo. Two persons can stay here at rates ranging from £40 ($78) to £60 ($117), including a full English breakfast and VAT. Some singles are available. A log fire in the lounge affords a warm welcome to this old coaching inn.

A Pattern of Pubs

The English public house—also known variously as the "local," the "watering hole," the "boozer," or the pub—is such a significant national institution that it has to get a bracket for itself. The pub represents far, far more than merely a place in which to drink.

For millions of Englishmen—and thousands of Englishwomen—it's the regular lunchtime rendezvous. For an even larger number, it also doubles as a club, front parlor, betting office, debating chamber, television lounge, or refuge from the family.

It is not, by and large, a good "pick-up" spot—but it's very nearly everything else.

The London establishments cover the entire social spectrum of the city, from the sleekest haunts to the plainest proletarian strongholds, from overstuffed Victorian plush palaces to neo-Scandinavian decor dreams. The range of entertainment is equally wide—from graveyard silence to epileptic rock bands, go-go girls, and even lunchtime and evening theater performances. Also popular in London are "drag" shows featuring female impersonators.

English pubs have a simultaneously greater and narrower scope than their foreign equivalents, the French bistro, the American bar, and the German Wirtshaus.

Their entertainment repertoire is larger than you'd find in Stateside bars. They cater to a wider range of social groups than their German counterparts. And the edibles they supply are more varied than those of a Parisian bistro.

Yet they only fulfill their pleasant functions during certain stingily measured periods, and the time you most feel in need of them is frequently the time they close their doors. With certain local variations, London's pubs are permitted to open only from 11:30 a.m. to 3 p.m., then from 5:30 p.m. (7 p.m. on Sunday) to 11 p.m. (10:30 p.m. Sunday). English wiseacres will remind you that *certain* pubs (like those around city markets) open and close earlier and you could thus *theoretically* extend your imbibing periods. But who the hell wants to chase around a city searching for a spot to have a quiet noggin in?

And don't let anyone persuade you that Britain's barbaric licensing laws are based on any traditional religious scruples. They aren't. All of them were introduced during the country's industrialization, and their one and only purpose was to get working people into their beds early enough to arrive bright-eyed at their factory benches next morning. Their social and financial betters were at liberty to drink themselves bowlegged until the wee hours in some private club, where the same liquors sold at triple prices.

And that situation has remained unchanged through a couple of World Wars and several socialist governments. Late-night restaurants and nightclubs will serve drinks at juiced-up prices until 2:30 in the morning. Hotel bars serve them to their residents entirely at the management's discretion. Only the poor, ordinary English wage-earner remains excluded. He or she still has to mount the water wagon at 11 p.m. sharp.

Now, having got that off our chests, we can proceed with some particulars on pubs.

To start with, they're eminently respectable institutions, which unescorted women tourists can frequent without the faintest hesitation.

London pubs serve almost every known drink concoction (with the possible exception of a really dry Martini), but their stock in trade is beer. And here you should be warned that standard English draft beer is (a) weak, and (b) most often served "with the chill off"—meaning lukewarm. To get something near your accustomed temperature level, ask for a "cold lager"—and put the accent on "cold."

Pub food varies as much as the decor. Most of them concentrate on lunches, and while a great many stick to a rather meager menu of sandwiches, sausages, and dubious "meat pies," some put on luncheon spreads that would have warmed old Dr. Johnson's glutton heart.

At last count, there were some 5000 pubs in metropolitan London, so the following survey represents no more than a few random samplings of the field. Perhaps you could try an exploration safari of your own—move on to possibly greener pastures next door after one drink. If repeated at length, the process evolves into a "pub crawl"—possibly Britain's most popular national pastime.

ON AND OFF FLEET STREET: Since Fleet Street is newspaper country and swarming with journalists, it's not surprising that it has pubs like some streets have cats.

Ye Olde Cock Tavern, 22 Fleet St., E.C.4 (tel. 353-9706), puts on exceptional lunches. The steak-and-kidney pie, at £2.40 ($4.68), is famous. The tavern was frequented by Charles Dickens in his Fleet Street days. "Ye Fare" is served from 12:30 to 3 p.m.

Old King Lud, 78 Ludgate Circus, E.C.4 (tel. 236-6610), was built in 1855 on the site of the Old Fleet Prison, and the former dungeons are now the cellars of this Victorian pub, one of the most interesting of its period in London, done in shades of green. Seating is on comfortable banquettes. Old King Lud was the home of the original Welsh rarebit, although it no longer features it. Instead, you'll find a selection of pâtés, including duck with orange as well as venison. On the ground floor there's a buffet bar, with salads and hot dishes going from £1.25 ($2.44) to £2

($3.90). Upstairs you can order steak with vegetables or salad, plus a dessert, for about £5.50 ($10.73). The bartender also serves Marlow Bitter. Tube: Blackfriars.

The George, 213 The Strand, E.C.4. (tel. 353-9238), just opposite the Law Courts, mixes press hawks and legal eagles in equal proportions. It boasts a wonderful 18th-century tower, theatrical playbills from the 1830s, oaken roof beams, a black and white timbered facade, and lashings of authentic atmosphere. In the second-floor restaurant you can order soup of the day at 85p ($1.66); sirloin steak, £5 ($9.75); or grilled lemon sole, £4.50 ($8.78). Tube: Aldwych.

AROUND PICCADILLY: **Cockney Pride,** Piccadilly Circus, W.1 (tel. 930-5339), is Victorian Cockney with a vengeance, including long-skirted waitresses and edibles advertised in barrow-boy slang. Cockney cuisine oddities include cottage pie at £1.25 ($2.44) and bangers and mash at £1.05 ($2.05). Tube: Piccadilly Circus.

Comedy, Panton Street, S.W.1 (tel. 930-4017), off Haymarket, is actually five bars and two restaurants in one building. Grandiose setting of scarlet plush and gilded mirrors, smoothly silent service, and outstanding meals are offered for medium prices. The Comedy specializes in two-course lunches for £3.75 ($7.31) downstairs or £7 ($13.65) for filet steak and dessert. The fare is more elaborate upstairs.

IN SOHO: **The French House,** 49 Dean St., W.1 (tel. 437-2799), is something of an oddity—a London pub run by a Frenchman, Monsieur Berlemont. It used to be unofficial headquarters of the French Resistance in exile during the war and still gets droves of French patrons. Outstanding wines by the glass are for sale.

OFF TRAFALGAR SQUARE: **The Sherlock Holmes,** 10 Northumberland St., W.C.2 (tel. 930-2644), is the gathering spot for "The Baker Street Irregulars." Upstairs you'll find a recreation of the living room at 221B Baker St. and such "Holmesiana" as the cobra of the *Speckled Band* and the head of the *Hound of the Baskervilles.* The downstairs is mainly for drinking, but upstairs you can order complete meals with wine. Main dishes are familiar and reliable, including veal Cordon Bleu at £5.80 ($11.31), or perhaps Dover sole meunière at £7 ($13.65). Desserts from the trolley cost from 60p ($1.17). There's also a good snackbar downstairs, with cold meats, salads, cheese, and wine sold by the glass if you wish. A plate of meat, a salad, and a glass of wine will cost around £2.20 ($4.49), which makes quite a nice luncheon stopover. Tube: Trafalgar Square.

IN CHELSEA: Artists and writers are traditionally attracted to this sector, and the pubs reflect their presence. Beards and jeans rub against velvet jackets, sometimes literally as well as figuratively.

Queen's Elm, 241 Fulham Rd. (corner Old Church Street), S.W.3 (tel. 352-9157), is the artists'-authors' "boozer" par excellence in Chelsea. It has to be above par in the beer and whisky line to keep its discerning patrons contented. Owner Sean Tracy autographs and sells his and customers' books.

King's Head & Eight Bells, 50 Cheyne Walk, S.W.1 (tel. 352-1820). As the name indicates, this is actually a fusion of two hostelries, both charming. The ground floor is fairly modern, but you can also drink in a romantic garden overlooking the Thames. Or go upstairs to the River Room restaurant. In the snackbar on the ground floor, you can get Cordon Bleu cookery at pub prices. In the River Room upstairs, the cuisine is both English and continental. In season, some specialties include sea trout, turkey coronation, and stuffed lamb cutlets. Year round you can order such delights as lasagne, shepherd's pie, or steak-and-kidney pie. One English critic wrote of the "elegant puds" (meaning desserts) served here. Among them are chocolate roulade and fresh fruit soufflés. You can dine here for £5 ($9.75). Always reserve a table. Try the cider here—mellow, but packing a considerable punch.

Trafalgar, 200 King's Rd., S.W.3 (tel. 352-1076), is a traditional pub, with darts, dominoes, and pool tables. It's very much a local hangout for the King's Road habitués. There's no dancing or entertainment, apart from DJ music on weekends. But it's a popular place, and an easy mixing ground of the young. Bar snacks run from 70p ($1.50) to £3 ($5.85). Hot and cold dishes are available during licensing hours at lunchtime and in the evening. A pint of beer goes for 70p ($1.37).

IN HAMPSTEAD: Hampstead is a residential suburb of London, and a desirable one. It stands high on a hill, its chic village houses bordering a wild heathland. Keats used to live here. For a pub crawl in Hampstead, take the Northern Line of the underground to the edge of the heath. Once there, drop in at—

The **Old Bull and Bush,** North End Way, N.W.3, which traces its founding back to the mid-1800s, although the present building dates from this century. Hogarth used to live nearby. But it was Florrie Forde's song that made the Old Bull and Bush one of London's best known pubs. In the center of the Heath, the pub is a gathering place of the young. Draft beer seems everybody's drink. With it, you can order sandwiches for around £1.05 ($2.05) and cold salads at £1.60 ($3.12).

ALL AROUND TOWN: Old King's Head, 18 Bear St., off Leicester Square, W.C.2, is a small, bright pub cum showcase. The former owner spent many years collecting matchbox covers; about 7000 of them are displayed in glass cases on the walls. Lunch, served daily except Sunday, features steak-and-kidney pie. Tube: Leicester Square.

The Grenadier, Wilton Row, S.W.1 (tel. 235-3400). Tucked away in a mews, this is one of London's numerous reputedly haunted pubs. Apart from the ghost, the basement also houses the original bar and skittle alley used by the duke of Wellington's officers on leave from fighting Napoleon. The scarlet front door of the one-time officers' mess is guarded by a scarlet sentrybox and shaded by a vine. The bar is nearly always crowded with male blue-bloods and their thin, pale girlfriends. Luncheons and dinners are offered daily, even on Sunday. In the stalls along the side you can order leek-and-potato soup, baked Virginia ham, and apple pie and cream. Snacks are available at the bar if you don't want a full meal. Lunch snacks at the bar range in price from £1 ($1.95) to £4 ($7.80) a plate. In the evening, only hot sausages are offered at 70p ($1.37). However, lunch or dinner in the small restaurant averages around £7 ($13.65).

The Prospect of Whitby, 57 Wapping Wall, E.1 (tel. 481-1095). Possibly the most famous pub in London, this riverside inn is more than 600 years old; it used to be the "Devil's Tavern" in the reign of King Henry VIII. It was frequented not only by Samuel Pepys and Charles Dickens, but also by the dreaded Judge Jeffreys, who used it as a grandstand to view the hanging of pirates at Execution Dock. It's hung with sailors' souvenirs from the Seven Seas, including stuffed crocodiles and native weaponry. The restaurant closes on Sunday and on Monday night. Reserve early if you plan to dine in the restaurant upstairs.

Ask for a bow window table with fine views over the Thames. Apart from its à la carte menu, the restaurant offers two set menus, at £9.50 ($18.53) and £11.50 ($22.43), including VAT, half a bottle of wine, a choice of several appetizers, and four main dishes, then a dessert (or cheese), and coffee. In the bar, you can order various meats, salads, and cheese, your selection stuffed into a large chunk of french bread with butter. Take the Metropolitan Line tube to Wapping. It's a five-minute walk from the station.

The **Golden Lion,** 25 King St., S.W.1. In elite St. James's, opposite Christie's auction rooms, this venerable and ancient hostelry is thronged with antique dealers, art experts, and art buyers on auction days. You can become a connoisseur of sorts by just eavesdropping.

ELEPHANT & CASTLE: South of the Thames, the following pub is easily reached by underground train to Elephant & Castle. From the station where you get off, it's a five-minute walk.

The **Goose and Ferkin,** 47-48 Borough Rd., S.E.1 (tel. 403-3590), is a pub which brews its own beer. The owner of this unique enterprise is David Bruce, who worked as a brewer for one of the big companies for many years until his chance came to buy the Goose and Ferkin. He obtained his own license to brew and set about producing his own beers. A large mirror proclaims "Bruce's Brewery, established 1979." He brews three special strengths, Borough Bitter, 50p (98¢), for a half pint, Dog Bolter, 55p ($1.07) for a half, and, for special occasions, Earth Stopper, 80p ($1.56) and only served in halves. Be warned: This one is a real potent brew, and your 80p worth is the equivalent of three measures of whisky in strength.

Food is also available in this lovely old London pub. Each day there is a different hot dish costing from around £1.85 ($3.61). Or you can order extra-large baps (bread buns) filled with your choice of meat and salad, costing from £1.10 ($2.15).

The whole operation is managed by the buxom Tint Watson and her husband Alistair. Son Neil is David's assistant brewer. From 8 p.m. onward, Crazy Jimmy plays the piano in the good old "knees up" style, and on Sunday at lunchtime the pub's group of Morris dancers entertain, another traditional item.

THE PUB INFORMATION CENTER: This unique organization was formed for the sole purpose of acquainting you with the pub of your dreams and vice versa. Just call at the Center, 2 Caxton St., S.W.1, Victoria, or use the 24-hour Dial-A-Pub telephone service (222-3232) for anything you might want to know pub-wise. You'll learn where to find history, nude dancers, select food, jazz combos, rock groups, gay pubs, vaudeville turns, drag shows, riverside pubs, market pubs, stockbrokers pubs, pubs where you can dance or pubs with folksingers. You name it, they'll tell you.

Jazz Pubs

Perhaps the most astonishing feature of the London entertainment scene is that you can hear far more live jazz in Britain's capital than in almost any American city. The quality varies, but the enthusiasm is on a standard high. Jazz here has become the most popular form of pub entertainment and at the moment you have at least 20 "boozers" flavoring their ale with live syncopation. Some of the outstanding samples are:

The **Bull's Head,** Barnes Bridge, S.W. 13 (tel. 876-5241), offers live jazz all week, with musical happenings that sometimes get very lively indeed. The modern jazz is said by many to be the best in town. Weekdays it attracts shoppers and fashion designers to its old English snackbar, which is a fine place to meet for lunch.

New Merlin's Cave, Margery Street, W.C.1 (tel. 837-2097), offers authentic '20s-style jazz on Thursday and Friday, the pop variety on Tuesday. Also grand-slam jazz concerts are given in a rear hall every Sunday lunchtime, often featuring guest celebrities who drop in casually and let fly.

Wine Bars

One of the most significant changes in English drinking habits has been the emergence of the wine bar. Many Londoners now prefer to patronize wine bars instead of their traditional pubs, finding them cleaner, the food better, and the ambience more inviting. Wine bars come in a wide range, some of them becoming discos at night. The oldest and most traditional wine bars are in—

THE CITY: Olde Wine Shades, 6 Martin Lane, Cannon Street, E.C.4 (tel. 626-6876), survived the Great Fire of 1666 and Hitler's bombs. It is the oldest wine house in the City, dating from 1663. Near the Monument, it is decorated with oil paintings and

19th-century political cartoons. Dickens used to patronize it. El
Vino, its owners, the famous City wine merchants, boast they
can satisfy anyone's taste in sherry. There is a restaurant downstairs, but you can order light meals upstairs, including Breton
pâté at £1 ($1.95) and french bread with ham "off the bone" at
£1.35 ($2.63). Sandwiches begin at 60p ($1.17). Hours are from
11:30 a.m. to 3 p.m. and from 5 to 8 p.m. Both men and women
must wear jackets, and men must also wear collars and ties.
Those wearing jeans or cords will not be served. The place is
closed Saturday, Sunday, and bank holidays. Tube: Monument.

Mother Bunch's Wine House, Arches F & G, Old Seacoal
Lane, E.C.4 (tel. 236-5317), lies underneath the arches of Ludgate Circus. In atmospheric vaults, you can enjoy a "well-
stocked larder," especially the best of baked hams and game pie.
Sherry, madeira, and port are served from the wood, beginning
at 85p ($1.66). Most table wines are priced at £1 ($1.95) by the
glass. Often featured are smoked ham off the bone and game pie.
Main lunchtime dishes cost about £2.25 ($4.39). The wine house
is open from 11:30 a.m. to 3 p.m. and from 5:30 to 8:30 p.m.
Monday to Friday. Tube: Blackfriars.

NEAR LEICESTER SQUARE: Slatters, 3 Panton St., S.W.1 (tel.
839-4649), off the Haymarket, is a split-level wine bar that serves
both a pretheater and an after-theater supper. If you admire the
paintings on the walls, you might want to make a purchase. All
are for sale. Some are originals, some are lithographs, and all
have theatrical or dance themes, executed and signed by Tome
Merrifield. Prices range from £30 ($58.50). Owner Kenneth Slat-
ter offers good food such as underdone pink roast beef, baked
ham, or chicken. A soup of the day is always offered, although
you may prefer the mackerel pâté. It's served with french bread.
A first-class cheese board is another feature. The average meal
price is £5 ($9.75) for three courses and 90p ($1.76) for a glass
of wine. Happy hour is from 8 to 10 p.m. when a bottle of wine
is £3.10 ($6.05) instead of £4.20 ($8.19). The house wine is from
France. The bar is closed Sunday, but open otherwise until midnight. Tube: Leicester Square.

NEAR COVENT GARDEN: The Counter, 4 Great Queen St.,
W.C.2 (tel. 405-6598), is owned by K. C. Sulkin, J. Bryan, and
D. Rudland—or KC, Joe, and David to their regulars. Upstairs
in the cream- and blue-colored restaurant, jitterbug, jazz, and

beebop is the theme, as the '40s and '50s live on. Live music accompanies your meal, selected from such appetizers as palma ham and melon, seafood avocado, or french onion soup. You can then follow with Dover sole, scallops and bacon, kebabs, steaks, or breast of chicken in puff pastry, followed by dessert. The average cost of a meal is £8 ($15.60). Downstairs in the quick-service Jazz Bar, snacks, such as southern fried chicken, eggs Benedict, and spare ribs with jacket potatoes, plus a salad, make up an average meal at a cost of about £4.50 ($8.78). A bottle of wine goes from £4.20 ($8.19). If you can remember to dance in the '40s style, the floor is all yours! Tube: Holborn.

MAYFAIR: **Downs Wine Bar,** 5 Down St., W.1 (tel. 491-3810), stands near the elegant Athenaeum Hotel, right in the heart of Mayfair. On a fair day, you'll find a handsome and sophisticated crowd of people here, occupying one of the sidewalk tables—a continental atmosphere. Inside, the wine bar is decorated in the modern style, with chrome and cane chairs as well as comfortable banquettes. Every evening you can attend a simple, admission-free disco in the basement. Some 100 wines, each bottled in the country of its origin, are offered. The chef's specialty is ham cooked in marmalade, costing £2.50 ($4.88) for a large platter with garnishes. On Sunday, a set lunch, again featuring the ham, is offered for £5 ($9.75), a good price for Mayfair. Hours are from 11:30 a.m. to 3 p.m. and from 5:30 p.m. to midnight daily, from noon to 3 p.m. and from 7 to 11:30 p.m. on Sunday. Tube: Green Park.

IN BELGRAVIA: **Bill Bentley's,** 31 Beauchamp Pl., S.W. 3 (tel. 589-5080), stands right on Beauchamp Place, the fashionable restaurant and boutique-lined block in the vicinity of Harrods department store. A small Georgian house, it is cozy and intimate, with a little patio out back. The wine list is varied and reasonable, including a good selection of bordeaux. A pub-style lunch, such as ham and a salad, costs £2.50 ($4.88), and hot main dishes include skate in black butter with capers at £4.10 ($8) and grilled lemon sole at £4.20 ($8.19). Hours are from 11:30 a.m. to 3 p.m. and from 5:30 to 11 p.m. daily; on Saturday, from 6:30 to 11 p.m.; closed Sunday. Tube: Knightsbridge.

CHELSEA: **Blushes,** 52 King's Rd., S.W. 3 (tel. 589-6640), is the nearest you'll get to a singles bar in London. This attractively decorated watering hole serves drinks and food all day from morning to midnight. The food is excellent and the service friendly. The average price for a meal and wine for two is from £8 ($15.60) to £12 ($23.40). At night there's a busy cocktail bar in the basement, where the barman, Spike, will mix any drink. Be prepared to be kept waiting before you get in. Tube: Sloane Square.

IN BLOOMSBURY: Entrecôte, 124 Southampton Row, W.C.1 (tel. 405-1466), is attractively decorated in an Edwardian style with an overlay of a French bistro. The house specialty, true to its name, is an entrecôte with french fries. Daily specials are offered as well. Sometimes coq au vin is featured. The wine list includes some Haut Médoc selections. Meal prices range from £5 ($9.75) to £8.50 ($16.58), and wine is priced at 80p ($1.56) a glass. A three-piece band plays nightly from 8 to 9 p.m.; during the rest of the time there's disco music to dance by on the cramped floor. Hours from Monday to Saturday are 11:30 a.m. to 3:30 p.m. and from 5:30 p.m. to 1 a.m. (to midnight on Sunday). Tube: Russell Square.

Tower Bridge

Chapter V

THE SIGHTS OF LONDON

THE MOMENT YOU HAVE to categorize the marvels of a sightseers' paradise like London, you find yourself in a predicament. What on earth do you put where?

Is Madame Tussaud's a museum or a show—when it happens to be both? Is the Commonwealth Institute educational, cultural, or entertainment—when it's all three?

It's almost as bad as trying to index "Love."

The system we're following is therefore somewhat loose around the edges. One group spills over into the next, the awesome nudging the banal, grandeur hobnobbing with irreverence. The sole purpose of our classification is to make the sightseeing process as digestible as possible for such a hunk.

In the first half of this chapter, for instance, you get an array of attractions sharing only one common denominator: they have to be seen in daytime. Most of them are free or viewable at a very nominal fee. But during the tourist season they are inclined to get rather thronged, so be prepared to participate in the hallowed English ritual of "queuing up."

Further on in the chapter we'll cover museums, for which London is justly famous, and also organized tours.

Toward the end of the chapter we'll head over to riverside sights along the Thames—and also touch on London sports.

Daytime Attractions

BUCKINGHAM PALACE: At the end of the Mall, a superbly smooth road running from Trafalgar Square, this massively graceful building is the official residence of the Queen.

You can see if Her Majesty is at home by whether the Royal Standard is flown at the masthead. You can't, of course, drop in for a visit (and getting an official invite isn't easy, even for ambassadors), but you can do what thousands of others do—peep through the railing into the front yard.

The palace was built as a red-brick country house for the notoriously rakish duke of Buckingham. In 1762 it was bought by King George III, who—if nothing else—was prolific. He needed room for his 15 children. From then on the building was expanded, remodeled, faced with Portland stone and twice bombed (during the Blitz). Today it stands 360 feet long in a 40-acre garden and contains 600 rooms.

Every summer morning at 11:30, Buckingham Palace puts on its most famous spectacle, the . . .

Changing of the Guard

This ceremony, which lasts half an hour, is perhaps the finest example of military pageantry extant. The new guard, marching behind a band, comes from either the Wellington or Chelsea Barracks and takes over from the old in the forecourt of the palace.

The troops are supplied by the Guards Division, Britain's elite equivalent of the United States Marines. They wear their traditional black bearskins and scarlet tunics, the different regiments distinguished by the plumes worn on the headdress: white for the Grenadiers, red for the Coldstreams, blue for the Irish, green and white for the Welsh. The Scots wear no plumes.

The drill movements are immensely intricate and performed with a robot precision that makes the ceremony seem like a kind of martial ballet, set to rousing music.

But don't get the idea that these are toy soldiers. The Guards date back to 1642, and since then they have fought on every battlefield Britain ever disputed—an endless gory chain stretching from Scotland in 1650 to Korea three centuries later. And those scarlet tunics were originally designed to hide bloodstains on their wearers.

At 11:30 a.m. on weekdays and at 10 a.m. on Sunday, another guard-changing takes place a few minutes' walk away, on the far side of St. James's Park, at the Horse Guards Parade, Whitehall, S.W.1.

This is performed by the even more spectacular Household Cavalry, in waving plumes and silver breastplates, mounted on superb black horses. The units concerned, the Life Guards and the Blues and Royals, are now armored regiments, but for peacetime ceremonies they still wear the uniforms in which they charged Napoleon's green-coated hussars.

Two other places in London also get ritual Guards protection —the Tower of London and the Bank of England, the latter as a result of the 18th-century "No-Popery" riots, during which anti-Catholic mobs threatened to tear the town apart and had to be subdued by means of 20,000 troops and some 300 dead.

TOWER OF LONDON: This forbidding, gray-brown giant with the sinister moats and even more sinister ravens could be the stone symbol of London's past. Even today, centuries after the last head rolled from Tower Hill, a shivery atmosphere of pending doom lingers over the mighty walls.

The Tower is actually an intricate pattern of different structures, built at various times and for varying purposes, most of them connected with expressions of royal power.

The oldest is the White Tower, put up by the Norman William the Conqueror in 1078 to keep the native Saxon population of London in check. Later rulers added other towers, more walls, and fortified gates, until the building became like a small town within a city.

Until the reign of James I, the Tower was also one of the royal residences. But above all, it was a prison for distinguished captives—usually their last.

Two of Henry VIII's unfortunate wives, Anne Boleyn and Catherine Howard, were locked up there before being taken out to the scaffold, as was Lady Jane Grey. The first Elizabeth spent a nightmare stretch in the Tower before she became queen—not knowing whether the next dawn would bring the headsman. She survived to become a remarkably capable monarch, but apparently never quite got over those nights.

That didn't stop her from dispatching her foremost lover, the earl of Essex, to the same prison and block she dreaded when he became silly enough to plot rebellion. The scaffold is gone, but a stone slab indicates the spot where it stood.

The Bloody Tower still stands where, according to the unproven story dramatized by Shakespeare, the two little princes were murdered by the henchmen of Richard III. And where Sir Walter Raleigh spent 13 years before his date with the executioner.

Only one American was ever locked in the Tower. A South Carolina merchant named Henry Laurens, who was also president of the Continental Congress. Captured at sea by the British in 1780, Laurens had 18 months behind those gray walls, until he was exchanged for the defeated Cornwallis.

Every stone of the Tower tells a story—mostly a gory one. On the walls of the **Beauchamp Tower** you can actually read the last messages scratched in by despairing prisoners.

But the Tower, besides being a royal palace, fortress, and prison, was also an armory, treasury, menagerie, and, for a few months in 1675, an astronomical observatory. In the White Tower you'll see rows of the original suits of armor worn by generations of medieval scrappers: ornate, cumbersome, and—for our dimensions—extremely small.

In the **Jewel House** lie England's Crown Jewels—some of the most precious stones known—set into the robes, sword, scepter, and crowns donned by each monarch at his or her coronation. They've been heavily guarded ever since the daredevil Colonel Blood almost got away with them.

The Tower is guarded by Yeoman Warders (plus electronic alarm systems). On state occasions, they carry halberds and wear scarlet and gold uniforms designed in Tudor times. At 10 p.m. every night, they elaborately lock the Tower in what is known as the Ceremony of the Keys. After that—until the arrival of the first sightseers in the morning—only the guards and the ghosts move around in those haunted battlements.

There are also the ravens. Six of them, all registered as official Tower residents and fed an exact six ounces of rations each per day. According to legend, the Tower will stand as long as those black, ominous birds remain there.

Take the tube to Tower Hill or bus 13 to Monument. The Tower is open Monday to Saturday, March 1 to October 30, from 9:30 a.m. to 5 p.m.; November 1 to February 28, 9:30 a.m. to 4 p.m.; on Sunday from March 1 to October 31, 2 to 5 p.m. The Jewel House is normally closed each year in February for maintenance. In July and August, the admission is £3 ($5.85) for adults, £1.50 ($2.93) for children. In January, February, November, and December, the admission is £2 ($3.90) for adults and £1 ($1.95) for children; in other months, £2.50 ($4.88) and £1.50 ($2.93), respectively. The admission to the Jewel House all year is 60p ($1.17) for adults and 30p (59¢) for children. Telephone 480-6593 for further information.

<u>**HOUSES OF PARLIAMENT**</u>: These are the spiritual opposite of the Tower, the stronghold of Britain's democracy, the assemblies which effectively trimmed the sails of royal power.

Strangely enough, both Houses (Commons and Lords) are set in the formerly royal **Palace of Westminster,** the king's residence until Henry VIII moved to Whitehall.

The present House of Commons was built in 1840, but the chamber was bombed and destroyed by the German air force in 1941. The 320-foot tower that houses Big Ben, however, remained standing and the famous clock continued to strike its chimes—the signature tune of Britain's wartime news broadcasts. "Big Ben," incidentally, was named after Sir Benjamin Hall, a cabinet minister distinguished only by his long-windedness.

The Palace of Westminster was closed to the public at the time this book went to press. It may be open during 1983. Check by calling 219-4272. But you can still watch an actual session of the Commons (equivalent of the U.S. Congress) from the "Strangers' Gallery." During crucial debates the exchanges get pretty peppery, although it's unlikely that you'll hear anyone of Churchill's pungency. (He once called the leader of the Opposition "that sheep in sheep's clothing.")

To be admitted to the Strangers' Gallery, you have to join a public queue outside St. Stephen's Entrance on the day in question. On normal days, the head of the queue is admitted from about 4:15 p.m. on Monday to Thursday, at 11:30 a.m. on Friday. But on days of important debates, there may be considerable delay before admission. It is easiest to get in in the evening, Monday to Thursday, from 6 to 9 p.m.

For admission to a session of the House of Lords—which is lavishly Gothic but politically somewhat dull—queue at the St. Stephen's Entrance Tuesday and Wednesday at 2:30 p.m., Thursday at 3 p.m., Monday at 2:30 p.m. (if sitting), and Friday at 11 a.m. (if sitting).

Westminster Hall, the oldest public building in London, was built by William Rufus in 1097. He intended it to be "but a bedroom" of the real palace he was going to erect, but he was murdered three years later.

The hall frequently doubled as a courthouse. Sir Thomas More (the *Man for All Seasons*), the gunpowder-plotting Guy Fawkes, and the obstreperous King Charles I, were all tried and sentenced to death there.

Even today the hall is stupendously large. During a 15th-

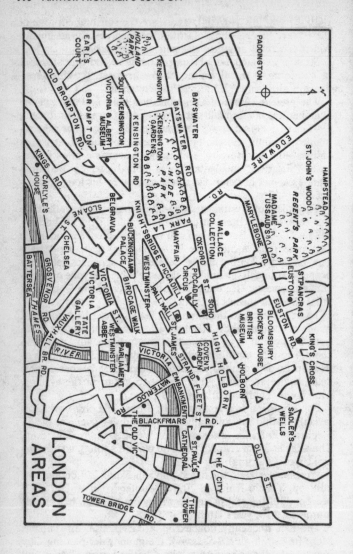

century flooding, rescuers actually rowed around it in boats.
Across the road from the hall rises—

WESTMINSTER ABBEY: With its square twin towers, superb archways, and Early English Gothic splendors, the abbey is one of the greatest examples of ecclesiastical architecture on earth. But it is far more than that—it is the shrine of a nation, symbol of everything Britain stood for and stands for, the edifice in which most of her rulers were crowned and many lie buried, along with the nameless bones of the Unknown Warrior.

King Edward the Confessor, whose bones lie there, rebuilt the abbey in 1065 just before his death. The next year, 1066, saw both the last of the Saxon kings, Harold who died at the Battle of Hastings, and the first of the Normans, William the Conqueror, crowned in the abbey. Little now remains of King Edward the Confessor's abbey, as rebuilding in the Gothic style was started by King Henry III and completed shortly before the dissolution of the monasteries by King Henry VIII, but it has remained the Coronation Church.

Next to Edward's tomb stands the Coronation Chair, with the ancient Scottish relic known as the Stone of Scone beneath the seat. Just before the present Queen Elizabeth's coronation, some Scottish nationalists kidnapped the stone, but were persuaded to return it in time for the crowning.

The entire abbey is crammed with such treasures, some truly priceless, some curious. There are the strange waxworks, showing the wax images of important personalities which were carried in their funeral processions, including Lord Nelson and the duchess of Richmond—who achieved immortality by posing as the figure of Britannia you see on British pennies.

There is Poet's Corner, with monuments to the British greats from Chaucer to Dylan Thomas and one American, Henry Wadsworth Longfellow. Also you'll find the graves of such familiars from U.S. history books as Major André and Gen. John Burgoyne.

A memorial stone for Sir Winston Churchill was laid in 1965. The abbey is open to visitors daily from 8 a.m. to 6 p.m. On Sunday visitors are admitted between the hours of service, but no organized touring groups are allowed. The Royal Chapels are closed to visitors on Sunday, but the nave, cloisters, and Exhibition of Treasures are always open. For information, telephone 222-5152.

Sun — 8   Matins   Evens   1030 1140 1500 1755 organ   18.30 Eve
Comm   extra

MADAME TUSSAUD'S: This building on Marylebone Road, at Baker Street Station (tel. 935-6861), is not so much a wax museum as an enclosed entertainment world. A weird, wonderful, moving, sometimes terrifying collage of exhibitions, panoramas, stage settings, snackbar, and gift shops, it manages to be most things to most people—most of the time.

Madame Tussaud learned her art in France, attended the court of Versailles, and personally took the death masks from the guillotined heads of Louis XVI and Marie Antoinette, which you'll find among the exhibits. Her original museum was founded in Paris in 1770 and moved to England in 1802. Since then, her exhibition has been imitated in every part of the world, but never with anything like the realism and imagination that marks the genuine Madame Tussaud's in London. The exhibition is a legion of famous and infamous personalities fashioned to uncanny likeness. Madame herself modeled the features of Benjamin Franklin, whom she met in Paris. All the rest—from George Washington to John F. Kennedy, from Mary Queen of Scots to Liza Minnelli—receive the same painstaking finish that makes you want to swear you can see them breathing.

The best-known portion is the **Chamber of Horrors.** There's an old, untrue legend that the management has a standing offer of £100 to anyone willing to spend a night there—alone. Even if this were true, we doubt if they'd be rushed by takers. Take a look and see why.

An entirely new Chamber of Horrors opened in 1980. There, in a kind of underground dungeon, stands a genuine gallows (from Hertford prison), with other instruments, and victims, of the death penalty. The shadowy presence of Jack the Ripper lurks in the gloom as you walk through a Victorian London street; George Joseph Smith can be seen with the tin bath in which he drowned the last of his three brides; and Christie conceals another murdered body behind his kitchen wall. Dr. Crippen, the poisoner, and his accomplice, Ethel le Neve, stand trial in the dock, and Mrs. Pearcey raises a poker to a crying baby in its pram. Many of their peers are displayed nearby.

For the first time, present-day criminals are portrayed within the confines of prison. As you walk among them, their eyes follow you—they move—or do they? Anyway, we'd forgo that £100.

Our favorite showpiece is the **Battle of Trafalgar,** fought out daily on the ground floor. You step right into the lower gun deck of Nelson's flagship *Victory,* and you're in the midst of it— among the half-naked sweating gun crews, the blinding white smoke, the acrid smell of gunpowder and burning riggings, the cracklings of flames, screams of the wounded, and deafening thunder of brass cannon (the gunfire on the sound track is the real thing). Then, with sounds of battle still in your ears, you descend into the gloom below the waterline, where Nelson—the victor—lies on his deathbed.

Next door to Madame Tussaud's is the copper-domed **Planetarium.** A huge, complex apparatus projects the night skies onto the dome, showing and dramatizing space movements and events by means of lighting effects, music, sounds, and narration. Programs (sample title: "Journey through the Night") are given regularly throughout the day from 11 a.m. to 4:30 p.m.

In a new exhibition, wax figures of Ptolemy, Copernicus, Galileo, Newton, and Einstein appear in imposing three-dimensional structures representing their revolutionary discoveries in astronomy. Exciting effects include sound, light, and projection.

Take the tube to Baker Street. Admission to Madame Tussaud's is £2.75 ($5.36) for adults, £1.55 ($3.02) for children under 16. The Planetarium costs £1.50 ($2.93) for adults, 95p ($1.85) for children under 16.

A combined ticket includes admission to both Madame Tussaud's and the Planetarium for £3.75 ($7.31) for adults, £2.15 ($4.19) for children under 16. Both places are closed only on Christmas Day.

ST. PAUL'S CATHEDRAL: Partly hidden by nondescript office buildings on Ludgate Hill, yet shining through by the sheer power of its beauty, stands London's largest and most famous church. Built by Sir Christopher Wren in place of the cathedral burned down during the Great Fire of 1666, St. Paul's represents the ultimate masterpiece of his genius.

The golden cross surmounting it is 365 feet above ground, the golden ball on which it rests measures 6 feet in diameter, and looks like a marble from below. Surrounding the interior of the dome is the **Whispering Gallery,** an acoustic marvel in which the faintest whisper can be clearly heard on the opposite side.

The interior of the church looks almost bare, yet houses a vast number of monuments linked with Britain's history. The duke of Wellington (of Waterloo fame) has his tomb there, as have Lord Nelson and Sir Christopher Wren. At the east end of the cathedral is the **American Memorial Chapel,** honoring the 28,000 U.S. servicemen who fell while based in Britain in World War II.

Take the tube to St. Paul's Station. The cathedral is open from 8 a.m. to 6 p.m. from mid-April to September. The crypt and galleries, including the Whispering Gallery, are open only from 10 a.m. to 4:15 p.m. The rest of the year, the cathedral's hours are from 8 a.m. to 5 p.m., the crypt and galleries from 10 a.m. to 3:15 p.m. Guided tours, lasting 1½ hours and including the crypt and the other parts of St. Paul's not normally open to the public, take place daily at 11 a.m. and 2 p.m. when the cathedral is open and cost £2.50 ($4.88) for adults, £1.25 ($2.44) for children.

KENSINGTON PALACE: Once the residence of British monarchs, Kensington Palace has not been the official home of reigning kings since the death of George II in 1760. The palace had been acquired less than 100 years before by William of Orange as an escape from the damp royal rooms along the Thames. Since the end of the 18th century, the palace has been a residence for various other members of the royal family. It was here in 1837 that a young Victoria was aroused from her sleep with the news that her uncle, William IV, had died and that she was now queen of England. Here, too, the late Queen Mary was born. In Victoria's bedroom and anteroom you can view a nostalgic collection of Victoriana, including some of her childhood toys and a fascinating old dollhouse.

In the apartments of Queen Mary II, wife of William III, you can admire a striking piece of furniture—a 17th-century writing cabinet inlaid with tortoise shell. Paintings from the Royal Collection literally line the walls of the apartments.

The palace is open to the public from 9 a.m. to 5 p.m. Monday through Saturday and from 1 to 5 p.m. on Sunday. Admission is 80p ($1.56) for adults and 40p (78¢) for children from April to September. From October to March, charges are lowered to 40p (78¢) for adults, 30p (39¢) for children. The palace gardens are open daily to the public for leisurely strolls around the Round Pond. One of the most famous sights here is the controversial Albert Memorial to Victoria's consort, one of the most lasting tributes to the questionable artistic taste of the Victorian era. For more information about the palace, telephone 937-9561.

THE COMMONWEALTH INSTITUTE: This vast, colorfully designed pavilion could be described as a miniature World's Fair. On Kensington High Street, W.8, it houses 60,000 square feet of exhibits illustrating the history, wildlife, art, scenery, and living styles of the countries belonging to the Commonwealth.

The list is pretty impressive—from Australia and Singapore to a cluster of West Indian nations and Zimbabwe, with about 40 other nations in between. The institute plays host to many cultural events, including dance, drama, music, visual art exhibitions, and festivals. Many of these events are free. Special services are offered to visiting groups (no charge is made), and there's a restaurant called Flags, a bar, and a coffeeshop. There's also a library and book/souvenir shop.

Take the tube to Kensington High Street, or bus 9 or 73. The institute is open six days a week from 10 a.m. to 5:30 p.m.; on Sunday from 2 to 5 p.m. Admission is free.

DICKENS'S HOUSE: From the mighty to the modest—at 48 Doughty St. in Bloomsbury stands the simple abode in which Charles Dickens wrote *Oliver Twist* and finished the *Pickwick Papers* (his American readers actually waited at the docks for the ships that brought in each new installment). The place is almost a shrine of Dickensiana, containing his study and reading desk, his manuscripts, and personal relics.

Take the tube to Russell Square. The house is open Monday to Saturday from 10 a.m. to 5 p.m. Admission is 75p ($1.46) for adults, 60p ($1.17) for students, 35p (68¢) for children.

BANQUETING HOUSE: The feasting chambers in the Palace of Whitehall are probably the most sumptuous eateries on earth. Unfortunately, you can't dine there unless you happen to be a visiting head of state. Designed by Inigo Jones and decorated with—among other things—original paintings by Rubens, these banqueting halls are dazzling enough to make you forget all about food. Among the historic events that took place here was the beheading of one of its most enthusiastic trenchermen, King Charles I. Also the restoration ceremony of Charles II, which took place here, marked the return of monarchy after Cromwell's brief Puritan-republican Commonwealth. It is closed on Monday from October to March and Good Friday. However, it is open Tuesday to Saturday from 10 a.m. to 5 p.m.; on Sunday from 2 to 5 p.m. Admission is 40p (78¢) for adults, 20p (39¢) for children under 16. For more information, telephone 212-4785. Tube: Trafalgar Square.

THE STOCK EXCHANGE: London has now replaced New York as the world's leading money mart, and investors watch its stock exchange with more or less bated breath. One of the world's most famous money centers—as well as the most modern—the trading floor gives you a glimpse of brokers and jobbers in furious action. Guides explain what the hustle and bustle means, and later you're shown a film in an adjoining cinema, which gives you an impressive insight into the world of high finance. The Visitors' Gallery entrance is in Old Broad Street, and the nearest underground station is Bank. Admission is free, and visiting hours are weekdays from 9:45 a.m. to 3 p.m.

This has been a very cursory glance at London's daytime attractions, skimming over only a fraction of what the city has to offer.

There are many more: the **Guildhall,** King Street, where the Corporation of London does its official banqueting: **Dr. Johnson's House,** 17 Gough Square, where the formidable Doc plus six secretaries composed his famous dictionary; the **Design Centre,** 28 Haymarket, where Britain displays her finest modern craftsmanship; the grim **Old Bailey,** Newgate Street, the central criminal court where you can watch the most dignified form of justice being meted out; the **Temple,** Middle Temple Lane, the hub of the country's legal system; **Carlyle's House,** 24 Cheyne Row, Chelsea, where the authoritative and opinionated author of the *French Revolution* lived for 49 years; the church of **St. Martin-in-the-Fields,** the **Bank of England,** the **Palace of St. James, Keats's House** . . . we could go on for the entire length of this book.

However, since daytime activities should include the outdoors, we've had to leave some space for . . .

THE PARKS OF LONDON: They deserve an entire chapter to themselves—the greatest, most wonderful system of "green lungs" of any large city on the globe. London's parklands are not as rigidly artificial as those of Paris, yet are maintained with a loving care and lavish artistry that puts their American equivalents to shame.

Above all, they've been kept safe from land-hungry building firms and city councils and still offer patches of real countryside right in the heart of the metropolis. Maybe there's something to be said for inviolate "royal" property, after all. Because that's what most of them are.

Largest of them—and one of the biggest in the world—is **Hyde Park**. With the adjoining Kensington Gardens, it covers 636 acres of central London; velvety lawns interspersed with ponds, flowerbeds, and trees. At the southeastern tip, near Marble Arch, is Speakers Corner, where any orator can declaim on any subject under the sun. He or she had better be good at it, however, as the audience is great on heckling and usually more sardonic than impressed. *on Sunday*

Hyde Park was once a favorite deer hunting ground of Henry VIII. Running through the width is a 41-acre lake known as the Serpentine, where you can row, sail model boats, or swim—providing you're not accustomed to Florida water temperatures. Rotten Row, a 1½-mile sand track, is reserved for horseback riding and on Sunday attracts some skilled equestriennes.

Kensington Gardens, blending with Hyde Park, border on the grounds of Kensington Palace. Kensington Gardens also contain the famous statue of Peter Pan, with the bronze rabbits which toddlers are always trying to kidnap. Unfortunately it also harbors the ghastly Albert Memorial—but you don't have to look.

East of Hyde Park, across Piccadilly, stretch **Green Park** and **St. James's Park,** forming an almost unbroken chain of landscaped beauty. This is an ideal area for picnics, and you'll find it hard to believe that it was once a festering piece of swamp near the leper hospital. There is a romantic lake, stocked with a variety of ducks and some surprising pelicans—descendants of the pair which the Russian ambassador presented to Charles II back in 1662.

Regents Park covers most of the district by that name, north of Baker Street and Marylebone Road. Designed by the 18th-century genius John Nash to surround a palace of the prince regent which never materialized, this is the most classically beautiful of London's parks. The core is a rose garden planted around a small lake alive with waterfowl and spanned by humped Japanese bridges. In early summer the rose perfume in the air is as heady as wine.

Regents Park also contains the Open Air Theater (see our entertainment chapter) and the London Zoo (see children's section). Also—as at all the local parks—there are hundreds of deckchairs on the lawns in which to sunbathe. The deckchair attendants who collect a small fee are mostly college students on summer vacation.

The hub of England's—and perhaps the world's—horticulture is the **Royal Botanic Gardens, Kew,** by the Thames southwest of the city. These splendid gardens have been a source of delight to visitors, scientific and otherwise, for more than 200 years. The staff deals annually with thousands of inquiries, covering every aspect of plant science.

Immense flowerbeds and equally gigantic hothouses grow species of shrubs, blooms, and trees from every part of the globe—from the Arctic Circle to tropical rain forests. Attractions vary with the seasons. There's also the permanent charm of Kew Palace, home of King George III and his queen, which was built in 1631 and is open for inspection.

Take the District Line tube to Kew Gardens. Admission to the gardens is 10p (20¢). Admission to the palace is 50p (98¢) for adults, 30p (59¢) for children. The palace is open from April to September, from 11 a.m. to 5:30 p.m. daily. The gardens may be visited all year from 10 a.m. till 7 p.m. Monday through Friday, till 8 p.m. weekends in summer. They are closed Christmas Day and New Year's Day.

Syon Park

This one has to be treated separately because the attractions here are multiple and varied. First of all the park contains the **Great Conservatory.** A world-famous structure, one of the wonders of the early 19th century, it houses spectacular displays of plants and cacti. In the West Wing you walk through a huge tropical aviary, aflutter and atwitter with multicolored birds. Beyond lies the Aquarium with rows of illuminated tanks of fish and reptiles.

Also on the grounds stands **Syon House,** the London home of the dukes of Northumberland, mostly of Adam design. The house was built in 1547. Most of the interior is from the 18th century. It's been compared to "standing right in the middle of a jewel box." Syon House was a monastery until suppressed by Henry VIII. It was in the original house that Catherine Howard, fifth wife of Henry VIII, was imprisoned prior to her beheading. The house may be visited from noon to 5 p.m. from Good Friday until the end of September. It is closed every other Friday but Good Friday, and every Saturday, because the duke is in residence during the summer. Adults are admitted to the gardens and house at a cost of £1.20 ($2.34), and children are charged 60p ($1.17).

Syon Park lies in Brentford, Middlesex, and was the creation of a gardening genius named Capability Brown. Take the train to Hammersmith, and bus 267. For information, telephone 01/560-0882.

Syon Park is also the site of **B. L. Heritage Motor Museum** and the **London Butterfly House,** diverse but most interesting collections in their own right.

Museums

London has more than 50 museums and exhibitions, and this count does not include the score of local museums run by suburban municipalities, nor the show houses connected with famous personalities, nor the various palaces and mansions which are museums in their own right.

If we tried to mention them all, we couldn't squeeze in much more than an expanded telephone listing for each. They include the **Percival David Foundation of Chinese Art,** the **National Maritime Museum,** a **Piano and Musical Museum,** the **Rotunda Museum** of firearms, the **Wellcome Institute of the History of Medicine,** the **Queen's Gallery,** showing Her Majesty's personal art collection, the **Jewish Museum,** the **Institute of Contemporary Arts.** . . . et cetera, et cetera, ad infinitum.

You can look up any of these if their specialty happens to coincide with yours. Here we have space only for a selection of the big leaguers, establishments which are internationally famous or unique or both. There are quite enough of these to keep you occupied for most of a rainy summer.

The Department of the Environment, 25 Savile Row, W.1 (tel. 734-6010), offers a **Season Ticket to History** to overseas visitors who write and enclose a fee. The ticket costs £6 ($11.70) for adults, £3 ($5.85) for children under 16, and is valid for one year. It is payable only by International Money Order (sterling only). With this ticket you're admitted to all sites under the care of the British government. These include Stonehenge, the Tower of London, the Banqueting House in the Palace of Whitehall, and Hampton Court Palace. The ticket can be purchased at the Department of the Environment (St), AMBH Store, Room 32, Building 1, Victoria Road, South Ruislip, Middlesex HA4 ONZ, or at any of the ancient monuments which have custodians.

If you're planning to tour the rest of the country, you might also be interested in an **Open to View** ticket which includes free admission to more than 500 properties in Great Britain. These include Edinburgh Castle, Churchill's Chartwell, Woburn Abbey, Hampton Court Palace, and Windsor Castle. The ticket sells for $19 (U.S.) for adults, $9.50 (U.S.) for children. In the United States, inquire at BritRail Travel International Inc., 630 Third Ave., New York, NY 10017; 333 North Michigan Ave., Chicago, IL 60601; or at 510 West 6th St., Los Angeles, CA 90014.

THE BRITISH MUSEUM: Great Russell Street, W.C.1. This immense museum, set in scholarly Bloomsbury, grew out of a private collection of manuscripts purchased in 1753 with the proceeds of a lottery. It grew and grew, fed by legacies, discoveries, and purchases until it became one of the world's largest museums, containing literally millions of objects.

It is utterly impossible to swallow this museum in one gulp, so to speak. You have to decide on a particular section, study it, then move on to another, preferably on another day.

The Egyptian room, for instance, contains the Rosetta Stone, whose discovery led to the deciphering of hieroglyphics; the Duveen Gallery houses the Elgin Marbles (a priceless series of sculptures from the frieze of the Parthenon); the Assyrian Transept has the legendary Black Obelisk, dating from around 860 B.C.

The treasure trove embraces the contents of Egyptian royal tombs (including bandaged mummies), the oldest land vehicle ever discovered (a Sumerian sledge), fabulous arrays of 2000-year-old jewelry, cosmetics, weapons, furniture and tools, Babylonian astronomical instruments, and winged lions that once guarded the palaces of ancient Nineveh.

The museum is open Monday to Saturday from 10 a.m. to 5 p.m.; on Sunday from 2:30 to 6 p.m. It is closed on Good Friday, December 24, 25, and 26, New Year's Day, and May 1. Admission is free.

THE BRITISH LIBRARY: In the east wing of the British Museum are the exhibition galleries of one of the world's great libraries. Strolling through the Manuscript Saloon with its notable collection of autographs, you'll see the signatures of Disraeli, Cromwell, Sir Walter Raleigh, Pepys, Newton, Wren, Milton, Fielding, Swift, Pope, and, of course, Dr. Johnson.

In the Grenville Library is the *Benedictional* of St. Ethelwold, bishop of Winchester (963-984 A.D.). It is considered one of the most outstanding medieval works of art in England.

In the King's Library is exhibited a First Folio (1623) of the tragedies and comedies of William Shakespeare. Displayed also is the *Gutenberg Bible,* the first substantial book ever printed with movable type. There is also a display of priceless Oriental manuscripts.

Other outstanding works in the galleries include the *Codex Sinaiticus,* a Greek version of the Bible written in the fourth century A.D.; Shakespeare's mortgage deed to the Blackfriars Gate House; Captain Scott's journals which tell of his attempt to reach the South Pole in his 1910–1912 expedition; and a memorandum of Admiral Nelson taken from his *Victory* logbook.

The *Lindisfarne Gospels* are a masterpiece, one of the great treasures from early Northumbria, written and illustrated about 698 A.D.

There is a letter that Nelson wrote to Lady Hamilton two days before he died in the Battle of Trafalgar.

Documents relating to Magna Carta include the Articles of the Barons, demands accepted by King John at Runnymede in June 1215. Also you'll find John's seal of white wax and two of the four surviving exemplifications of Magna Carta issued over his seal.

Opening times for the British Library are the same as for the British Museum. Admission is free.

NATIONAL GALLERY: Extending along the northwest side of Trafalgar Square, this stately neoclassical building (together with the **National Portrait Gallery** behind it) contains an unrivaled collection of paintings, covering every great European art school over seven centuries.

It does not represent modern painting (there are other galleries for that), but for sheer skill of display and arrangement it surpasses even its counterparts in Paris, New York, Madrid, and Amsterdam.

All of the British greats are gathered here—Turner, Constable, Hogarth, Gainsborough, Reynolds—and shown at their finest. The Rembrandts include two of his immortal self-portraits (at age 34 and 63), while Peter Paul Rubens has adjoining galleries.

The Italian Renaissance shows Leonardo da Vinci's *Virgin of the Rocks,* Titian's *Bacchus and Ariadne,* Giorgione's *Adoration of the Kings,* and unforgettable canvases by Bellini, Veronese, Botticelli, Tintoretto, and Michelangelo.

Then there are the Spanish giants: El Greco's *Agony in the Garden,* and portraits by Goya and Velázquez. The Flemish-Dutch school with Vermeer, Pieter de Hooch, two of the Brueghels, and van Eyck. An immense array of French works stretch into the late 19th-century impressionists and postimpressionists, with Degas, Renoir, Cézanne, Manet, and Monet.

A particularly charming item is the peep-show cabinet by Hoogstraten in one of the Dutch rooms . . . like spying through a key hole.

The museum is open Monday to Saturday from 10 a.m. to 6 p.m., on Sunday from 2 p.m. to 6 p.m.; admission is free. An excellent catalog, almost indispensable for touring the gallery, can be purchased upon entering. Tube: Charing Cross.

TATE GALLERY: Millbank, S.W.1. Fronting the Thames near Vauxhall Bridge in Pimlico, the Tate looks like a smaller and more classically graceful relation of the British Museum. Considered the most prestigious gallery in Britain by many, it houses the national collections covering traditional British art from the 16th century on, plus an international array of moderns.

The Tate thus falls into two separate portions—traditional and contemporary. Since it is very difficult to take in all the exhibits, we'd suggest that you concentrate on whichever section interests you more.

The older works include Hogarth, Turner, Blake, Stubbs, Gainsborough, Reynolds, and Constable; the moderns Picasso, Braque, Matisse, Beardsley, Salvador Dali, Munch, Chagall, Modigliani, Bacon . . . you name him, he's there.

There are also the sculptures, including masterpieces by Epstein, Henry Moore, Rodin, and Maillol (two examples are Rodin's *The Kiss*—attacked by the grubby-minded as "obscene" when first shown—and Marini's *Cavaliere,* equally well known).

The range of exhibits reaches into the realm of pop art and minimal art, and the most fascinating part of the gallery is frequently the "current exhibition."

Admission to the general gallery is free, but for special exhibitions a charge of approximately £1 ($1.95) is made. You can dine at the Tate Gallery Restaurant on such classic dishes as Hindle Wakes and Windsor veal pie. Meal prices are around £8.50

($16.58) to £9 ($17.55), although you can eat for less. It is essential to book a table.

Take the tube to Pimlico. Buses 77 and 88 stop outside. The gallery is open Monday to Saturday from 10 a.m. to 6 p.m.; on Sunday from 2 to 6 p.m.

VICTORIA AND ALBERT MUSEUM: Cromwell Road, S.W.7 (tel. 589-6371). Despite its ponderous label, this museum in South Kensington is one of the liveliest and most imaginative in London. It's named after the queen and her consort, but not run in their spirits.

The general theme here is the decorative arts—but the theme is adhered to in a pleasantly relaxed fashion.

There are, for instance, seven "cartoons" (in the artistic, non-Disney sense of the term) by Raphael, painted for Pope Leo in 1516. An entire room, domed and gilded like a church, is devoted to early medieval art in every aspect: from carvings of Christ in wood to silver candlesticks and ivory caskets.

Islamic art is represented by stunning carpets from Persia and intricate arabesques from every part of the Muslim world. In complete contrast, there are suites of English furniture and ornaments dating back to the 16th century, and a superb collection of portrait miniatures, including the one Hans Holbein made of Anne of Cleves for the benefit of Henry VIII, who was again casting around for a suitable wife.

Among the treasures displayed are the Eltenberg Reliquary (Rhenish, second half of the 12th century); the Early English Gloucester Candlestick; the Byzantine Veroli Casket; the Syon Cope, made in the early 14th century; a marble group, *Neptune with Triton,* by Bernini; and another rare portrait miniature by Hans Holbein the Younger of Mrs. Pemberton.

Take the tube to South Kensington. The museum is open Monday through Thursday, and Saturday from 10 a.m. to 5:50 p.m.; on Sunday from 2:30 to 5:50 p.m.

MUSEUM OF LONDON: At the corner of London Wall and Aldersgate Street, just north of St. Paul's, E.C.2, is a new museum, bringing the former collections of the Guildhall Museum of the City of London and the London Museum at Kensington Palace under one roof, plus much additional material. For the first time, visitors are able to trace the history of London from prehistoric times to the present through relics, costumes, household effects, maps, and models. The main galleries occupy about 50,000 square feet, on two floors surrounding an inner courtyard.

Exhibits are arranged so that visitors can begin and end their chronological stroll through 250,000 years at the main entrance to the museum. The pièce de résistance is the lord mayor's coach, built in 1757 and weighing in at three tons. The gilt and red, horse-drawn vehicle is like a fairytale coach. Visitors can also see the Great Fire of London in living color and sound; a Roman dinner, including the kitchen and utensils; a cell in Newgate Prison made famous by Charles Dickens; and, most amazing of all, a shop window with pre-World War II prices on the items.

The museum is open Tuesday through Saturday from 10 a.m. to 6 p.m.; on Sunday from 2 to 6 p.m. Admission is free.

IMPERIAL WAR MUSEUM: Lambeth Road, S.E.1. This, one of our few sights situated south of the Thames, is a block the size of an army barracks, greeting you with the two separate 15-inch guns from the battleships *Resolution* and *Ramillies*.

The large domed building, built in 1815, was the former Bethlem Royal Hospital for the insane, or "Bedlam." Perhaps this is the right place to house the relics of two World Wars. War may be lunacy, but there's no doubt that it has a macabre fascination all its own—like a rattlesnake among flower beds.

In the lower galleries are aircraft, all originals, from the mothlike wire-and-canvas Camels of 1917 to the cockpit section of the fuselage of a 1944 Lancaster bomber, and the experimental blob that was a Nazi jet fighter. Displayed are the machine guns with which they blasted each other out of the sky, from sleek Parabellums to bulky Vickers. And the photos—those incredibly young-looking aces with 30, 50, 90 kills to their credit.

For those with naval interests, the galleries also house an Italian "human torpedo," and a German one-man submarine.

The army is portrayed with almost every weapon from its arsenal. Rows of guns include the German antitank, that dreaded French 75, the stubby finger of death that was a heavy British howitzer. There are also grenades, every type of steel helmet and gas mask, mortar bombs, and an infinite variety of sub, light, heavy machine guns. And along the walls are photos of what these things can do to humans and their habitations.

In addition, the museum has an extensive art collection, which includes paintings by such well-known war artists as Paul Nash and Stanley Spencer.

The museum is reached by tube to Lambeth North or Elephant & Castle, and is open Monday to Saturday from 10 a.m. to 5:50 p.m.; on Sunday from 2 to 5:50 p.m. Public film shows take place on weekends at 3 p.m. and on certain weekdays during school holidays and on public holidays. Various special exhibitions are mounted at different times. The museum is closed on Good Friday, Christmas Eve, Christmas Day, Boxing Day, and New Year's Day.

COURTAULD INSTITUTE GALLERIES: Woburn Square, W.C.1, contain the following collections: The Lee collection of Old Masters; the Gambier-Perry Collection of Early Italian paintings and sculptures, ivories, majolica, and other works of art; the great collection of French impressionist and postimpressionist paintings (masterpieces by Monet, Manet, Degas, Renoir, Cézanne who is represented by eight paintings, Van Gogh, Gauguin) brought together by the late Samuel Courtauld; the Roger Fry collection of early 20th-century English and French painting; the Witt collection of old master drawings; the Spooner collection of English watercolors, and the recent bequest of the Princes Gate Collection of superb old master paintings and drawings, especially Rubens, Michelangelo, and Tiepolo. The galleries are air-conditioned, and the paintings are shown without glass. Times of opening: weekdays from 10 a.m. to 5 p.m.; on Sunday from 2 to 5 p.m. Admission is £1 ($1.95) for adults, 50p (98¢) for students or children. The galleries are near Euston Square, Goodge Street, and Russell Square underground stations.

WALLACE COLLECTION: Manchester Square, W.1 (tel. 935-0687). Gathered in a palatial setting (the modestly described "Town House" of the late Lady Wallace) are a contrasting array of artists and armaments. The former (mostly French) include Watteau, Boucher, Fragonard, and Greuze, as well as such classics as Frans Hals's *Laughing Cavalier* and Rembrandt's portrait of his son, *Titus.*

The arms, European and Oriental, are shown on the ground floor and are works of art in their own right. Superb inlaid suits of armor, some obviously more for parade than battle, are exhibited together with more businesslike swords, halberds, and magnificent Persian scimitars. The crescent sabres were reputedly tested by striking the blade against a stone, then examining it for even the minutest dent. If one was found, the sword was rejected.

The paintings of the Dutch, English, Spanish, and Italian schools are outstanding. The collection also contains one of the most important groups of French 18th-century works of art in the world, including furniture from a number of royal palaces, Sèvres porcelain, and gold boxes.

Take the tube to Bond Street or Baker Street or buses to Oxford Street (Selfridges). It is open weekdays from 10 a.m. to 5 p.m.; on Sunday from 2 to 5 p.m. Closed Christmas Eve, Christmas Day, Boxing Day, New Year's Day, Good Friday, and the first Monday in May

HAYWARD GALLERY: Opened by the queen in 1968, this gallery, South Bank, S.E.1, presents a changing program of major exhibitions, organized by the Arts Council of Great Britain. The gallery forms part of the **South Bank Arts Centre,** which also includes the Royal Festival Hall, the Queen Elizabeth Hall, the Purcell Room, the National Film Theatre, and the National Theatre. Admission to the gallery varies according to exhibitions, with cheap entry on Monday and Tuesday through Thursday evening. Opening hours are Monday through Thursday from 10 a.m. to 8 p.m.; on Friday and Saturday from 10 a.m. to 6 p.m.; on Sunday from noon to 6 p.m. The gallery is closed between exhibitions, so check the listings before crossing the Thames.

SCIENCE MUSEUM: Exhibition Road, S.W.7. This museum traces the development of both science and industry, particularly their application to everyday life—meaning that there's a minimum of "pure science."

Exhibits vary from models and facsimiles to the actual machines. You'll find Stephenson's original *Rocket,* the tiny locomotive that won a race against all competitors and thus became the world's prototype railroad engine. The earliest motor-propelled airplanes, a cavalcade of antique cars, steam engines from their crudest to their most refined form. Greatest fascinators are the working models of machinery (visitor-operable by push buttons). The most recent galleries are "Exploration" and "Printing and Paper." Take the tube to South Kensington or bus 14. The museum is open on weekdays from 10 a.m. to 6 p.m.; on Sunday from 2:30 to 6 p.m.

PUBLIC RECORD OFFICE MUSEUM: Chancery Lane, W.C.2 (tel. 405-0741). Contrary to its dry-as-dust title, this little museum can make your eyes pop. For here, under glass, are the last will and testament of Shakespeare, an astonishing letter from George Washington addressing King George III as "my great and good friend," the preaching license issued to John Bunyan (of *Pilgrim's Progress* fame), the signed confession of Guy Fawkes admitting his "Gunpowder Plot" to blow up Parliament, plus correspondence from Napoleon, Catherine the Great, and Marie Antoinette. Greatest treasure is the Domesday Book, the two volumes compiled as a result of a general survey of England ordered by William the Conqueror in 1085.

Take the tube to Chancery Lane. The museum is open Monday to Friday from 1 to 4 p.m. However, it is closed on public holidays.

WELLINGTON MUSEUM: Apsley House, 149 Piccadilly, W.1. This was the mansion of the duke of Wellington, one of Britain's greatest generals and one of her prime ministers. The "Iron Duke" defeated Napoleon at Waterloo, but later, for a short period, had to have iron shutters fitted to his windows as a protection from the mob, but his temporary unpopularity soon passed.

The house is crammed with art treasures, military mementos, and a regal china and porcelain collection. You can admire the duke's medals, the array of field marshal's batons, the battlefield orders, plus three original Velázquez paintings among a score of other greats. One of the features of the museum is a colossal marble statue of Napoleon in the vestibule. It was a present from the grateful King George IV.

Take the tube to Hyde Park Corner. It is open Tuesday, Wednesday, Thursday, and Saturday from 10 a.m. to 6 p.m.; on Sunday from 2:30 to 6 p.m. Admission is free.

NATIONAL ARMY MUSEUM: Royal Hospital Road, Chelsea, S.W.3. We may abhor war in all its forms, but there's no doubt that it makes for fascinating viewing. The National Army Museum occupies a building adjoining the Chelsea Hospital (a thoughtful combination, this, but not intentional).

Whereas the Imperial War Museum is concerned only with the two World Wars, the National Army Museum tells the colorful story of British armies from 1485. Here you'll find the rainbow uniforms British soldiers carried to every corner of the world and many of the items they brought back. Included is the regional flag of a Connecticut unit captured in the War of 1812. The skeleton of Napoleon's favorite charger is here, too. Displayed also is the actual battle order which—through its hazy wording—launched the lunatic and heroic Charge of the Light Brigade at Balaklava. In all, here are weapons, the gear, the colors and medals Britain's soldiers wore, and some of the magnificent paintings that glorified them.

Take the tube to Sloane Square. The museum is open weekdays from 10 a.m. to 5:30 p.m.; on Sunday from 2 p.m. to 5:30 p.m. It is closed on New Year's Day, Good Friday, December 24 through 26, and the May bank holiday.

NATIONAL POSTAL MUSEUM: King Edward Building, King Edward St. E.C.1. This museum attracts philatelists and even vaguely kindred spirits. Actually part of the Post Office, it features permanent exhibitions of the stamps of Great Britain and the world and special displays of stamps and postal history, changing every few months according to certain themes.

For example, a recent exhibition featured a history of postcards from 1870 to 1981. Exhibits ranged from official post office cards of Queen Victoria through picture postcards to modern post office pictorial cards.

The museum is open from 10 a.m. to 4:30 p.m. Monday through Thursday; to 4 p.m. on Friday. Admission is free. Take the tube to St. Paul's.

LONDON TRANSPORT MUSEUM: A collection of historic vehicles is displayed in a spendid Victorian building which formerly housed the Flower Market at Covent Garden, 39 Wellington St., W.C.2 (tel. 379-6344). The museum shows how London's transport system evolved, and exhibits include a representative collection of road vehicles, featuring a reconstruction of George Shillibeer's Omnibus of 1829.

Nearly two centuries of London's public transport are represented by these historic buses, trams, trolleybuses, locomotives, rolling stock, posters, models, working exhibits, and audio-visual displays. A steam locomotive which ran on the world's first underground railway, a knifeboard horse bus, the "B" type motor bus, London's first trolleybus, and the Feltham tram are of particular interest. One of the features of the exhibition is the number of participatory exhibits which are unique and popular with visitors. These allow visitors to operate the controls of a tube train, a tram, a bus, and full-size signaling equipment.

In addition, there's a London Transport Shop at the St. James's Park underground station (just beyond the ticket barrier, but still within the station complex; the station is on both the Circle and District lines).

The museum is open every day of the year except Christmas and Boxing Day from 10 a.m. to 6 p.m. Admission charges are £1.60 ($3.12) for adults, 80p ($1.56) for children.

Organized Tours

Given unlimited time, the stamina of a veteran jogger, plus permanent good weather, the ideal way to see the sights of London would, of course, be on foot. And there are sections—such as Soho and the actual City—which can't be seen any other way. At least not properly.

But if you have to budget your time and still want to get as much London as possible for your money, there's an enormous variety of touring arrangements at your fingertips, including by bus, by car, by boat.

We'll give you a quick rundown of a few sample tours. Each of them has several variations, expanding or telescoping the amount of sightseeing involved. If the particular tour we happen to mention doesn't quite suit your particular schedule, the organization involved will be glad to list alternatives.

LONDON'S WEST END AND THE CITY: If you want a detailed look at the city's sights, then **London Transport** offers two highly regarded conducted coach tours.

For a look at the West End, a three-hour tour is offered, passing Westminster Abbey (guided tour), Houses of Parliament, Horse Guards, Changing of the Guard at Buckingham Palace, Trafalgar Square, and Piccadilly Circus.

London Transport's other popular three-hour tour is of the City, and includes guided trips to the Tower of London and St. Paul's Cathedral. The fare for the Westminster and Changing of the Guard tour is £6 ($11.70) for adults and £4.50 ($8.78) for children under 14. For the City and Tower tour, the cost is £8 ($15.60) for adults, £5.50 ($10.73) for children under 14. The City tour leaves at 2 p.m. Monday through Saturday from

March to October. For about three months during the summer the tour also runs on Sunday.

These two tours are also combined to form the London Day tour, which costs £15 ($29.25) for adults and £11 ($21.45) for children under 14, including lunch.

The tours begin at Victoria Coach Station, at the corner of Buckingham Palace Road and Elizabeth Street. To reserve seats, go the London Transport Travel Information Centres at: St. James's Park, Piccadilly Circus, King's Cross, Euston, Oxford Circus, or Victoria tube station. Reservations cannot be made over the phone.

LONDON, MORNING AND AFTERNOON: Three separate tours are offered by all the major motorcoach companies, including **Evan Evans Tours Ltd.,** 7 York Way, N.1 (tel. 837-1280). They are made in the latest motorcoaches with fully reclining seats. The following two tours cost respectively: £4.50 ($8.78) for adults, and £3 ($5.85) for children; £5.80 ($11.31) for adults, and £3.50 ($6.83) for children.

The **Evan Evans Morning Tour** (every day) starts at 9:30 a.m. and returns at 12:30 p.m. It takes in Trafalgar Square, the Houses of Parliament, a visit to Westminster Abbey, Buckingham Palace, and (weather permitting) a look at the Changing of the Guard. The return drive is via **Hyde Park.**

The **Afternoon Tour** (every day) leaves at 2:15 p.m. It goes past the Law Courts and down Fleet Street, then visits St. Paul's Cathedral. Then it goes on through the center of the City for a guided trip through the Tower of London. On the return journey, it visits the Old Curiosity Shop, which served as model and inspiration for Dickens's book.

Evan Evans runs a full-day tour too, as well as jaunts out to Windsor, the Shakespeare Country, Oxford, Stonehenge, and many other destinations.

LONDON BY NIGHT: A selection of outings is offered by **Frames,** 11 Herbrand St., W.C.1 (tel. 837-3111).

A London Evening drive, departing from 11 Herbrand St., is featured throughout the year. April through October, it leaves every Monday and Friday at 7:30 p.m.; November through March, it leaves every Saturday at 7 p.m. The adult fare, including a stop at a Thames-side pub and an observation tour of London without interior visits, is £5.50 ($10.73).

Another evening tour includes a River Thames cruise which leaves Herbrand Street at 7 p.m. every Wednesday and Sunday, May through September. Adult fare is £15 ($29.25), inclusive of buffet supper.

CANAL CRUISES: The London canals, which were once major highways, are a world very few visitors get to see. Since the Festival of Britain in 1951, some of the traditional painted canal boats have been resurrected for Venetian-style trips through these waterways.

One of them is the *Jason,* which takes you on a 90-minute trip through the long Maida Hill tunnel under Edgware Road, through Regents Park, the Mosque, the Zoo, Lord Snowdon's Aviary, past the Pirate's Castle to Camden Lock and returns to Little Venice. The season begins Good Friday and lasts through September. During April and May, the boats run at 2 and 4 p.m. In June, July, August, and September, there is an additional trip during the afternoon, but always telephone first. Refreshments are served on all trips. The fare is £1.75 ($3.41) for adults, 85p ($1.66) for children.

To inquire about bookings, get in touch with **Jason's Trip,** opposite 60 Blomfield Rd., Little Venice, W.9 (tel. 286-3428). Advance booking is essential in season.

Also offered are one-way trips to Camden Lock on Saturday and Sunday to enable passengers to view the fascinating flea market and craft shops. Passengers may finish the trip there or return to Little Venice on a later boat.

LONDON BY CAR: This is the easiest way to do your sightseeing. Your driver/guide picks you up at your hotel (if requested, he or she will come within 30 minutes of your booking) and deposits you back at your front door at the end of your tour. Chances are the guide will be an Oxford or Cambridge student or graduate, an extrovert, and the most knowledgeable leader you've ever had anywhere. Prices quoted are per car, not per person, and the company supplies them in three sizes: small (1 to 2 passengers), medium (2 to 3 passengers), and large (4 to 5 passengers).

For a half-day tour of London a small car costs £35 ($68.25); a medium, £40 ($78); and a large vehicle, £47 ($91.65). If you're interested, get in touch with **Undergraduate Tours,** 6 South Molton St., W.1, off Oxford Street (tel. 629-5267). Tube: Bond Street.

The Homes of the Great

There is, unfortunately, no conducted tour catering to one of the most popular pursuits for visitors: viewing the birthplaces or working abodes of great historical figures. The map of London is peppered with them, but only the home of Charles Dickens gets included in the regular sightseeing jaunts.

Over the years the Historical Society has marked most of these sites with the characteristic blue and white plaques that now adorn thousands of London buildings, telling you which celebrity lived there, when, and for how long. But you still have to track them down for yourself. We have therefore compiled a selective list of some of the most sought-after sites, with the idea of saving you some leg work. But please remember that the following is merely a sampling from a register that could be as big as a city telephone book. We're bound to have left out somebody's particular hero, and for this we apologize and plead lack of space.

William Blake, artist and poet, 74 Broadwick St., Soho.

James Boswell, biographer of Dr. Johnson, 122 Great Portland St., W.1.

Elizabeth Barrett Browning, poet, 50 Wimpole St., W.1.

Robert Browning, poet, 19 Warwick Crescent, W.2.

Samuel Taylor Coleridge, poet, 71 Berners St., W.1.

Daniel Defoe, author of *Robinson Crusoe,* 95 Newington Church St., N.16

Benjamin Disraeli, statesman, 19 Curzon St., W.1.

George Eliot (actually Mary Ann Cross), novelist, 4 Cheyne Walk, S.W.3.

Benjamin Franklin, statesman and scientist, 36 Craven St., W.C.2.

Thomas Gainsborough, painter, 82 Pall Mall, S.W.1.

John Galsworthy, novelist, Grove Lodge, Hampstead.

Mahatma Gandhi, statesman, Kingsley Hall, Powis Road, E.3.

George Frederick Handel, composer, 25 Brook St., W.1.

John Keats, poet, Keats House, Keats Grove, N.W.3.

Rudyard Kipling, poet and novelist, 43 Villiers St., W.C.2.

Horatio Nelson, naval hero, 103 New Bond St., W.1.

Isaac Newton, scientist, 87 Jermyn St., W.1.

Florence Nightingale, pioneer of modern nursing, 10 South St., N.W.1.

Dante Gabriel Rossetti, artist and poet, 16 Cheyne Walk, Chelsea.

Percy Bysshe Shelley, poet, 20 Nelson Square, S.E.1.

Arthur Sullivan, composer (Gilbert and Sullivan), 58 Victoria St., S.W.1.

William Makepeace Thackeray, novelist, 36 Onslow Square, S.W.7.

John Wesley, founder of Methodism, 47 City Rd., Finsbury.

Richard Whittington, London's most celebrated mayor and cat owner, 20 College Hill, E.C.4.

Finally we have the astonishingly famous address of a man who never was: 221b Baker Street, as most people know, was the place where Sherlock Holmes occupied "furnished lodgings." But a startling number of folks never accepted the fact that the pipe-puffing sleuth didn't exist outside the imagination of his creator, Arthur Conan Doyle. The company actually on the premises, the Abbey National Building Society, has a special switchboard operator to answer the 60 or more calls a week from people wanting to become clients of the illustrious detective. She tells most of them that Mr. Holmes is currently out of the country and therefore can't take their case. "And Dr. Watson?"

"Oh, he is with him, naturally."

Along the Thames

There is a row of fascinating attractions lying on, across, and alongside the River Thames. All of London's history and development is linked with this winding ribbon of water. The Thames connects the city with the sea, from which it drew its wealth and its power. And for centuries the river was London's highway and main street.

Some of the bridges that span the Thames are household words. London Bridge, which—contrary to the nursery rhyme —has never "fallen down," but has been dismantled and shipped to the United States, ran from the Monument (a tall pillar commemorating the Great Fire of 1666) to Southwark Cathedral, parts of which date back to 1207.

Its neighbor to the east is the still-standing Tower Bridge, one of the city's most celebrated landmarks and possibly the most photographed and painted bridge on earth. Despite its curiously medieval appearance—two fortress-like towers facing each other —it was built in 1894 and is something of an engineering marvel. The main traffic deck, over which around 10,000 vehicles pass daily, consists of two giant leaves, each weighing 1000 tons. They are hinged at the ends and can be hoisted up, drawbridge fashion, to allow ships to pass through. The lifting operation, repeated several times a day, takes 1½ minutes and is well worth watching. Take the tube to Tower Hill, or bus 42 or 78.

The piece of river between the site of the old London Bridge and <u>Tower Bridge</u> marks the city end of the immense row of docks stretching 26 miles to the coast. Although most of them are no longer in use, collectively they have long been known as the Port of London.

But the Thames meant more to London than a port. It was also her chief commercial thoroughfare and a royal highway, the only regal one in the days of winding cobblestone streets. Every royal procession was undertaken by barge—gorgeously painted and gilded vessels, which you can still see at the National Maritime Museum in Greenwich. All important state prisoners were delivered to the Tower by water—it eliminated the chance of an ambush by their friends in one of those narrow, crooked alleys surrounding the fortress.

When Henry VIII had his country residence at Hampton Court, there was a constant stream of messenger boats shuttling between his other riverside palaces all the way to Greenwich. His illustrious daughter, Queen Elizabeth I, revved up the practice to such a degree that a contemporary chronicler complained he couldn't spit in the Thames for fear of hitting a royal craft.

The royal boats and much of the commercial traffic disappeared when the streets were widened enough for horse coaches to maintain a decent pace. But a trip up or down the river today will give you an entirely different view of London from the one you get from dry land. You'll see exactly how the city grew along and around the Thames and how many of her landmarks turn their faces toward the water. It's like Manhattan from a ferry.

There are pleasure launches sailing from Charing Cross and Westminster piers from April to September. You can take them upstream, past the Houses of Parliament, to Kew, Richmond, and Hampton Court. The downstream journey takes about 50 minutes and ends at Greenwich. For inquiries, telephone 930-2074.

SHIPS ON THE RIVER: For anyone with even the faintest nautical bent, there's a fascinating collection of craft permanently moored along the river. Each is totally different from the other and you could spend an entire day inspecting the contrasting marine worlds they represent.

The Maritime Trust's **Historic Ship Collection** is at St. Katharine's Dock, E.1 (tel. 730-0096), which has been for some years the home of the old *Nore* lightship. That vessel has now been joined by the Thames sailing barge *Cambria,* a schooner, an East Coast herring drifter, a steam coaster, the *Robin,* and now the R.R.S. *Discovery,* the royal research ship which was removed from its berth at Victoria Embankment.

The Trust provides walk-around guide leaflets to help visitors interpret what they see, and souvenirs are sold aboard the *Cambria.* While the *Discovery* is in dock, it will be possible to see restoration work carried out on her massive timbers by tradition-al shipwrights and riggers. There are plenty of places for a snack lunch or a pint in a pub, and, of course, the Tower of London is just across the road. The ships are open daily from 10 a.m. to 5 p.m. (until dusk in winter), charging an admission of £1.50 ($2.93) for adults, 50p (98¢) for children.

Permanently moored opposite the Tower of London lies H.M.S. *Belfast,* one of the largest cruisers ever constructed for the Royal Navy and the last of that fleet's "big gun" ships. After a hectic career in two wars (she was crippled by magnetic mines, fought the German battleships *Tirpitz* and *Scharnhorst,* bom-barded the Normandy beaches on D-Day, battled alongside the U.S. Seventh Fleet off Korea in 1951), *Belfast* was destined for the junkyard. Saved from such a fate by a public subscription that raised the necessary funds, she got her specially dug berth near Tower Bridge and now acts as a floating museum.

Almost the whole of the ship has been carefully restored and opened to the public. There are more than seven decks to be explored. The gun turrets, the bridge, the engine and boiler rooms, and dozens of other spaces are there for you to see. In addition, many exhibitions are provided.

Access is from London Bridge underground or by ferry from Tower Pier. H.M.S. *Belfast* (tel. 407-6434) is open every day from 11 a.m. to 5:50 p.m. (till 4:30 p.m. in winter). The admis-sion fee, which is put toward maintenance of the ship, is current-ly £1.80 ($3.51) for adults, half price for children. The address is Symon's Wharf, Vine Lane, Tooley Street, S.E.1.

TWO SHIPS AT GREENWICH: Two other ships, both world famous, are at Greenwich, four miles east of London. You can make the trip faster by train from Charing Cross, but the leisure-ly journey downriver from Westminster Pier is definitely more enjoyable. The river launch chugs you past a full-length view of the imposing County Hall—London's equivalent of City Hall—the Royal Festival Hall, and the immense Shell Centre.

Rising from the Victorian Embankment is a tall white stone obelisk, popularly misnamed "Cleopatra's Needle." The pillar is, in fact, far older than Cleopatra and once stood in front of the temple of Heliopolis, erected sometime between 1600 and 1500 B.C. In 1878 it was presented to Britain by the khedive of Egypt and brought here in a ship specially fitted for the purpose. On its reerection by the Thames, the Victorians couldn't resist adding some contemporary objects to the interior of the foundation stone. To wit: a Bible, a straight razor, several morning newspapers, a baby's feeding bottle, and a box of hairpins, presumably to impress whoever would excavate the site with the splendors of 19th-century civilization.

At Greenwich Pier, now in permanent drydock, lies the last and ultimate word on sailpower—the *Cutty Sark*. Named after the witch in Robert Burn's poem "Tam o'Shanter," she was the greatest of the breed of clipper ships which carried tea from China and wool from Australia in the most exciting ocean races ever sailed. Her record stood at a then unsurpassed 363 miles in 24 hours.

Launched in Scotland in 1869, the sleek, black three-master represented the final fighting run of canvas against steam. And although the age of the clippers was brief, they did outpace the steamers as long as there was wind to fill their billowing mountain of sheets.

On board the *Cutty Sark,* you'll find a museum devoted to clipper lore, plus all the fittings that made her the fastest thing at sea.

The admission is 80p ($1.56) for adults, 40p (78¢) for children. The vessel may be boarded weekdays from 11 a.m. to 6 p.m. and on Sunday from 2:30 to 6 p.m. It closes at 5 p.m. in winter.

Next to the clipper—and looking like a sardine beside a shark—lies the equally famous *Gipsy Moth IV*. This, in case you don't remember, was the ridiculously tiny sailing craft in which Sir Francis Chichester circumnavigated the globe—solo! You can go on board and marvel at the sheer minuteness of the vessel in which the gray-haired old seadog made his incredible 119-day journey. His chief worry—or so he claimed—was running out of ale before he reached land. The admission to go aboard is 25p (49¢) for adults, 15p (29¢) for children under the age of 14. The *Gipsy* keeps the same hours as the *Cutty Sark,* and is usually closed on Friday.

The Sporting Scene

London can be as exciting for sports enthusiasts as for theater fans. That is, if they happen to be *British* sports enthusiasts.

The trouble is that Britain's two main sporting obsessions— soccer and cricket—are respectively unknown and incomprehensible to the average American visitor.

Soccer is the national winter sport. The teams which set British pulses racing—Chelsea, Leyton Orient, Tottenham Hotspurs —sound like so many brands of cheese spread to a Statesider.

In summer there is cricket, played at Lord's or Oval Cricket Ground in London. During the international test matches between Britain and Australia, the West Indies or India (equivalent in importance to the World Series), the country goes into a state of collective trance, hanging glassy-eyed on every ball as described over the radio or TV.

Cricket is a game of infinite skill and subtlety and—to the initiate—a source of unending delight and occasional bursts of high passion. (The closest England and Australia ever came to going to war against each other was during the so-called body-line cricket scandal of the 1930s.) But it is not what you might call a fast game. Decisions fall in a matter of hours (unless postponed by rain) and our average American may be slumbering peacefully by the time the last embattled wicket topples.

Luckily, there are a number of sports and events that can be shared by all transatlantic visitors.

At the **All England Lawn Tennis & Croquet Club** at Wimbledon, you can see some of the world's greatest tennis players in action. The annual championship Fortnight comprises the last week in June and the first in July, with matches lasting from 2 p.m. till dark. Although the British founded the All England Lawn Tennis & Croquet Club back in 1877, they now rarely manage to win against the Australian and American late-comers to the game. Take the tube to Southfields Station, then a special bus from there. The gates open at noon.

Attracting all equestrians is the annual **Horse of the Year Show** in the Wembley Arena. This takes place in October and consists of six days of jumping, harness driving, mounted games, and school riding of the highest order.

The **Royal International Horse Show,** one of the greatest equestrian events in the world, is held at Wembley Arena the third week of July. High jumping, riding teams, men's and women's championships, and team competitions make up the program. Matinees are at 2 p.m., evening shows at 7 p.m. Take the tube to Wembley Park.

Within easy reach of central London, there are horse-racing tracks at **Kempton Park, Sandown Park,** and the most famous of them all, **Epsom** where the Derby is the main feature of the summer meeting. Entrance to the courses for a day's racing can be as little as £1.50 ($2.93), but, of course, you pay more for a seat in the grandstand or on one of the most prestigious racedays. There is not racing every weekend, so you should telephone **United Racecourses** at Epsom (tel. 03727/26311) for information of the next meeting. You can drive yourself or, if you want to travel by rail, phone 928-5100 in London for details of train services.

London's stadium for greyhound and speedway racing is the giant **White City,** Wood Lane, W.12, which can accommodate 50,000 spectators. Check the newspapers for the current event, then take the tube to White City Station.

Finally, we come to a spectacle for which it is difficult to find a comprehensive tag. The **Royal Tournament,** which takes place in mid-July for a two-week run. It's one of London's longest running shows. For more than 100 years, this military tattoo has been thrilling the public with its special blend of color, pageantry, and seat-edge excitement. It's a cross between a military and a sporting display put on by the three British services, plus foreign visiting displays.

The show includes the massed bands of the Royal Air Force presenting stirring music, the Royal Navy field gun competition, the Royal Air Force with their dogs, the Royal Marines in action, the King's Troop Royal Horse Artillery, the Red Caps with their act combining motorcycles, and many other spectacular acts.

There are two performances daily, at 2:30 and 7:30 p.m., at Earl's Court, Warwick Road, S.W.5. There are no performances on Sunday and no matinees on Monday. Seats cost from £2 ($3.90) upward. For tickets and other information, write to the Royal Tournament, Horse Guards, Whitehall, London S.W.1., U.K. (tel. 930-6000.)

Chapter VI

THE THEATERS OF LONDON

LONDON TODAY IS THE theatrical capital of the world by any criterion you want to apply. It shows both more and better plays than any other city, enjoys a standard of acting unequalled anywhere, and holds a wide lead in both the traditional and the experimental forms of stagecraft.

This is partly, but only partly, due to a theatrical tradition going back 400 years. The city's first theater, in the Fields at Shoreditch, opened in 1576 under the patronage of Queen Elizabeth I. The following year saw the debut of the Curtain, and 1598 the most famous of all—the Globe. This was Shakespeare's and Marlowe's stage, and as long as the shrewd, tough, and efficient Queen Bess ruled England, the legitimate theater held its own against such rival attractions as bullbaiting, cockfighting, and public executions.

But from then on, the nation's dramatic glory suffered periodic declines which almost extinguished it—the first under Cromwell's official puritanism which banned *all* stage performances (along with the celebration of Christmas) as "heathenish and un-Godly."

In more recent times, the causes lay in the social and moral rigidity Britain had acquired along with her Empire. At the turn of our century, France became the country with the best theater. In the 1920s Germany took the lead. During the '30s the focus shifted to the United States, while England floundered in the most dismal theatrical shallows of her history—and turned out her worst movies to boot.

This doesn't mean that the country at any time lacked great playwrights, actors, or directors. But her stage and film craft had become largely removed from real life. It tended to reflect little beyond the stilted formalism of a thin upper-middle crust who went to the theater to admire their own petrified reflection in a kind of polite distortion mirror.

Attempts in earthier directions were rigorously sat upon by an official called the lord chamberlain, who had unlimited powers of censorship and used them like the proverbial "Little Old Lady from Dubuque." This Mandarin figure was responsible for the creation of London's theater clubs, which—being private rather than public stages—were outside his jurisdiction. One such club was specially founded to present Arthur Miller's *A View from the Bridge* to English audiences, who would have been deprived of this masterpiece otherwise.

The Great Thaw occurred some time during the mid-1950s, although it was more like a volcanic eruption. The pressures of talent, creativeness, and expressive urges had been building up ever since the war. Now they broke loose in a veritable lava stream of stage and film productions, which flooded the globe, swept away most of London's dusty theatrical mores, and swung open the gates of a second Elizabethan dramatic era.

Britain hasn't looked back since. The tide is still running, originality still rampant. No one can say for how long. So our advice is to use your stay in London for a theater orgy—you may never get opportunities like this again.

London's live stage presents a unique combination of variety, accessibility, and economy. No other city anywhere can currently boast a similar trio of advantages.

Variety is assured by the sheer number of productions on view, London currently has more than 35 active theaters—and this figure does not include opera, ballet, amateur stages, or the semiprivate theater clubs mentioned earlier.

Accessibility, of course, is linked with the enormously wide choice available to patrons. With the exception of one or two smash hits, for which advance booking is advisable, you can literally walk up to any box office five minutes before the opening curtain and buy whatever seat you fancy. Compare this to the woes of Broadway, which features only two types of plays—those that flop and those you can't get into. Strangely enough, things are much tighter in the movie realm. You frequently have to book ahead or "queue up" for major film releases.

Finally, there's economy. London theater prices are—by U.S. standards—almost unbelievably cheap. The **Leicester Square Ticket Booth,** Leicester Square, W.C.2, sells theater tickets on the day of a performance for half price, plus a 50p (98¢) service charge. It is open from noon to 2 p.m. for matinee performances and from 2:30 to 6:30 p.m. for evening performances. The staff there has a wide range of seats available. Ask for the show you want to see, and they will offer you alternatives if they don't have tickets available. Obviously, tickets for "hits" are not available often. There is a long queue, but it moves quickly, and it's well worth the effort if you want to take in a lot of theater when you're in London. Saving money is important, naturally. Many of the shows for which tickets are available are well displayed at the booth, so you can make up your mind on what to see as you wait in the queue.

Apart from this, many London theaters offer additional trimmings in the shape of licensed bars on the premises and hot coffee brought to your seat during intermissions.

London theaters generally start and finish earlier than their American cousins. Evening performances are between 7:30 and 8:30, matinees (Wednesday and Thursday) are at 2:40, Saturday at 5:45. For a complete listing of live shows and performance times, pick up the *Entertainment Guide* available gratis in most hotel lobbies, or pay 40p (78¢) for a handy weekly publication called *What's On In London*.

The Theaters

Since it is quite impossible to describe all of London's live theaters in this space, we'll just pick out a few choice selections for your benefit. Don't forget—these are merely gleanings from a treasure trove:

ADELPHI: The Strand, W.C.2 (tel. 836-7611). This theater offers light comedies and musicals, mainly, but not exclusively. Performances are at 7:30 p.m. on weeknights, 4 p.m. and 7:45 p.m. on Saturday. Matinees are on Thursday at 3 p.m. Take the tube to Trafalgar Square.

DRURY LANE, THEATRE ROYAL: W.C.2. (tel. 836-8108). This is one of the oldest and most prestigious establishments in town, crammed with traditions, not all of them venerable. Nell Gwynne, the rough-tongued, well-stacked Cockney wench who became King Charles's mistress, used to have her orange pitch under the long colonnade in front. Nearly every star of the London stage heaven played here at some time. It has a wide-open repertoire, but leans toward musicals. Shows are at 8 p.m. Monday to Saturday, with matinees at 3 p.m. on Wednesday and

Saturday. Take the tube to Covent Garden. Guided tours of this historic theater may be arranged through George Hoare, general manager.

FORTUNE: Russell Street, W.C.2 (tel. 836-2238). Like the Drury Lane, this is part of the ancient and odd theater concentration around Covent Garden. It offers general plays and occasional revues. Shows are at 8 p.m. on weeknights, 5:30 and 8:30 p.m. on Saturday.

GLOBE: Shaftesbury Avenue, W.1 (tel. 437-1592). Only a name connection with Shakespeare's playhouse (which was down by the Thames), this is one of a row of theaters in the same street, leading off Piccadilly Circus. Dramas and comedies are presented. Check the daily press for shows and times of performances. Take the tube to Piccadilly Circus.

HER MAJESTY'S: Haymarket, W.1 (tel. 930-6606). Big, plush, and ornate, this is one of London's traditional homes for top musicals, standing in what used to be *the* street for mustached "toffs" and scarlet women. Shows weeknights are at 8 p.m. and cheaper matinees are presented Wednesday and Saturday at 3 p.m. Take the tube to Piccadilly Circus.

MERMAID: Puddle Dock, E.C.4 (tel. 236-5568). Although this is one of London's newest theaters (reopened 1981), it stands on hallowed stage ground. Shakespeare's Globe rose on the opposite Bankside, and he bought a house in an adjoining alley for £140. The Mermaid is an entire complex: two riverside restaurants, a coffee bar in the foyer, two other bars adjacent, and a bookstall selling Mermaid souvenirs. Shows range from classics to comedies and musicals. After you take the tube to Blackfriars Station, it's one minute's walk to the right.

NATIONAL THEATRE: South Bank, S.E.1 (tel. 928-2252). This is the home of Britain's National Theatre, one of the greatest stage companies on earth. Not one, but three theaters, each radically different in design, all under the same roof, offer a wide mixture of plays: new works; revivals of ancient and modern classics; contemporary foreign plays; experimental drama. The theaters are the Olivier, the Lyttelton, and the Cottesloe. The

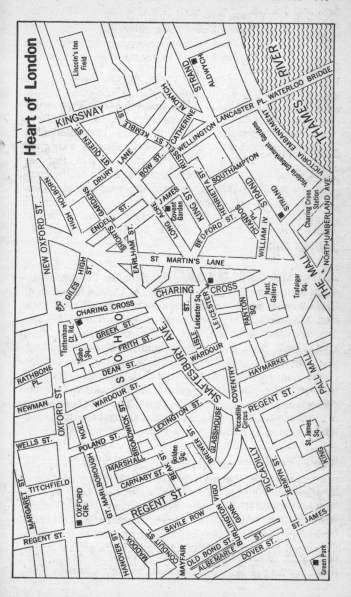

building, with its bars, restaurant, buffets, foyers, river walks and terraces, is a full-time theater center presenting—alongside its main work—short, early-evening performances, poetry, live foyer music, and exhibitions. It's more than worth the tube ride to Waterloo Station.

OPEN AIR: Regents Park, N.W.1 (tel. 486-2431). As the name indicates, this is an outdoor theater, right in the center of Regents Park. The setting is enchanting, and the longest theater bar in London provides both drink and food. Performances are given in June, July, and August only, evenings at 7:45 p.m., matinees on Wednesday, Thursday, and Saturday at 2:30 p.m. Presentations are mainly Shakespeare, usually in period costume. Also, Sunday concerts are presented. Both seating and acoustics are excellent. If it rains, you're given tickets for another performance. Prices are from £2 ($3.90) to £6 ($11.70). Nearest tube is Baker Street.

ROYAL SHAKESPEARE COMPANY: Barbican Theatre, Barbican Centre in the City (tel. 628-8795). The London repertoire of the company, whose headquarters are in Stratford-upon-Avon (tel. Stratford 292271), doesn't rely on the Bard alone, but also presents other first-raters, such as Ben Jonson, Brecht, Ibsen, and O'Neill. It has its own magnificent playhouse in Stratford, but performs in London as well, at its magnificent new London home. The program is changeable, with up to three or four plays in a week, so consult the newspapers. Take the tube to Barbican, Moorgate, Liverpool Street, or St. Paul's. The company also has a studio theater, the Pit, in the Barbican, showing new works and classics.

ROYAL COURT: Sloane Square, Chelsea, S.W.1 (tel. 730-1745). This theater ushered in the New Wave of British stagecraft when it presented John Osborne's (then) sensational *Look Back in Anger* in 1956. It now houses twin companies. The "Theatre Upstairs"—60 steps up—is a theater concentrating on experimental plays, open to the public. The main theater downstairs features dramas and comedies and is open to the general public. Shows are at 8 p.m. weeknights, 5 and 8:30 p.m. on Saturday. Take the tube to Sloane Square.

Vaudeville

Virtually extinct in America, the variety stage not only lives but flourishes in London. Streamlined and updated, it has dropped most of the corn and preserved all of the excitement of the old vaudeville fare.

Top house in the field (not merely in London but in the world) is the **Palladium,** Argyle Street, W.1 (tel. 437-7373). It's hard to capsule the prestige of this establishment in a paragraph. Performers from Britain, Europe, and America consider that they have "arrived" when they've appeared here. Highlight of the season is the "Royal Command Performance" held before the queen, which includes an introduction of the artists to Her Majesty. It's amazing to watch hardboiled showbiz champions moved close to tears after receiving the royal handshake.

The Palladium has starred aces such as Frank Sinatra, Shirley MacLaine, Andy Williams, Perry Como, Julie Andrews, Tom Jones, Sammy Davis, Jr., and so on, like the Milky Way of stardom. Second-line program attractions are likely to include, say, "Los Paraguayos" and the Ukrainian Cossack Ensemble. Ticket prices, usually in the £2.50 ($4.88) to £8 ($15.60) range, and showtimes vary. Tube: Oxford Circus.

Variety on a somewhat more modest scale is the keynote at the **Victoria Palace,** Victoria Street, S.W.1 (tel. 834-1317). Near Victoria Station, it presents comedy, variety, and light entertainment, all at popular prices.

Music Hall

So far we have deliberately avoided the theater clubs. First because the abolition of the lord chamberlain's censorship has made them redundant, and second because of the (very minor) formalities involved in joining them.

But there is one which is simply too enjoyable to miss. That is the **Players Theatre,** Villiers Street, Strand (tel. 839-1134).

Tucked away behind Charing Cross Station, this playhouse presents Victorian music hall. Not takeoffs or imitations, but the real thing, authentic from the costumes to the backdrops. And the effect on modern, allegedly blasé, audiences is overwhelming. This might just possibly be your best night in London.

The entire setting is delightful. You can start by having a sumptuously old-fashioned dinner in the adjoining restaurant, which forms part of the club. Or get snacks (liquid or biteable) served at your table during the show. The stage is a piece of pure

Pub Theater

In 1969 a "new" movement developed in London's theatrical world, which was delightful but certainly not new in terms of stage history. Live theater penetrated the pubs. Within a year the movement gathered such momentum that a string of pubs began to display regular playbills alongside their beer ads. Saloon regulars who normally wouldn't have dreamt of theater going, picked up their pint mugs and slipped into the auditorium, and frequently became devoted fans and critics.

There is no uniformity about either the material presented or the premises involved. The former ranges from wildly experimental efforts by unknown young playwrights to established classics. The latter from elaborately decorated and lit stages to pretty primitive backroom assemblies. But that's part of the movement's peculiar charm. You never know what you're going to get, the monetary risk is minimal— seat prices average around 50p (98¢) for students, £1.50 ($2.93) for adults—and you don't even have to buy a drink to see the show. Some pubs feature lunchtime performances only, others put on another, often different, play at night as well. Phone beforehand and find out what's on and when. It's an experience you shouldn't miss, since you're not likely to find it anywhere else.

The line-up of public houses doubling as theaters changes frequently and abruptly: at this writing some of the most interesting examples are:

Orange Tree, 45 Kew Rd., Richmond (tel. 940-3633). A veteran among pub theaters, the Orange Tree proved immensely popular with the locals and soon began to draw patrons from all over London. It began purely as a lunchtime venture, but is now putting on evening performances as well. The tube runs on a direct line to Richmond.

The Bush Theatre, Shepherds Bush Green, W.12 (tel. 743-3388). This theater operates above the Bush Hotel Pub, reached by a staircase from the bar. One of the most innovative theaters in the field of contemporary drama, it presents solely new works by the best contemporary writers. The theater is fully air-conditioned. Tickets cost £2.80 ($5.46). Membership at an annual subscription of 40p (78¢) entitles you to bring three guests to any performance. Tube: Shepherds Bush.

Victorian, but the emcee—here called the "chairman"—is in a class quite his own. He introduces each act, tells anecdotes, keeps up a running patter of remarks and asides to and about the audience, trades insults with the patrons (and he takes as good as he gives), and ceremonially welcomes "Visitors from the Colonies"—meaning Americans, Canadians, Australians, and suchlike.

The acts are the immortal music hall melodies and lyrics—and you'll be surprised at their immortality. You'll know at least half of them, except that you probably didn't suspect them of being 90 or so years old.

You can join the Players by filling out a form and paying a temporary membership fee of £6 ($11.70) for one week, £12 ($23.40) quarterly. Then you have to wait 48 hours for the membership to become effective. Incidentally, memberships must be paid in sterling. After that *you* go in free, but you have to pay £3.25 ($6.34) for each guest you bring. Dinner, from £8 ($15.60), is served in the restaurant from 6:45 p.m. (book a table ahead). The show starts nightly at 8:30 p.m. There's a new program every fortnight, and after the performance the stage is cleared for dancing until midnight.

If you don't want to go through the formalities of membership, you can enjoy music-hall-type shows at **Aba Daba,** 328 Gray's Inn Rd., W.C.1 (tel. 722-5395), near the King's Cross underground station. Unlike Players, Aba Daba is not a private club, and its admission charges to the general public are £3.50 ($6.83) per person. In winter the club is especially popular, and reservations are suggested. It's more like a pub than a supper club, although in addition to drinks from its well-stocked bar, you can also order typically British meals. Decorated in red, Aba Daba seats more than a hundred guests at tiny tables. On show nights about half a dozen performers entertain, exchanging banter with members of the audience. This music hall presents shows on Thursday, Friday, and Saturday nights.

Movies

The films shown in London are much like those you'd see in any large American city, but with a stronger international flavor. Screenings, however, are not continuous and the last performances start around 8 p.m., so you'd better consult a newspaper for the exact showtimes. Prices vary according to seats—all of them considerably cheaper than at home. And don't forget that movie theaters are called cinemas.

London has a dozen or so real movie palaces in the old meaning of the term, gigantic citadels with plush loges, grand buffets, and triple curtains. But her prime piece is the kind of ultra-modern movie mansion you might expect to find in Hollywood —but won't.

The **Cinecenta** is a streamlined, black-and-white block in Panton Street, off Leicester Square, S.W.1 (tel. 930-0631), housing four superb theaters under one roof. They share one sleekly plush lobby, but each runs a separate program, always including at least one European film. Tube: Leicester Square.

Opera and Ballet

You might be getting a little tired of superlatives, but in this particular chapter it's unavoidable. For in the operatic and ballet field as well as in straight theater, the British currently lead the world.

In a way this is rather strange, because historically neither singing nor dancing has been a particular English talent. But over the past couple of decades (and with a strong influx of foreigners), both have developed in an almost breathtaking fashion.

The central shrine is the **Royal Opera House**, a classical building in Bow Street, actually the northeast corner of Covent Garden. Covent Garden was London's first square, originally laid out by Inigo Jones as a residential piazza. Until a few years ago the whole area was a thriving fruit and vegetable market, originally started by the nuns selling surplus stocks from their convent garden. In the 16th century, the area became fashionable to live in and was soon to become one of the centers of London nightlife. The first theater was built on the present site in 1732. The existing opera house, one of the most beautiful theaters in Europe, was built in 1858 and is now the home of the Royal Opera and Royal Ballet, the leading international opera and ballet companies. Newspapers give full details of performances. Ticket prices vary according to presentations, from £5 ($9.75) to £31 ($60.45). For seat reservations, telephone 240-1066.

The **Barbican Centre**, The Barbican, in the city, E.C.2, is newly built and reckoned to be Western Europe's largest art and exhibition center. It was created to make a perfect setting in which to enjoy good music and theater from comfortable and roomy seating.

The theater is now the home of the Royal Shakespeare Company which, of course, performs a wide range of works other than the plays of the immortal Bard. The Concert Hall is the permanent home of the London Symphony Orchestra and host to visiting players.

There are often lunchtime concerts when the admission is £2.50 ($4.88) for the 45 minutes or so. Otherwise, seats are priced from £2.80 ($5.46) to £9 ($17.55) for the evening performances. Matinees in the theater start at £1.75 ($3.41) to £7 ($13.65), and in the evening seats are from £1.75 ($3.41) to £9 ($17.55).

The following numbers will be useful—box office for seats for concerts and theaters (tel. 628-8795); 24-hour information service on performances is provided by calling 928-9760 for concerts and 628-2295 for theaters.

There are a number of bars and a self-service café and wine bar which are open from 9 a.m. until 10:30 p.m. Monday to Saturday (and from noon to 10:30 p.m. on Sunday). Called the Waterside Café, it has views over the artificial lake. In good weather patrons can sit on the terrace in the open air.

The main restaurant, the Cut Above, also overlooks the lake. It's a more formal place with a Carvery which is open from noon to 3 p.m. and from 6 p.m. until last orders at half an hour after the end of a performance. The cost of a meal where you can carve as much or as little as you want from the succulent joints of meat is £8.50 ($16.58). For table reservations, phone 588-3008.

English National Opera (formerly Sadler's Wells), London Coliseum, St. Martin's Lane, W.C.2 (tel. 836-3161), features a wide range of opera—from Wagner and Verdi to Berlioz and Richard Strauss—usually in English. Ticket prices start as low as £2 ($3.90). Upper Circle seats, which are more preferable, begin at £3.50 ($6.83).

The **Sadler's Wells Theatre** (tel. 837-1672) is on Rosebery Avenue, E.C.1. Apart from its resident company, Sadler's Wells Royal Ballet, it also plays host to other outstanding British and international opera, ballet, and dance companies. Prices fluctuate from £1.50 ($2.93) to £11 ($21.45). Take the underground to Angel Station (Northern Line). The theater is a three-minute walk from the stop. By bus, take no. 19 or 38 from Piccadilly; no. 19, 38, or 172 from Holborn. To the Angel, take no. 4, 30, 43, 73, 104, 214, 277, or 279. From Waterloo, you can take bus no. 171 or 188 and change at Holborn.

The **Royal Festival Hall** (for a description, see further on) features a succession of top foreign dance groups. Check your *Entertainment Guide* for current attractions. Among past presentations there have been the Bolshoi and Kirov Companies, Ballet Folklorico de México, D'Oyly Carte Opera Company, the Mazowsze Dance Company of Poland, and London Festival Ballet. But for nine months of the year, the Royal Festival is a concert hall with a different concert every night of the week. Tickets cost from £1 ($1.95) to £4 ($7.80).

The **Holland Park Court Theatre** is a charming open-air stage in Holland Park, W.8, close to the Commonwealth Institute, and it really has the air of a court theater in some Renaissance palace yard. There is a weekly program in June and July of opera and drama. Shows begin at 8 p.m. nightly, at 2:30 p.m. for Saturday matinees. For program inquiries and ticket prices, telephone 633-1707, although be warned that no advance bookings are accepted. Tube: Kensington High Street.

Concerts

London's oldest established concert auditorium is the Royal Albert Hall, Kensington Gore, S.W.7 (tel. 589-8212). Dating back to 1871, the building is a fine example of Victorian architecture on a grand scale. The design of the auditorium makes it equally suitable for meetings, conferences, tennis and badminton tournaments, boxing, wrestling, and a multitude of other activities apart from its renowned musical events. During the eight-week season of BBC Promenade concerts held each summer, up to 7000 people gather together under this great dome and yet there is still an intimate atmosphere that has to be experienced to be appreciated. Ticket prices vary with the programs. Tube: South Kensington, Kensington High Street, or Knightsbridge.

In recent years, the musical focal point has shifted to a superbly specialized complex of buildings on the South Bank side of Waterloo Bridge. This Cultural Centre—including pleasure gardens and the National Film Theatre—houses three of the most stylish, comfortable, and acoustically perfect concert structures in the world: the **Royal Festival Hall**, the **Queen Elizabeth Hall**, and the **Purcell Room.**

The complex was started in 1950 and completed 15 years later, giving London's music lovers some sorely needed relief from the gargantuan gruesomeness of the Albert Hall. Here the foyers are architectural works of art, offering sweeping views of the Thames from several levels. The auditorium is an isolated inner shell, allowing a purity of sound that would even have satisfied Toscanini. There are three streamlined coffee bars on the premises, a cafeteria, and a very plush restaurant.

The musical offerings come in a vast variety of forms—from the London Philharmonic Orchestra and the Bach Festival Ensemble to opera, films, and stage productions. The Queen Elizabeth Hall also presents poetry readings, solo concerts, contemporary theater, and exhibitions. On the same day, the South Bank complex can cater to a taste spectrum ranging from chamber music to a panel discussion by the Drama Brain Trust.

For inquiries, ring 928-3002. Ticket prices vary according to the attraction offered. Take the tube to Waterloo Station and leave by the Festival Hall exit, following the ample signposts.

Ticket Agents

Herewith you are given a selection of agencies selling tickets for all London theaters and some movie houses, concerts, and sporting events. Otherwise, you can also purchase tickets over the phone by giving the number of your American Express card, then picking up the tickets half an hour before curtain.

Keith Prowse, 90 New Bond St., W.1 (tel. 493-6000).

Edwards & Edwards, Palace Theatre, Shaftesbury Avenue, (tel. 437-4695).

Kent Theatre Tickets, Hilton Hotel, Park Lane (tel. 493-4406).

Simpson (Piccadilly) Ltd., 203 Piccadilly (tel. 734-2002).

Webster Girling, 211 Baker St., N.W.1 (tel. 935-6666).

Parade at Buckingham Palace

Chapter VII

LONDON AFTER DARK

MIDNIGHT RUNS THROUGH the length and width of London's nightlife like an invisible Iron Curtain. The entire world of bright lights, in fact, can be divided into Pre and Post Midnight.

The division is achieved partly by the pub closing hour (11 p.m.) and the cessation of public transport (around midnight). But is is subtly reinforced by a tangled coil of bylaws, unwritten rules, precedents, and traditions laid down for one express purpose: to get the lower (i.e., working) orders into bed at what local magistrates still term "a respectable hour," so they would be bright and lively at work the next morning. The original purpose went the way of bloomers and spats, but the regulations remained, others were added, half of them were ignored, until the whole thing came to resemble a jigsaw puzzle of paragraphs assembled with the singular aim of driving travel writers to distraction.

Take the matter of clubs. In every other metropolis, from Buenos Aires to Tokyo, a club means the same thing and requires no further explanation. Not so in London. Here a club can mean virtually anything, depending on where it is, what it does, and how long it does it. A club can be a rigidly exclusive institution, vetoing prospective members like candidates for the diplomatic service. Or it can be as wide-open as a Reno gambling parlor, blithely disregarding its own rules as well as those laid down by the law—and getting away with it.

You cannot formulate an overall picture with the word "club"; each has to be dealt with individually. Some "nightclubs," for example, are clubs in name only, like their American counterparts. Others take their tag dead serious and rigorously exclude strangers, no matter how affluent. Some clubs stick to precise opening and closing hours, others regard them as a practical joke. Some clubs . . .

Anyway, this will give you an idea of the general situation. Which amounts to the fact that there is no *general* situation, only an encyclopedic mass of half-remembered, rarely enforced, occasionally applied ordinances with which you learn to live like you can learn to live with hayfever.

But don't let the above mislead you into thinking that London is in any way short of nightlife. It's there in vast quantities, except that some of it takes a little finding.

Geographically, about 90% of the bright lights burn in the area roughly defined as the West End. There are no great outer patches like Paris's Montmartre, San Francisco's North Beach, or Chicago's Old Town. The core of this region is Piccadilly Circus which, with Coventry Street running down to Leicester Square, resembles Broadway. To the north lies Soho—chockablock with entertainment in various hues of scarlet. To the east the theaterland of Covent Garden, to the south Trafalgar Square, and to the west the fashionable and expensive night world of Mayfair.

With a few widely scattered exceptions, this area encompasses all the nightlife of interest to visitors, most of the attractions within easy walking distance of each other. But there are a few peculiarities you should be warned about.

The midnight curtain mentioned earlier operates against *simple* nighttime pleasures. It prevents you, for instance, from just dropping into a place for a drink (you must have something to eat with a drink served after 11). It doesn't prevent you, after hours, from paying a cover charge (frequently disguised as a membership fee) and enjoying a stage show, taking a spin on a dance floor, trying your luck at a gambling table, eating a five-course meal, and drinking yourself into oblivion.

If this sound slightly wacky to you, be assured that it sounds precisely the same to some 20 million-odd English people who, being English, would rather die than change it.

In London, a complete night out in a smart establishment, including dinner, floorshow, and dancing, might set you back about £22 ($42.90) per person—although you can get much the same food and entertainment in several establishments for around £12 ($23.40) a head just as easily.

Most of the places we'll visit in the course of this chapter are well below the higher price quoted above. Many of them have some kind of frontdoor mumbo-jumbo that passes as membership enrollment. What it amounts to is a so-called temporary membership, which satisfies the letter (if not the spirit) of the law and enables you to get in without delay. Most nightclub admissions for overseas visitors (bring along your passport) range from £1 ($1.95) up to about £6 ($11.70). In many cases the temporary membership fee is deducted from the cost of dinner. There is, however, no hard and fast rule.

At this point, however, we'll add a word for the benefit of male travelers. London's club world is full of "hostesses." Their purpose is to make you buy things—from drinks to dolls and cigarettes—and they can shoot up your tab to much more than you intend to spend.

London's recognized meeting spots, particularly for the younger set, are the ballrooms and discos, neither of which employ hostesses.

Now, moving from generalities to particulars, let's start swinging with . . .

Some Top Clubs
(splurge price)

Eve, 189 Regent St., W.1 (tel. 734-0557), is London's longest established late nightclub. Doyen of London's nightlife, owner Jimmy O'Brien launched it in 1953. Strip cabaret and erotic entertainment (at 1 a.m.) has replaced the floorshows previously presented. Dancing is to disco alternating with live music of a high standard. Eve is open Monday to Friday from 10 p.m. to 3:30 a.m. Admittance is by membership only. There is an annual subscription of £5 ($9.75), but a special temporary membership for overseas visitors, valid for one night only, is available for £1 ($1.95). Only one person in a party need be a member, and overseas visitors may be admitted on application without waiting the customary 48 hours. There is an entrance fee or cover charge of £5 ($9.75) for a member and each guest. An à la carte menu is offered throughout the night and an all-in champagne supper until midnight. This includes the entrance fee, an apéritif, a three-course meal, a half bottle of champagne, brandy, and coffee, all for £29.50 ($57.53). All prices include VAT. Charming and attractive young women, many of whom speak more than one language, are available as dining or dancing partners for unaccompanied men.

The **Royal Roof Restaurant,** Royal Garden Hotel, Kensington High Street, W.8 (tel. 937-8000), lies on the top floor of the hotel, is elegant and refined, and overlooks Kensington Gardens and Hyde Park. From your table you will see the lights of

Kensington and Knightsbridge, with a view of London's West End skyline. In a romantic candlelit aura, you can enjoy a three-course dinner for between £18 ($35.10) and £22 ($42.90), with a £2 ($3.90) entertainment charge. Joe Stein and his International Royal Roof Violins will serenade you at your table and, if you wish, you may dance the night away to the sounds of their quartet. The Royal Roof Restaurant is open from 8 p.m. until 2 a.m. Monday to Saturday. Reservations are necessary.

The **Talk of the Town** theater-restaurant, Leicester Square, W.C.2 (tel. 734-5051), is the chief "entertainment factory" of Great Britain, a slick showbiz extravaganza that attracts top-drawer talent. Five hours of continuous entertainment are offered from 8 p.m. to 1 a.m.

For those nervous about the tabs and hidden charges in London supper clubs, the Talk of the Town is a good bet, as it offers an inclusive price of £18.45 ($35.98), including VAT and service, for a three-course dinner and the show. On Friday and Saturday nights, the tariff is raised to £21.75 ($42.41) per person, including VAT and service. The entertainment involves a spectacular revue, with a large West End cast. Most tables have a clear view of the stage, as the restaurant is a remake of a theater, the old Hippodrome, with rows of tables set on a stepped-up ledge of the mezzanine. The theater-restaurant is open Monday through Saturday but closed on Sunday.

l'Hirondelle, Swallow Street, off Regent Street, W.1 (tel. 734-6666). Rather misnamed, for it doesn't in the least resemble the streamlined, functional swallow, the Hirondelle puts on some of the most lavishly gorgeous floorshows in town. What's more it lets you dine, drink, and dance from 7:30 in the evening till 3:45 a.m. without the ceremonial "temporary memberships." Neither does it charge an entrance fee. The shows are really full-scale revues and come on at 11 p.m. and 1:30 a.m. Dancing is from 8 p.m. to two live bands. Dancing/dining partners are available. There is a minimum charge of £5.75 ($9.26) for nondiners. Otherwise, a three-course table d'hôte dinner costs from £15 ($29.25), and bottles of wine range from £13 ($25.35) up. Tube: Piccadilly.

Other Cabarets
(less expensive)

At 27 Gerrard St., W.1, in Soho, the **Boulogne** (tel. 437-3186) is a gorgeously decorated Edwardian restaurant that became a show spot as an afterthought. Founded in 1852, the Boulogne catered to generations of silk-hatted, cane-twirling Mayfair toffs who regarded it as a French oasis in London's culinary desert. The cuisine is still French and the decor still scarlet-plush Edwardian, but a few other details have changed considerably. The owners put on a sparkling, spangled, leg-swirling cabaret twice nightly at 10:30 p.m. and 1:30 a.m. The young women are scintillating and we feel sure that even the crustiest Edwardian gent would have approved of the establishment's resident belly dancer.

Dining and dancing goes on from 7 p.m. till dawn. The average meal with wine for two persons goes for about £30 ($58.50). The cabaret here, by the way, is no impromptu series of song and dance acts, but an elaborately staged show, often with guest stars from the legitimate theater. The one we watched boasted one solitary male amid the array of femininity.

Cockney Cabaret and Music Hall, 18 Charing Cross Rd., W.C.2 (tel. 408-1001), recaptures the atmosphere of a Victorian music hall. At the whisky and gin reception, you'll have the cockles of your heart warmed and learn about "Mother's ruin" (large gins). The lively waiters and waitresses join the guests to sing along to the sounds of a honky-tonk piano. An East End meal, three courses of Cockney nosh, is served. Music to sing and dance mark the evening. The show is divided into two parts, featuring cabaret with both production numbers and solo performances. Seven nights a week you can join in the revelry at a cost of £10.75 ($20.96) inclusive, plus a £2 ($3.90) supplement on Saturday. The club is open from 7:15 p.m.

Ballrooms

Although the straight dance hall is by now almost defunct in America, it continues to draw crowds in London. There are several reasons for this survival, all of them having to do with the boy-meets-girl syndrome.

As places for casual encounters, the ballrooms are unbeatable. The music is not so loud that you can't hear each others' names, the illumination is bright enough to see whom you're meeting, and the floors sufficiently large for actual dancing—as distinct from the postage stamp that passes for it in the discos. The hunters of both sexes usually prowl in pairs, but will split up as readily as amoebas when opportunity beckons.

The **Café de Paris,** on Coventry Street, off Piccadilly Circus,

W.1 (tel. 437-2036), is the grandest of institutions, and still basks in a rosy glow of nostalgia. Opened in 1924, it was once the chicest nitery in the Empire, patronized by the prince of Wales (the late duke of Windsor) and on one occasion counted four reigning kings in its audience. Merle Oberon worked there as a dance hostess, Marlene Dietrich and Noël Coward topped the floorshows, and Robert Graves wrote a book about it.

Today the Café is still plush, chandelier-blazing, and large enough to land a plane on the dance floor. But instead of the aristocratic smart set, patrons today consist largely of regular folks who like to dance rather than to "be seen." They get to do so on a truly superb maple floor, to continuous music. The floor is bathed in changing "mood lights" and surrounded by gilded balustrades. One band alternates with disco for dancing seven nights a week. Admission ranges from £1.80 ($3.51) to £3 ($5.85), depending on the night. It's always cheaper before 9:30 p.m. and most expensive on Friday and Saturday nights. Women are admitted free on Tuesday night. A reasonable three-course meal is about £8 ($15.60), including a glass of wine and coffee. Drinks are available at the bar. The nostalgia is on the house. The Café also has tea dancing from 3 to 5:45 p.m. to live and recorded music seven days a week. Admission at that time ranges from £1.25 ($2.44) to £1.85 ($3.61).

The **Empire Ballroom,** Leicester Square, W.C.2 (tel. 437-1446), is another dance giant of the type now virtually extinct in the United States. Vast and plushly ornate, it operates on several levels centering around a magnificent dance floor. Liquid refreshment is dispensed from no fewer than five bars, and the sign above the entrance says "Disco Dancing" in 14 languages (we counted).

The Empire, the largest dance hall of its type in Europe and situated in the heart of London's most famous entertainment area, was the scene of the World Disco Dancing Championship in 1978 and 1979. Every night of the week, the best in live bands, groups, and DJs are featured. A wine bar operation is also open here in the evenings. Dancing is Monday to Thursday from 8 p.m. to 2 a.m., on Friday and Saturday from 8 p.m. till 3 a.m. According to the day of the week and the time (early is cheaper, of course), admission prices range from £2.50 ($4.88) to £4 ($7.80). Both disco and live groups are regularly featured.

Bars and Bierkellers

Here we come to a series of hybrid hostelries—somewhere between pubs and cabarets—but constituting a distinct species of their own. They are springing up like mushrooms all over town and absolutely defy exact classification. We're including some samples in this survey, because they happen to be among the coziest, most stimulating, and least expensive fun spots in London. Unfortunately, we have space for only these. But there are plenty more where they came from.

The **Swiss Bierkeller,** Grand Building, Trafalgar Square, W.C.2, keeps English pub hours, but otherwise is a patch of old Helvetia transplanted bodily to London. This is a real cellar—stone floor, wooden benches and tables, rows of barrels on wall shelves, candles flickering in bottlenecks—specializing in powerful Swiss Hürlimann brew and a rollicking accordion minstrel. Alpine snacks, poetic combinations of smoked meat and sharp cheeses, are available, and the potent and very good Swiss draft beer flows. Tube: Trafalgar Square.

The **Holsten Bierkeller,** 34 Brook St. (off Bond Street), W.1 (tel. 629-2471), is something like a German cousin of the above, except that it stays open till midnight. It is in Mayfair, near Claridges Hotel. Brick cellar walls and Gothic partition windows, strong lager beer and stronger "schnapps," plus groups of strumming, fiddling, and squeezing musicians take care of the *Gemütlichkeit* angle. The menu, however, is considerably more extensive and includes genuine sauerbraten—slices of beef marinated in red wine. The popular German Liebfraumilch is only £5.10 ($9.95) a bottle. The cellar is open from 11:15 a.m. to 3 p.m. and from 5:30 to 11 p.m. daily except Sunday.

The **Rheingold Club** thrives in a century-old wine cellar at Sedley Place, just off 361 Oxford St., W.1 (tel. 629-5343). The live music is an even melange of the latest pop, soft Latin, even German drinking songs, and Viennese waltzes. The nightly cabaret occasionally offers big-time guest stars, but most of the entertainment is created by the patrons. The Rheingold has a particular attraction for the racing set, and you can pick up some sound tips by eavesdropping on their table talk. The temporary membership you get at the door includes one free admission and costs £5 ($9.75) for men, £4 ($7.80) for women.

The club prides itself on offering a substantial German dish called *eisbein*— pickled knuckle of pork cooked in sauerkraut with pease pudding and boiled potatoes, all for £3.50 ($6.83). It also has a strong German draft beer at 60p ($1.17) for a half pint, and excellent German and French wines, from £4 ($7.80) for a simple Qualitatswein to £7.50 ($14.63) for an Auslese.

The cabaret comes on at midnight. The club is open Monday and Tuesday from 7:30 p.m. to 1:30 a.m., on Wednesday and Thursday till 2 a.m., and on Friday and Saturday till 2:30 a.m. It's closed on Sunday. Take the tube to Bond Street.

And now, let's hop over to Greece.

Bouzouki and Folk

The **Elysse,** 13 Percy St. (tel. 636-4804), boasts the biggest roof garden restaurant in London and is bursting with Greek atmosphere. Run by the three Karageorgis brothers, who also participate in the cabaret, the place is alive with the strains of Hellenic strings and redolent with the aroma of Balkan cooking.

The twice-nightly shows feature Greek dancing and singing, mixed with some astonishing feats of wine-glass balancing while swaying to the rhythmic clapping of the musicians. If you dug *Zorba,* this place will send you. The full and fragrant meal costs around £17 ($33.15) per person, including a bottle of wine. The club is open nightly from 6:30 p.m. until 3:30 a.m. (on Sunday to 2 a.m.). Dancing to music by a quartet is from 9 p.m. The Greek cabaret shows are staged at 11 p.m. and again at 1 a.m. (on Sunday at 10:30 p.m. and again at 12:15 a.m.).

Folk music is getting as scarce in London as in New York, but a few strongholds survive. One of the most genuine and least commercialized is **Bunjies Cellar,** 28 Litchfield St., W.C.2 (tel. 240-1796), off Charing Cross Road and next to the famous Ivy Restaurant. The cellar tag is real, and the whole place as cozy, sloppy, and friendly as you'd expect from a den of modern troubadors. The front portion, decorated with theatrical posters, serves as a coffeehouse. You only pay for what you order, and there's no beverage stronger than Coke.

The cellar, where the singers and guitarists perform, charges £1 ($1.95) for admission. It's usually packed with enthusiastic youngsters, humming or smiling in unison, and it stars a different singer every night. The place is open from noon to midnight, except on Saturday when it offers a late-night blues-and-rock session from midnight until 2 a.m. The kitchen, which serves wholefood vegetarian meals, prices its most expensive dish at £1.60 ($3.12).

Jazz

Mention the word "jazz" in London and people immediately think of **Ronnie Scott's Club.** This citadel of Europe's aficionados is a svelte three-story establishment at 47 Frith St., Soho, W.1 (tel. 439-0747), crowded on weeknights, bursting at the seams on weekends. But don't let the throng discourage you. This is one of the—perhaps *the*—greatest jazz dispensary outside America and worth braving any size mob for. Featured on almost every bill is an American band, often with a top-notch singer. The best English and American groups are booked. It's in the heart of Soho, a ten-minute walk from Piccadilly Circus via Shaftesbury Avenue, and worth an entire evening. You can not only saturate yourself in the best of jazz, but get reasonably priced drinks and dinners as well.

There are three separate areas: The Main Room, the Upstairs Discotheque, and the Downstairs Bar. You don't have to be a member, although you can join if you wish. The nightly entrance fee is, on average, around £5 ($9.75) for members, £6.50 ($12.68) for nonmembers, depending on who's appearing. If you have a student ID you are granted considerable reductions on entrance fees, providing you come before 9:30 p.m. Monday through Thursday, without making a reservation beforehand. Drinks cost around 80p ($1.56) for whisky.

The Main Room is open Monday to Saturday from 8:30 p.m. to 3 a.m. You can either stand at the bar to watch the show or sit at tables, where you can order a three-course dinner from around £9 ($17.55).

The Downstairs Bar is more intimate, a quiet rendezvous where you can meet and talk with the regulars, usually some of the world's most talented musicians.

The Upstairs Discotheque has sculptured foam seating, and in this part of the club you can either dance or drink. On most nights a live band is featured.

Although considerably less plush and cheaper, the **100 Club** is considered a serious rival of the above among many dedicated jazz gourmets. At 100 Oxford St., W.1 (tel. 636-0933), the 100 Club sprinkles disco-dance nights among its cavalcade of bands which include Mr. Acker Bilk and his Paramount Band, Ken Colyer's Jazzmen, Chris Barber's Jazz Band, and Max Collie's Rhythm Aces.

Sessions go from 7:30 p.m. till midnight weeknights, till 1 a.m. on Friday and Saturday. Admission prices vary according to who's playing, and hover between £2 ($3.90) and £3 ($5.85).

Without membership, you'll pay an additional 50p (98¢). Tube: Tottenham Court Road.

Discos

The discos originated in Paris just after the war, but were taken up enthusiastically by the rest of Europe and by North America. London, strangely enough, was one of the last cities to catch the bug, but has since more than made up for lost time.

For the past few years, discos have been springing up and closing down in London with such bewildering rapidity—besides changing their names, their image, character, and patrons—that a list compiled now is liable to be hopelessly out of date by the time this book appears. Yet the "discs" play such a vital part in London's nightlife that to ignore them would mean to eliminate nearly half the fun spots in town.

So, with the perils of instant obsolescence in mind, here's a fractional survey of the disco field *at this moment.* We offer no guarantee that the picture will be the same, say, a week from next Wednesday.

One of the dilemmas in trying to classify these ephemeral establishments is that many of them have totally forgotten their original concept. A disco was meant to be a place where you danced or listened to recorded music—hence the name. But a solid proportion now offer live bands, floorshows, movies, gaming tables, and what-have-you, while still insisting on their original title.

Whatever we choose to tag them, London now has more of their breed than Paris and New York combined—and the ranks are still swelling.

The following, therefore, is merely a sample patchwork of the field.

La Valbonne Club, at 62 Kingly St. (off Regent Street), W.1 (tel. 439-7242). The decor is modern, with mirrors and futuristic furniture. Masses of flashing and changing colored lights make a feature of the dance floor. There is a 100-inch video screen, showing a multitude of pictures. A light machine flashes words and sentences on the walls. Of the three bars, one is a quieter cocktail lounge, the others merely places to drink. Disco music is noisy and heavy on the beat. Admission to this fun palace of lights is £3 ($5.85) for women and £4 ($7.80) for men from Monday through Wednesday. On Thursday, everybody pays £4 ($7.80). However, from Thursday through Saturday, admission goes up to £5 ($9.75) per person. There is an à la carte menu, with a basic meal costing about £8 ($15.60), plus the cost of your drinks.

Samantha's is one of a breed of nightclub discos whose function is as difficult to pin down as its ethnic label. It's a delightful bit of everything—dance dive, restaurant, cabaret, bar, pool hall —but above all it is one of London's most durable discos, dating from the early '60s. At 3 New Burlington St., W.1 (tel. 734-6249), just off Regent Street, Samantha's swings six nights a week from 8:30 p.m. to 3:30 a.m. (closed on Sunday). The place features top live recording groups, and a dance floor that's hectic, with masses of multihued lights and a disc jockey operating his equipment from inside a Mark I E-type Jaguar. You'll find an endless cavalcade of cosmopolitan lads and lasses, some of them wearing the most bewitchingly zany togs you're likely to see anywhere in Europe.

The ear-shattering disco music is confined to the main dance floor, and mercifully does not penetrate into the other areas of Samantha's, which include snackbars, a smaller dance floor, Samantha's Playroom (for pinball and pool enthusiasts), and, for a complete change of atmosphere—literally—Sir Harry's Bar, where you can sip drinks or dine in a tropical setting of cane and garden furniture and wall hangings of animal skins and heads. The entrance fee to Samantha's is £7 ($13.63) per couple, which permits you to wander freely among the bars, dance areas, and game rooms. You'll pay an average of £1.50 ($2.93) for drinks, although the "super cocktails" in Sir Harry's will cost slightly more.

Le Beat Route, 17 Greek St., W.1 (tel. 734-1470), is a luxurious club with both live and disco music, open every day except Sunday. Top recording artists make personal appearances here. There's a superb sprung dance floor, as well as a pool room with its own bar. Admission is £3.50 ($6.83). It opens at 9 p.m., closing at 3:30 a.m.

Music Hall Showboat

The luxury catamaran *Naticia* leaves Lambeth Pier nightly at 7 for a four-hour cruise on the Thames, returning at 11 p.m. There is a bar for a drink while you watch the landmarks slip by, then dinner is either a supper basket with chicken, scampi, or some such, or a three-course meal with wine. At that time a first-class oldtime music hall program entertains you. Advance booking is essential. Phone **Catamaran Cruisers Ltd.,** Westminster Pier, S.W.1 (tel. 839-2349). The supper basket menu costs about £13 ($25.35), and the full dinner goes for £18.50 ($36.08) for the evening.

Strip Shows

Once upon a time, Britian's film censors were kept busy snipping the bare patches out of those "daring" French movies, and London's stage regulations permitted braless belles only on condition that they didn't move a limb while thus exposed.

All this might just as well have happened in the last century for all the relevance it has today. For the sheer acreage of undress currently on view in London outshows anything in Paris, New York, San Francisco, or Hamburg. Only Toyko might be on the same par.

Some of this clothes-shedding mania is undoubtedly a reaction to the years of Mother Grundy's dictatorship, when even a semitransparent nightgown had to be struck out of a play as "bordering on the indecent." But by now it has gone past the saturation point. London's entertainment world, in fact, is in danger of being smothered by a pink tidal wave of nudity, lapping into every nook and cranny of the West End and sweeping before it every other brand of amusement.

Entire blocks of Soho now consist of little else but strip shows, sometimes two in one building. Along Frith Street, Greek Street, Old Compton Street, Brewer Street, Windmill Street, Dean and Wardour Streets, and the little courts and alleys in between, the disrobing establishments jostle cheek by jowl. Big ones and small ones, fancy and dingy, elaborate and primitive, they all sport outsize photos of the inside attractions, gloriously exotic names, and bellowing spruikers to draw your attention in the right direction.

The basic commodity is the same, but the packaging varies considerably. Some of the large—and fairly expensive—places are regular theaters, putting on lavish productions, complete with musical scores, choreography, trained dancers, and intricate, if insufficient, costuming.

At the other extreme are dozens of cellar dens, holding a few rows of creaking chairs, a torn curtain, and a few boards knocked together as a stage. The women appearing there can neither dance nor strip gracefully, but they can take their clothes off.

Regarding their acts, you'd better forget what you know about

American burlesque. There's no trace of humor, no slapstick gags with girdles, no wisecracking with the boys in the front row, and no fans and fluttering pigeons. Here, the stripping is total, minus modesty gimmicks such as flickering strobe lights or climactic blackouts. The women go through a series of vaguely undulating movements and strip right down to their skins. And that's that.

The big, plush establishments, of course, have regular and highly paid casts, and among the most spectacular is the **Raymond Revuebar,** Walker's Court, Brewer St., W.1 (tel. 734-1593). Proprietor Paul Raymond is considered the doyen of strip society and his young, beautiful, hand-picked women are considered among the best in Europe. The stage show, Festival of Erotica, is presented three times nightly, Sunday included, at 7, 9, and 11 p.m. There are licensed bars, and patrons may take their drinks into the theater. The price of admission is £7.50 ($14.63), and there is no membership fee. Whisky is around £1.20 ($2.34) per large measure.

The **Nell Gwynne Club,** 69 Dean St. (entrance in Meard Street, W.1 (tel. 437-3278), is smaller, but its shows are—if anything—more spectacular. The girls range from pinky-white to ebony-black, they can not only dance but dance well, and their costumes are minor miracles of the art of covering a minimum amount of surface with a maximum amount of embroidery. Casts are large, the erotic ballets remarkably ingenious, and seating arrangements luxurious.

The club is open Monday to Friday from 5:30 to 11 p.m., with continuous striptease from 6 p.m. (shows at two hour intervals). Admission is £5 ($9.75).

Nell Gwynne patrons are admitted free to the **Comedy Store,** at the same address. Otherwise, individual patrons pay £3 ($5.85) Wednesday through Friday, and £4 ($7.80) on Saturday. There's dancing to disco with live shows by up-and-coming (some arrived) comedians at 11 p.m. on Wednesday, Thursday, and Friday. There are also shows at 8 p.m. on Friday and Saturday (again at midnight on Saturday). Drinks cost £2 ($3.90) for a double. In addition, there are light snacks, pizzas, chicken in the basket, and scampi, at about £5 ($9.75) per person.

Gambling

London was a gambling metropolis long before anyone had ever heard of Monte Carlo and when Las Vegas was an anonymous sandpile in the desert. From the Regency period until halfway into the 19th century, Britain was more or less governed by gamblers. Lord Sandwich invented the snack named after him so he wouldn't have to leave the card table for a meal. Prime Minister Fox was so addicted that he frequently went to a cabinet meeting straight from the green baize table.

Queen Victoria's reign changed all that, as usual, by jumping to the other extreme. For more than a century, games of chance were so rigorously outlawed that no barmaid dared to keep a dice cup on her counter.

The pendulum swung again in July 1960, when the present queen gave her Royal Assent to the new "Betting and Gaming Act." According to this legislation, gambling was again permitted in "bona fide clubs" by members and their guests.

Since London's definition of a "club" is as loose as a rusty screw in a cardboard wall, this immediately gave rise to the current situation, which continues to startle, amaze, and bewilder foreign visitors. For the fact is that you come across gambling devices in the most unlikely spots, such as discos, social clubs, and cabaret restaurants. All of which may, by the haziest definition, qualify as "clubs."

Many London gambling clubs offer very pleasant trimmings in the shape of bars and restaurants, but their central theme is unequivocally the flirtation with Lady Luck.

There are at least 25 of them in the West End alone, with many more scattered through the suburbs. And the contrasts between them are much sharper than you find in the Nevada casinos.

However, we can no longer make specific recommendations. Under a new law, casinos aren't allowed to advertise, which in this context would mean appearing in a guidebook. It isn't illegal to gamble—only to advertise that you do. Most hall porters can tell you where you can gamble in London.

You will be required to become a member of your chosen club, and in addition you must wait 24 hours before you can play at the tables—then strictly for cash. Most common games are roulette, blackjack, punto banco, and baccarat.

Chapter VIII

A LONDON SHOPPING SPREE

WHEN PRUSSIAN Field Marshal Blücher, Wellington's stout ally at Waterloo, first laid eyes on London, he allegedly slapped his thigh and exclaimed: "Herr Gott, what a city to plunder!"

He was gazing at what, for the early 19th century, was a phenomenal mass of shops and stores, overwhelming to Herr Blücher's unsophisticated eyes. Since those days, other cities have drawn level with London as shopping centers—but none has ever surpassed her.

London's shopping world today is a superbly balanced mixture of luxury and utility, of small, personalized boutiques and giant department stores, of junk-heaped market stalls and breathtakingly elegant specialty shops.

As for bargains—that magic word in every traveler's dictionary—they are everywhere, but likely to be limited by the U.S. Customs regulations.

According to the latest rules, you—and everyone traveling with you—are entitled to bring back $300 worth of foreign-made merchandise without paying U.S. duty. This applies only to goods actually accompanying you. You can quite legitimately stretch that amount by mailing gifts back from abroad. No gift, however, can be worth more than $25, and you are not permitted to send more than one present per day to the same address.

Many London shops will help you beat the whopping purchase tax levied on much of England's merchandise. By presenting your passport, you can frequently purchase goods tax-free—but only on condition that:

● You either have your purchase sent directly to your home address or

● Have it delivered to the plane you're taking back.

The huge purchase taxes imposed on so-called luxury goods are responsible for the extremely high cost of items like wines, spirits, tobacco, cigarettes, and gasoline.

When bargain-hunting, zero in on those goods which are manufactured in England and liable to cost a lot more when exported to America. These are—above all—men's and women's suits, woolens, tweeds, overcoats, scarves, tartans, bone china, cutlery, and prints, plus specialties like antiques, rare books, and those magnificent old world and city maps in most bookstores.

Shopping Districts

London stores keep fairly uniform hours, mostly shorter than their American equivalents. The norm is a 5:30 p.m. closing, with a late Wednesday or Thursday night, until 7 p.m. Most central shops close Saturday around 1 p.m. They don't, however, go in for the French-style lunch-hour closing.

Any minor hindrances are more than compensated for by the tact, courtesy, and patience you'll meet in English shops, coupled—in some of the smaller establishments—with an almost courtly sense of pride and craftsmanship.

London's retail stores tend to cluster in certain areas, a hangover from the times when each guild or craft had its own street. This is what gives a London shopping spree its special flavor—you head in a certain direction to find a certain style of merchandise.

Herewith, we present a very rough outline of the main shopping districts (not including the "Two Singular Shopping Districts" which we shall detail below):

REGENT STREET: Curving down elegantly from Oxford Circus to Piccadilly Circus, this stylish thoroughfare is crammed with fashionable stores, selling everything from silks to silverware. It has both department stores and boutiques, but the accent is on the medium-size establishment in the upper-medium price range.

OXFORD STREET: *The* shopping drag of the metropolis, runs from St. Giles Circus to Marble Arch, an endless, faceless, totally uninspiring but utility-crammed band of stores, stores, and yet more stores. It contains six of London's major department stores, apart from just about every kind of retailing establishment under the sun.

PICCADILLY: Unlike the circus, the street Piccadilly is distinctly in the upper bracket, specializing in mouthwatering automobile showrooms, travel offices, art galleries, plus London's poshest grocery store, Fortnum & Mason.

BOND STREET: Divided into New and Old, Bond Street connects Piccadilly with Oxford Street and is synonymous with the luxury trade. Here are found the very finest—and most expensive—of tailors, hatters, milliners, shoe stores, sporting goods, and antiques.

KNIGHTSBRIDGE: Together with Kensington and Brompton Roads, this forms an extremely svelte shopping district south of Hyde Park. It's patronized for furniture, antiques, jewelry, and Harrods department store.

THE STRAND: Stately, broad, and dignified, the Strand runs from Trafalgar Square into Fleet Street, is lined with hotels and theaters, and a selection of specialty stores you could spend a whole day peeking into.

Shopping Arcades

Running off the above streets are a dozen or so arcades, housing some of the most exclusive and intriguing shops and boutiques in London. The best known arcade of all is the . . .

BURLINGTON ARCADE: This is a glass-roofed, Regency-style passage leading off Piccadilly, looking like a period exhibition. It has been celebrated in several music hall ditties (to wit: "I'm Burlington Bertie, I rise at ten thirty, and I saunter along like a toff . . .").

Lit by wrought-iron lamps, decorated with clusters of ferns and flowers, it makes shopping feel like strolling through a classy hotel lobby. Goods here, naturally, aren't cheap. The small, smart stores specialize in lines such as high fashions, jewelry, Irish linen, camera equipment, stationery, pipes and smoking accessories, and model soldiers.

Top Department Stores

London has some 25 department stores, nearly all of them in the centers listed above. Shopping emporiums tend to look alike the world over, but London boasts at least two for which you'll find no parallels anywhere. Some American counterparts may be larger, some Parisian ones may be older, and some German and Scandinavian ones more streamlined, but both of the following enterprises have a unique touch of their own that no one has so far succeeded in copying.

Harrods, Brompton Road, Knightsbridge, S.W.3, is London's —indeed Europe's—top store. Harrods is really an institution, and visitors to the city come to view it as a sightseeing attraction, like the Tower of London. Some of the goods displayed for sale are works of art and so are the departments displaying them. The sheer range and variety of merchandise is dazzling—from silver and pewter ware to clothing, from food to furs, from pianos to delicatessen. Every department seems to have had a different architect, but each one unmistakably carries Harrods distinctive stamp of the best in quality, taste, and decor. Now they even have a genuine pub on the premises.

It's called "The Green Man," and is the only in-store one in London. Other departments include an American Ice Cream Parlor, the first in-store one in the country; a jewelry department, "Collingwood at Harrods"; a fantastic sports department called "Olympic Way," a huge complex which has brought together sports equipment and fashionable sports clothing and accessories for dozens of different sports in one department; and "Way In Living," an extension of the store's "Way In" Department for the younger set.

Much more economical, however, is **Selfridges,** on Oxford Street, W.1 (tel. 629-1234), one of the biggest department stores in Europe, with more than 550 divisions selling everything from artificial flowers to groceries. The specialty shops are particularly enticing, with good buys in Irish linen, Wedgwood, leather goods, silver-plated goblets, cashmere and woolen scarves. There's also the Miss Selfridge Boufique, for the young or those who'd like to be. To help you travel light, the Export Bureau will air-freight your purchases to anywhere in the world, completely tax free. On the ground floor, the London Tourist Board will help you find your way around London's sights with plenty of maps, tips, and friendly advice.

The world's most elegant grocery store, **Fortnum & Mason Ltd.,** 181 Piccadilly, W.1 (tel. 734-8040), down the street from the Ritz, draws the carriage trade, the well-heeled dowager from Mayfair or Belgravia who comes seeking such tinned treasures as pâté de foie gras or a boar's head. She would never set foot in a regular grocery store, but Fortnum & Mason, with its swallow-tailed attendants, is no mere grocery store: it's a British tradition dating back to 1707. In fact, the establishment likes to think that Mr. Fortnum and Mr. Mason "created a union surpassed in its importance to the human race only by the meeting of Adam and Eve."

In the Mezzanine Restaurant, you can mingle at lunch with the caviar and champagne shoppers. The "country cousin" (cheddar and cottage cheese blended with egg on brown bread) costs £2.80 ($5.46); a Danish pastry, 60p ($1.17). The pastries are calorie loaded but divine. The chocolate and confectionery department is on the ground floor. The Fountain Restaurant has both store and street entrances (Jermyn Street), and is open from 9:30 a.m. until 11:30 p.m. Monday to Saturday for the benefit of theater-goers. The St. James's Room Restaurant on the fourth floor is open during normal store hours.

Two Singular Shopping Streets

If London has unique department stores, it also has a couple of equally unique streets. The first one achieved such legendary fame abroad that you owe yourself a visit. We're talking, of course, about . . .

CARNABY STREET: A short, narrow thoroughfare in the west section of Soho, it skyrocketed into prominence in the '60s with the advent of the Beatles, Twiggy, and the psychedelic pop scene. On a summer day, it still gets so crowded with tourists that you can barely see the shop windows. It's crowded, yes, but exciting, pulsating, alive with young people. Even if you don't buy anything (and the street is simply littered with shops), stop in and stare at the sales people, walking testimonials to the youth-oriented way of life.

On the fashion scene, there's **Aristos,** a pop-colored, garment-crammed treasure trove, at 31 Carnaby St., W.1. It sells original designs (only a few of each) of remarkably good workmanship and at very moderate prices. Aristos is now one of the leading names on the London fashion scene and has become known both in the British press and on British TV.

A further, much larger establishment at 72 Oxford St., W.1,

offers a variety of accessories, including jewelry, shoes, hand-bags, knitwear, as well as the full Aristos collection of women's fashion outerwear, covering every occasion from day and sports-wear to the most luxurious and sophisticated designs for evening wear. For information, you can telephone the head office at 580-2652.

KING'S ROAD: The formerly village-like main street of Chelsea, although still the cutting edge for fashion trends, has undergone yet another metamorphosis—the trendies of the '70s who re-placed the hippies of the '60s have been pushed aside by the punk scene. Numerous stores sporting American clothes, even Frye boots, have sprung up along its length.

King's Road starts at Sloane Square (with Peter Jones' classy department store) and meanders on for a mile before losing its personality and dissolving into drabness at a sharp bend appro-priately known as World's End.

Along the way, you'll see the tokens of Chelsea's former claims to fame—cozy pubs, smart nightclubs and discos, coffee bars, cosmopolitan restaurants, and possibly the most casually attractive of London's "Beautiful People."

The leap of King's Road to the mod throne in the late '60s came with the advent of designer Mary Quant, who scored bull's eyes on the English as well as the world's fashion target. Ms. Quant is no longer there, but what seems like a myriad others have taken her place.

At 82 King's Rd. (tel. 584-0150) and at 124 King's Rd. (tel. 589-6942), are two branches of **Irvine Sellars** stores. Called **Mates,** they cater to women with the latest fashion ideas on their minds. You'll find other branches of this immensely successful chain all over the city.

At no. 93 stands a unique establishment, the **Boutique Le Bistingo** (tel. 351-1799). The idea of clothing as well as feeding your customers is certainly appealing. This is one of London's leading boutiques for French and Italian imports, including such name designers as Valentino, David, and Yves St. Laurent. Americans and Canadians make a bee-line to buy those designer jeans and silk shirts.

More and more, however, King's Road is becoming a lineup of markets and "multistores," large or small conglomerations of in- and outdoor stands, stalls, and booths fulfilling half a dozen different functions within one building or enclosure. They're springing up so fast that it's impossible to keep them tabulated. By the time this book appears there may be several more (or several fewer), but the trend is what counts and the outline below will give you an idea of the tremendous variety already in action.

Biggest of them all is the **Chelsea Village Market** at no. 77, a mish-mash of souvenir, fashion, antique, jewelry, edibles, drinkables, and wearables jammed into a partly outdoor, partly sheltered market area that also features roving minstrels, foot-loose clowns, street artists, and huge happy throngs of gazers, listeners, and buyers.

Longest established is the **Chelsea Drugstore,** 49 King's Rd., S.W.3 (tel. 730-8838), an incredible melange of commerce and entertainment. One portion is a real drugstore, selling everything you'd expect from its Stateside counterparts as well as T-shirts, sweatshirts, posters, button badges, clothing, and jewelry. But from 7:30 to 11 at night the place turns into a far-out disco with go-go girls who—from Monday to Thursday—gyrate topless. This puts it somewhat ahead of the U.S. originals.

Street Markets

Markets are considerably more ancient than shops as a retailing medium. Most of the Old World's large cities began as market towns, and in London you still have a few thriving survivors of the open-air trading tradition. They're great fun to visit, even if you don't plan on buying anything. But we're willing to bet that you'll go home with something . . . anything.

PETTICOAT LANE: The most popular of London markets, this functions only on Sunday mornings. There's furious bargaining for every conceivable kind of object, from old clothing to brand-new "antiques," the air vibrating with voices, canned and human. It's no place for hangover victims, but a gas otherwise. Take the tube to Liverpool Street Station.

PORTOBELLO ROAD: A magnet for collectors of virtually everything, this Saturday event occasionally turns up real treasures at bargain prices. Only don't take the stallholder's word for it that the mildewed fiddle he's holding is a genuine Stradivarius left to him in the will of his Italian great-uncle. It might just as well have been "nicked" from an East End pawn shop. You can browse around jewelry, weapons modern and antique, toys, kitchenware, scientific instruments, china, books, old cigarette cards, movie posters, magazines long defunct, watches, pens, music boxes. . . . Anyway, take the tube to Ladbroke Grove, then turn east—and the best of finder's luck to you.

GRAY'S ANTIQUES: On Davies Street and Davies Mews, W.1, just south of Oxford Street on a triangular point formed by South Molton Street and Davies Street, an old building has been converted into booths and stalls, with independent owners renting space. The term "antique" is stretched here to cover items from oil paintings to, say, the 1894 edition of the *Encyclopaedia Britannica.* Also sold are snuff boxes, old silver, brasses, furniture, jewelry, maps, and Victorian ornaments. Most of the wares are perfectly genuine, and some of them go at equally genuine bargain rates. You can spend anything from a pound to £500, and the fun of browsing and discovering is free.

ALFIE'S ANTIQUE MARKET: This is one of the cheapest covered markets in London, and it's where the dealers come to buy. It's at 13-25 Church St., N.W.8 (tel. 723-6066). Alfie's is named after the father of Bennie Gray, the owner of Gray's and Gray's Mews and former owner of the Antique Hypermarket, Kensington, and Antiquarius. The market contains more than 150 stalls, showrooms, and workshops on 20,000 square feet of floor.

BERWICK STREET MARKET: This may be the only street market in the world that is flanked by two rows of strip clubs, porno stores, and adult movie dens. Don't let that put you off, however. Humming six days a week in the scarlet heart of Soho, this array of stalls and booths sells probably the best and cheapest fruit and vegetables in town. It also sells ancient records that may turn out to be collectors' items, tapes, books, and old magazines. It's in action from 8 a.m. to 5 p.m. Monday through Saturday.

COVENT GARDEN: After four centuries the most famous market in all England—possibly all Europe—has gone suburban, **Covent Garden,** London's legendary fruit, vegetable, and flower market, has followed the lead of Les Halles in Paris and shifted to more contemporary but less colorful quarters south of the River Thames. The move relieves some of the wild congestion it generated, but a lot of memories are left behind.

In 1662 Samuel Pepys, a diarist, watched a Punch and Judy

show there and was so impressed that he brought Mrs. Pepys along for the next performance. And, of course, Professor Higgins met Eliza Doolittle under the portico of St. Paul's Church in Covent Garden. George Bernard Shaw spent weeks eavesdropping around the market to catch the sound of Eliza's 'orrible Cockney, which he then immortalized in *Pygmalion,* alias *My Fair Lady.* Generally the Garden porters approved of Shaw's rendering of their speech but faulted him on one point: during her memorable debut at a society tea, Eliza lets fly with, "Not bloody likely—I am taking a taxi." Which, apparently, was linguistically false. A real Cockney would have said, "No bloody fear."

The new Covent Garden has developed into an impressive array of shops, pubs, and other attractions. Judging from the already-existing enterprises in the area, the new Covent Garden will prove exciting for the visitor. After all, who would expect to find a kite shop in central London?

The following are places which have caught our interest.

The **Covent Garden General Store,** 111 Long Acre, W.C.2, offers a conglomeration of household items, ranging from pots, pans, glass and china, cups, mugs, and money boxes, to packing boxes, walking sticks, handbags, and shopping bags. It's ideal for browsing to find that odd souvenir which will have some use. Prices range from a few pence to several pounds, and they also sell herb teas, sea salt, spices, and country jam, as well as natural soaps.

At 21 Neal St., W.C.2 (tel. 836-5254), the **Natural Shoe Store** sells all manner of footware from thong sandals to climbing boots made of natural leather.

The **Neal Street Shop,** 29 Neal St., W.C.2, offers a vast selection of gifts, toys, and cards, which jostle with pottery, baskets, glassware, chinoiserie, and Victoriana.

At 23 Neal St., **China China** specializes in antique pottery, jewelry, and silver, as well as paintings on silk, feather or silk flowers, and small bamboo furniture.

The **Warehouse,** 39 Neal St., W.C.2, specializes in beads and stones, providing the fittings, clasps, and strings to make necklaces and earrings.

Naturally British, 13 New Row, W.C.2, specializes in items handmade in Britain, including handmade pottery from Devon and Cornwall, tweed and knitwear from Scotland, leather goods, wrought-iron work, and carved woodwork. A perfectly carved rocking horse will cost upward of £350 ($682.50), but a three-dimensional jigsaw puzzle monkey, dog, or cat will go for only about £9 ($17.55).

The Glasshouse, 65 Long Acre, W.C.2, sells beautiful glass and also invites visitors into the workshops to see the craftspeople producing their wares.

Penhaligon's, 41 Wellington St., W.C.2 (tel. 836-2150), is a Victorian perfumery established in 1870, holding a Royal Warrant to H.R.H. the Duke of Edinburgh. It offers a large selection of perfumes, after shave, soap, and bath oils for men and women. Perfect gifts include antique silver perfume bottles. Prices range from £5 ($9.75) for soap to £500 ($975).

And **Robert White & Sons,** 22 Tavistock St., W.C.2 (tel. 836-8237), will make you a full suit of armor to size for around £800 ($1560). These are the people who make theatrical jewelry. In the workshop in Neal's Yard, they'll make you a fine copy of the crown jewels at the cost of £4500 ($8775.00).

Behind the Warehouse off Neal Street runs a narrow road leading to the already-mentioned **Neal's Yard,** a mews of warehouses which seem to retain some of the old London atmosphere. The open warehouses display such goods as vegetables, health foods, fresh-baked breads, cakes, sandwiches, and, in an immaculate dairy, the largest variety of flavored cream cheeses you are likely to encounter.

At the top of Burleigh Street, off the Strand, beside the old Flower Market, is the **Covent Garden Flea Market.** This is a real browser's paradise, with its good, bad, and indifferent clothing, fruit, and vegetables—you name it. The stalls are mainly under cover, and stall holders range from the aristocratic through punk.

Shops Around Town

In case you don't know what a "bespoke" tailor is, he's someone such as **Manning, Morris & Stone,** 2 Savile Row, W.1 (tel. 734-9100), who builds a suit for—and only for—you. It will be a suit that includes all the little style touches you happen to fancy and nobody else has. The kind of suit that people recognize from behind as being—well, bespoke. They start at $650 (U.S.) to $700 and range upward for the very finest quality wool suits.

At the **Man's Shops** at the London Hilton Hotel, Park Lane, W.1 (tel. 493-8000), a man can equip himself sartorially from neck to ankles. The masculine boutique in the international arcade features subtly superb ties, cashmere and mink jackets, original shirts, alpaca slipovers with antelope suede fronts, cufflinks of crafted silver, and the latest in belt designs. The shop has lounge suits and silk suits by famous makers like Chester Barrie and Brioni of Italy, Aquascutum raincoats, cashmere and vicuna cardigans, magnificent silk dressing gowns from India, brocaded braces, and a range of allied items—all with that custom-built look that somehow blends with Park Lane.

André Bernard Hair International, one of the undisputed masters on the London hair-styling scene, operates exclusive salons at five fashionable addresses. Three are in hotels—the Savoy on the Strand, W.C.2, Claridge's in Davies Street, W.1, and the Berkeley at 41 Knightsbridge, S.W.3. The fourth establishment is in the Swan & Edgar Department Store at Piccadilly Circus, W.1., and the fifth is in the Debenhams Store, 334-348 Oxford St., W.1. Appointments are accepted Monday through Friday from 9 a.m. to 5:30 p.m., on Saturday to 12:30 p.m. except at Swan & Edgar and Debenhams where they are taken all day.

Sanford Brothers Ltd. (tel. 405-2352), the jewelers at 3 Holborn Bars, Old Elizabethan Houses, and 2 Fenchurch St., E.C.3, is a family firm that has been in business since 1923. They sell anything in jewelry, both modern and Victorian, silver of all kinds, and a fine selection of clocks and watches. The Old Elizabethan buildings are one of the sights of Old London.

The **Reject China Shops,** at 33, 34, and 35 Beauchamp Place, Knightsbridge, S.W.3, stand on the corner of Beauchamp Place, just around the corner from Harrods. These shops are known for their huge displays of fine bone china, crystal, earthenware, and gifts from some of Britain's leading manufacturers. First-quality or slight rejects are available at London's best prices. The shops are open seven days a week from 9 a.m. to 6 p.m.

Westaway & Westaway, opposite the British Museum at 65 Great Russell St., W.C.1 (tel. 405-0479), are a splendid substitute for a shopping trip to Scotland. They stock an enormous range of kilts, scarves, waistcoats (pronounced "weskits"), capes, dressing gowns, and rugs in authentic clan tartans. What's more, they're wonderfully knowledgeable on the subject of these minutely intricate clan symbols. They also sell superb—and untartaned—cashmere, camel-hair, and Shetland knitwear. Another branch is at 29 Bloomsbury Way, W.C.1 (tel. 405-0497).

Berk, at 46 Burlington Arcade, Piccadilly, W.1 (tel. 493-0028), is one of those irresistible "fancy shops" for which London is famous. The fancies here are woolen—sweaters, skirts, cardigans, kilts by the mile and by the clan, superb cashmere and pure camel-hair sets, hardy Scottish shetlands. The store is believed to have one of the largest collections of cashmere sweaters in London, at least of the top brands. And all this is displayed amid the 150-year-old Burlington Arcade, an attraction in its own right.

Astleys, 109 Jermyn St., S.W.1 (tel. 930-1687). This is a pipe-smoker's paradise, masculine to the core. Apart from selling superb pipes (some of them special freehand models) and virtually every conceivable blend of their own tobaccos, Astleys features a kind of pipe museum, consisting of antique smoking utensils which tell the history of the ancient and noble art of "tobacco drinking." Briar pipes start at £15 ($29.25) and go upward.

Taylor of London, 167 Sloane St., S.W.1 (tel. 235-4653), are originators of English flower fragrances since 1887. Beautiful gifts include bone china pomanders, potpourri, luxurious bathroom accessories, and perfumes of quality. Taylor of London makes personal deliveries in style—that is, in a horse-drawn carriage.

Gary Mark of London Ltd., 3 Station Approach Baker St., N.W.1 (tel. 935-3170), is a modern jewelry shop adjacent to Madame Tussaud's. Its owner, Gary M. Edel, sells the latest designs in gold and silver jewelry from Paris, Amsterdam, Rome, and London as well, with many exclusive styles at reasonable prices. The shop has an excellent reputation for design and value for money, and is so patronized by people worldwide when visiting London, and by Londoners themselves, that it is open every day. The shop also carries leather handbags, belts, and gloves, as well as Swiss watches and a wide collection of gifts. The latest store is at the luxurious Washington Hotel, Curzon Street, Mayfair, W.1, inside the hotel, selling jewelry, souvenirs, and electronic equipment at discount prices.

Christie's Contemporary Art, 8 Dover St., W.1 (tel. 499-6701), offers original etchings, lithographs, and screenprints by up-and-coming artists for around £30 ($58.50) to £60 ($117). You will certainly not end up with an absolute "pup," and your holiday purchase may turn out to be a first work of a second Picasso. The gallery also has the works of such masters as Henry Moore, David Hockney, Joan Miró, and John Piper. Each work is an original, numbered and signed by the artist, then stamped with Christie's seal of authentication before delivery. You can send for a catalogue or just go along.

Lillywhites Ltd., Piccadilly Circus, S.W.1 (tel. 930-3181), is Britain's biggest sports store with six floors of sports clothing, equipment, and footwear. Established in 1863 and Europe's most famous sports store, Lillywhites offers everything connected with sport, together with new and exciting ranges of stylish and fashionable leisurewear for both men and women. For overseas customers, the Lillywhites Special Orders and International Departments offer a worldwide service.

The **Welsh Craft Centre,** 36 Parliament St., S.W.1 (tel. 839-5056), is a gallery of things Welsh, ranging from hand-woven rugs, tapestries, and tweeds to Welsh lovespoons, brass miners' lamps, horse brasses, pottery, and stoneware.

St. Paul's Cathedral

Chapter IX

CHILDREN'S LONDON

IT'S HARD TO DRAW a clear distinguishing line between junior and senior brands of entertainment. In London it's almost impossible.

The British Museum, for instance, is definitely rated as an adult attraction. Yet we've watched group after group of kids stand absolutely spellbound in front of the Egyptian mummies, still completely absorbed long after their parents were champing at the bit to trot along.

Conversely, the Zoo is supposed to be primarily for the younger set. But we've seen dignified daddies become so hypnotized by the ant colony and the nest-stitching Indian tailor bird that they had to be literally dragged away by their brood.

One variation or another of the same scene is constantly enacted at the Tower, Madame Tussaud's, the *Discovery,* Billingsgate Market, Battersea Park, and a dozen other places.

We've seen small girls react with frozen unamusement to royal dollhouses that had their mothers cooing with delight. And we've observed those same little ladies aglow with enthusiasm before the oil painting of a particularly gruesome 17th-century massacre. Their spiritual brothers meanwhile disdained even to glance at a model car racetrack and preferred to give their total attention to the activities of a window cleaner.

All of which merely goes to prove that children are at least as individualistic in their tastes as adults. It also goes to make our classification job very difficult.

The attractions to follow are *not* meant specifically for children. They are general and universal fun places to which you can take youngsters without having to worry about either their physical or moral safety. There's nothing to stop you from going to any of them minus a juvenile escort. It is even possible that you'll enjoy them more thoroughly than any kid around.

The only exceptions are the children's tours listed at the end of this chapter. Those *are* designed—in fact, tailor-made—for the younger set.

THE LONDON DUNGEON: The premises at 34 Tooley St., S.E.1 (tel. 403-0606), simulate a ghoulish atmosphere designed deliberately to chill the blood while reproducing the conditions which existed in the Middle Ages. Set under the arches of London Bridge Station, the dungeon is a series of tableaux, more grizzly than Madame Tussaud's, depicting life in Old London. The rumble of trains overhead adds to the spine-chilling horror of the place. Bells toll and there is constant melancholy chanting in the background. Dripping water and live rats make for even more atmosphere.

The heads of executed criminals were stuck on spikes for onlookers to observe through glasses hired for the occasion. The murder of Thomas à Becket in Canterbury Cathedral is also depicted. Naturally, there's a burning at the stake, as well as a torture chamber with racking, branding, and fingernail extraction.

If you survive, there is a souvenir shop selling certificates which testify that you have been through the works.

The dungeon is open from 10 a.m. to 6 p.m. daily, charging £2.50 ($4.88) for adults, £1.25 ($2.44) for children.

BATTERSEA PARK: The park is a vast patch of woodland, lakes, and lawns on the south bank of the Thames, opposite Chelsea Embankment. It boasts just about everything that makes for happiness on a dry day: a tree-lined boulevard, magnificent fountains, and a children's zoo with baby animals.

THE UNICORN THEATRE CLUB: Based at the Arts Theatre, Great Newport Street, W.C.2, the Unicorn is a company producing eight or nine new plays per season, each one tailored for young people aged 4 to 13 years. (The age-range suitability is indicated on the program.) In addition it runs special workshops for children in improvisation, puppet-making, music, magic, makeup, scene-painting, and tumbling, and also presents visiting puppet shows, mime troupes, dance companies, films, and concerts.

Most of the plays are specially written for the Unicorn and range from modernized Punch and Judy larks (with human actors) to full-fledged three-acters depicting anything likely to stir junior's imagination. Productions are completely and smoothly professional and the workshops among the most stimulating in London, so much so that your youngsters are likely to become theater buffs for life after a session there. Anyone can buy a ticket for a play by paying a nominal temporary membership charge of 5p (10¢), and overseas visitors can become full members for four months for 60p ($1.17). Also provided are diaries and club information giving dates and details about forthcoming productions. For additional information telephone 240-2076.

CLUB ROW MARKET: In Sclater Street, Bethnal Green (tube to Bethnal Green), this is one of the most famous markets in London and a guaranteed fascinator for kids. It sells pets—parakeets to puppy dogs, goldfish to golden hamsters—the cages, bowls, and boxes to keep them in, and the food they eat. The S.P.C.A. keeps a sharply benevolent eye on the stalls, so the wee critters are comfortable and dangerously appealing. It operates only on Sunday from 9 a.m. to 1 p.m. And watch out you don't go home with a bunny rabbit.

LONDON ZOO: Run by the Zoological Society of London, Regents Park, N.W.1 (tel. 722-3333), with an equal measure of showmanship and scholarly know-how, this 36-acre garden houses 6000 animals, including some of the rarest species on earth, such as the two famous giant pandas, Ching-Ching and Chia-Chia. The most fascinating part of the collection is the separate houses reserved for particular species. The insect house (incredible bird-eating spiders, a cross-sectioned ant colony), the reptile house (huge dragon-like monitor lizards and a fantastic 20-foot python), and the latest additions, the Clore Pavilion for Small Mammals, the Sobell Pavilion for Apes and Monkeys, and the Lion Terraces.

Designed for the largest collection of small mammals in the world, the Clore Pavilion has a basement called "The Moonlight World," where special lighting effects simulate night for the nocturnal beasties, while rendering them clearly visible to onlookers. You can see all the night rovers in action—leaping bush babies, rare kiwis, fierce Tasmanian devils, giant Indian fruit bats with heads like prehistoric dogs.

Admission is £3.50 ($6.83) for adults, £1.50 ($2.93) for children 5 to 16; children under 5, free. It's open daily from 9 a.m.

in summer till 6 p.m. (the last admission half an hour before closing). Winter hours are from 10 a.m. Take the tube to Baker Street or Camden Town, then walk (or take bus 74 from Marble Arch or Baker Street).

WHIPSNADE PARK ZOO: Also owned by the Zoological Society, this is the unbarred big brother of the above, covering 500 acres of landscape in the Chilterns hills of Bedfordshire. There are no cages, only patches of natural bush and scrubland placed inside wide enclosures and paddocks, allowing the furred, fanged, or hoofed inhabitants maximum freedom. Owing to the spread of the layout, this is hard on your legs, but wonderful for your camera. You can tell the folks at home you've been on safari. Exhibits include a water mammals spectacle displaying dolphins, a steam railway, an African animal preview, and animals of Asia. Cars are admitted in summer for £2.50 ($4.88) in summer and in winter for £1.25 ($2.44). In addition, you must pay £2.75 ($5.36) for adults, £1.50 ($2.93) for children. Take the train from St. Pancras Station to Luton, then bus 43 to Whipsnade Park. The zoo is open daily from 10 a.m. to sunset.

NATURAL HISTORY MUSEUM: Cromwell Road, S.W.7, is the home of the national collections of living and fossil plants and animals, minerals, rocks, and meteorites, with lots of magnificent specimens on display. Traditional displays are being replaced by exciting new exhibitions designed to encourage people of all ages to enjoy learning about modern natural history. Exhibitions already open include "Human Biology—An Exhibition of Ourselves," "Dinosaurs and Their Living Relatives," "Man's Place in Evolution," "Introducing Ecology," and "Origin of the Species."

   Admission is free. The museum is open weekdays from 10 a.m. to 6 p.m.; on Sunday from 2:30 to 6 p.m. Take the tube to South Kensington.

BETHNAL GREEN MUSEUM: Cambridge Heath Road, E.2. (tel. 980-2415). This establishment has dolls, dolls, and more dolls, plus everything associated with them. Strictly speaking, it displays toys over the past century, but the accent is definitely on dolls. The variety of dolls is staggering, some of them dressed in period costumes of such elaborateness that you don't even want to think of the price tags they must have carried.

With the dolls go dollhouses, from simple cottages to miniature mansions, complete with fireplaces and grand pianos, plus carriages, furniture, kitchen utensils, and household pets. It might be wise to explain to your children beforehand, that—no, none of them is for sale.

In addition, the museum displays optical toys, a toy theater, marionettes, puppets, and a considerable exhibit of soldiers and warlike toys of both World Wars, plus trains and aircraft. On the upper floor is decorative art of the 19th century, ranging from the 1830s to art nouveau. Often special activities for children are presented; telephone for information.

The museum is open weekdays from 10 a.m. to 6 p.m.; on Sunday from 2:30 p.m. Admission is free. Take the tube to Bethnal Green. Closed on Friday.

PENNY ARCADES: This may seem an astonishing item to include in a children's chapter, but—hold it—London's arcades are like nothing you see in the States. Whereas the American versions represent litter-strewn receptacles for bored juveniles and servicemen, the London variations are FUN. Clean fun. However, persons under 18 are not admitted unless accompanied by an adult.

There are literally hundreds of them, ranging from plain to near-palatial. Many are found in and around Leicester Square. Some contain chandeliers and carpets. The play gadgets give you a pretty good run for your money.

Some of the skill and thrill machines are marvels of ingenuity, including miniature racetracks with whizzing cars, jumping horses, and bubbling speedboats. In some tank shooting games, you control and aim a revolving turret. In remarkably realistic submarine periscopes, you direct torpedos at moving battleships. Aerial duels can be viewed through the cockpit of a fighter plane. In driving tests the road and traffic hazards unwind on a screen in front of your steering wheel. The controls of an airliner can be used for a safe landing.

These arcades also house some genuine gambling machines, paying off in pennies or tokens. But they take second place to the just-fun contraptions.

HAMPSTEAD HEATH: This is the traditional playground of the Londoner, the 'Appy 'Ampstead of Cockney legendry, the place dedicated "to the use of the public forever" by special Act of

Parliament in 1872. Londoners might just possibly tolerate the conversion of, say, Hyde Park into housing estates or supermarkets, but they would certainly mount the barricades if Hampstead Heath were imperiled.

This 800-acre expanse of high heath entirely surrounded by London is actually a chain of continuous park, wood, and grassland, bearing different names in different portions. It contains just about every known form of outdoor amusement, with the exception of big-game hunting.

There are natural lakes for swimmers (who don't mind goosebumps), bridle paths for horseriders, athletic tracks, hills for kite flying, and a special pond for model yachting. You can catch bream and pike in several lakes, paddle your own boat on others, feed the squirrels or admire the interiors of two beautiful 17th-century mansions converted into museums.

At the shore of Kenwood Lake, in the northern section, is a concert platform devoted to symphony performances on summer Saturday evenings. Waterlow Park, the northeast corner, has the Grass Theatre, where ballets, operas, and comedies are staged over a five-week season in June and July.

At Easter, Whitsun, and August bank holidays, the heath becomes riotous with the noise and tunes of two fun fairs going full-blast, and even sophisticated Londoners make it a point of dropping in on them. It's all part of a tradition, as deeply rooted as orderly "queuing" and Christmas decorations.

If you're history minded, you can stand for a moment on top of Parliament Hill on the south side. It was from that vantage point that the ancient British Queen Boadicea and her daughters watched the burning of the Roman camp of Londinium, which her tribesmen had put to the torch in A.D. 61.

Take the tube to Hampstead or Belsize Park.

THE LITTLE ANGEL THEATRE: 14 Dagmar Passage, N.1. This is especially constructed for and devoted to the presentation of puppetry in all its forms. It is open to the general public, and between 200 and 300 performances are given here every year. The theater is the focal point of a loosely formed group of about 20 professional puppeteers who work there as occasion demands, sometimes presenting their own shows and often helping with the performances of the resident company.

In the current repertory, there are 25 programs. These vary in style and content from *The Soldier's Tale,* using eight-foot-high figures, to *Wonder Island* and *Lancelot the Lion,* written especially for the humble glove puppet. Many of the plays, such as Hans Christian Andersen's *The Little Mermaid,* are performed with marionettes (string puppets), but whatever is being presented you'll be enthralled with the exquisite lighting and skill with which the puppets are handled.

The theater is beautifully decorated and well equipped. There is a coffee bar in the foyer and a workshop adjacent where the settings and costumes, as well as the puppets, are made. To find out what's playing and book your seats, call 226-1787. Performances are at 11 a.m. on Saturday, when the seats are £1 ($1.95) for children, £1.25 ($2.44) for adults; and at 3 p.m. on Saturday and Sunday, when the cost is £1.25 ($2.44) for children, £2 ($3.90) for adults.

Take the tube to Angel Station, then walk up Upper Street past St. Mary's Church until you come to Cross Street, Dagmar Passage being just off here. Buses 19, 30, 38, 4, and 73 pass within short distances of the theater. Ask for the Cross Street stop, Islington.

POLLOCK'S TOY MUSEUM: 1 Scala St., W.1, is probably the most curious museum in London. A wee white corner house, it's like something out of Hans Christian Andersen, crammed to the bursting point with antique playthings.

Each of the three stories has its specialties. On the ground level, the museum is a shop displaying old-fashioned toys and dolls you can buy. One steep flight up is the world of toy theaters —Victorian wood and cardboard stages, colorful and ornate like wedding cakes, Balinese shadow screens, 19th-century French "living pictures." Another flight up are the dolls—from wooden Dutch to china English, not forgetting original American teddy bears.

In between is a vast array of miniature kitchen stoves, tin soldiers, ships, horses, and "flying machines," plus playtime rarities like magic lanterns dating from 1866, clockwork cars from 1902, and a working British bathtub submarine from 1904.

Admission is 30p (59¢) for adults, 15p (29¢) for children. It is open from 10 a.m. to 5 p.m., Monday through Saturday. Closed Sunday. Take the tube to Goodge Street Station, then it's a minute's walk to the corner of Whitfield and Scala Streets.

NATIONAL MARITIME MUSEUM: Romney Road, Greenwich. Down the Thames at Greenwich, about six miles from the city, the Maritime Museum stands in a beautiful park and has a special claim to fame, aside from its contents. Through one wing of this building runs the zero meridian of longitude, which is how we got the term "Greenwich Mean Time." The working Royal Observatory, which coined it, has since been moved, but the meridian is still there—invisible but marked by a brass strip across the Old Royal Observatory courtyard.

A great many astronomical instruments still mingle with the navigation gadgets—it's easy to see the connection. Otherwise, the building harbors the glory that was Britain at sea. The wooden ships, the brass cannon, the iron men; the relics, models, and paintings telling the story of a thousand naval battles and a thousand victories. Also the price of those battles—among the exhibits is the uniform which Lord Nelson wore when he was struck by a French musket ball at the very moment of his triumph at the Battle of Trafalgar.

Admission is free. Weekday visiting hours in summer are from 10 a.m. to 6 p.m.; on Sunday from 2 to 5:30 p.m. The museum is closed Monday. You can take a Thames launch downstream from Westminster Pier or the train from Charing Cross Station to Maze Hill.

Children's Tours

There comes a time in the affairs of parents abroad when life would appear distinctly brighter for a temporary respite from the offspring. Catering to just that contingency is . . .

JUNIOR JAUNTS: 4A William St., S.W.1 (tel. 235-4750). Operating as a branch of a Knightsbridge employment agency, this service takes parties of kids 5 to 15 years of age on tours of London for the day. It currently offers a choice of 12 different tours and is constantly adding new excursions to the list.

Lasting from 10 a.m. to 4 p.m., the jaunts cover various batches of attractions tailored to a wide range of juvenile tastes—from visits to Regents Park Zoo by canal boat, to Carnaby Street and the Tower of London, to Greenwich by river, to the Planetarium, the Changing of the Guards, R.R.S. *Discovery,* or a police station, to pottery lessons in Chelsea, or ice skating or boating on the Hyde Park Serpentine.

The guides are highly experienced teachers and ex-air hostesses, and the standard fee of £17 ($33.15) includes transport, admission fees, and a picnic lunch. Visits are adjusted entirely to the interests of the children. Children are picked up at their hotel and returned.

VISITORS WELCOME LTD.: 17 Radley Mews, W.8 (tel. 937-9755). This organization, founded in 1960, looks after children for the day or puts them up (very comfortably) for the night, in case the parents want to go on a short excursion or holiday by themselves. The staff also meets at the airports children or students who are coming to visit friends or study in England.

The staff consists of level-headed young women, eminently capable of coping with whatever crises might arise. Charges (for single children or two of a family) vary according to the time of day or night. During daylight hours, these are approximately £4 ($7.80) per hour.

Trafalgar Square

Chapter X

ONE-DAY EXCURSIONS FROM LONDON

YOU COULD SPEND the best part of year—or a lifetime—exploring London, without risking either boredom or repetition. But since your stay is probably limited, we'd advise you to tear yourself away from Big Ben for at least a day or two.

For the Thames metropolis is surrounded by some of the most memorable spots on earth, entire clusters of scenic resorts, historic sites, cultural and religious shrines, and just-plain-fun places, all within comfortable commuting range.

The only trouble is that there are too many of them.

There's Shakespeare's town of Stratford-upon-Avon, the pilgrimage city of Canterbury, Churchill's country home at Chartwell, the Tudor turrets of Hampton Court, dozens of "stately mansions"—and resident dukes—awaiting your inspection, Windsor Castle of Queen Victoria's memory, the fabulous flowers of Syon Park, the great universities of Oxford and Cambridge, the roaming wild animals of Woburn Abbey, Runnymede of Magna Carta fame—the roll call goes on and on.

The small county of Hampshire alone contains the medieval cathedral city of Winchester, the great seaport of Southampton, the New Forest nature preserve with deer and shaggy wild ponies, and the 800-year-old Mottisfont Abbey, all within a 70-minute train ride of London.

Stratford-upon-Avon

Starting with the farthest and most famous, this small town in Warwickshire lies 91 miles from London. The train from Paddington Station takes you there in 2½ hours.

As you probably know, Shakespeare was born there in 1564, and returned to marry and live there after his wild and creative years in London had earned him enough money to settle down as the solid bourgeois he was at heart.

You can trace his life story in Stratford, from his birthplace on Henley Street to his tomb in the Holy Trinity Church. There's still an aura of old Elizabethan England among Stratford's timbered inns and 16th-century houses with their oddly protruding upper story. And the Avon is still the same gentle river in which young Will, the tanner's son, admired the reflection of his sprouting beard.

The Bard was first honored at a "birthday celebration" in Stratford in 1769. Ever since, Will has drawn a steady stream of tourists to his hometown. By the way, in Stratford—especially to the prospering innkeepers and shop owners—don't put forth the theory that Francis Bacon really wrote those plays.

All the Shakespearian properties are open from 9 a.m. till 6 p.m. on weekdays (on Sunday from 2 to 6 p.m.; Shakespeare's Birthplace and Anne Hathaway's Cottage from 10 a.m.), from April to October. In the winter season, they remain open weekdays from 9 a.m. to 4 p.m. On off-season Sundays, only the two most visited attractions, Shakespeare's Birthplace and the Cottage of Anne Hathaway remain open (the hours are from 1:30 to 4:30 p.m.).

It's recommended that you go first to **Shakespeare's Birthplace,** on Henley Street. The Elizabethan dramatist was born there on April 23, 1564, the son of a "whittawer" or glove maker. Since 1847, when fans of the Bard raised the pounds and purchased the property, the house has been operated as a national shrine. A museum on the premises reveals his "life and times." Built to honor the 400th anniversary of the writer's birth, the Shakespeare Center next door was dedicated as a library and study center in 1964. An extension to the original building, opened in 1981, provides a reception center for visitors to the Birthplace. It contains some notable artistic features.

It's recommended that you purchase a comprehensive ticket admitting you to all five trust properties. The cost is £2.20 ($4.29) for adults, 90p ($1.76) for children. If visited separately, the birthplace costs 90p ($1.76) for adults, 30p (59¢) for children.

For many, the chief magnet here is **Anne Hathaway's Cottage,** in the small hamlet of Shottery, outside of Stratford. Poor Anne had to remain behind when her roving husband wandered off to London in 1587 to pursue his career as a playwright and actor at the Blackfriars and Globe Theatres. At the cottage made of what the English call "wattle and daub," Miss Hathaway, the daughter of a yeoman farmer, lived before her marriage to Shakespeare. Of the furnishings remaining, the "courting settle" evokes the most interest.

If the weather is good, the best way to reach Shottery is from Evesham Place in town (the strolling path is marked), traversing a meadow. Otherwise, a bus leaves from Bridge Street in Stratford.

At the so-called **New Place** on Chapel Street, Shakespeare retired in comfort in 1610. His reputation was already secured, his purse full, although, we suspect, he could hardly imagine the fame that would one day come to him. He was to live there in peace for six years, enjoying the esteem and respect of the townspeople, in spite of his "scandalous" career in the theater. He died in 1616 at the age of 52.

The house which he purchased for his retirement was destroyed, but you can walk through the gardens (entered through the home of Thomas Nash, a man who married Shakespeare's granddaughter, Elizabeth Hall). Of chief interest in the garden is a mulberry tree, said to have been rooted from a cutting of a tree that Shakespeare planted.

Although often ignored by the casual visitor, **Mary Arden's House** is a delight, built in the charming Tudor style. Shakespeare's mother, who, like his wife, was the daughter of a yeoman farmer, lived here in Wilmcote, a village about three miles outside of Stratford. A farming museum is accommodated in the barns.

In the "Old Town," the **Hall's Croft Festival Club** is another timbered Elizabethan building, the home of Susanna, Shakespeare's daughter, and her doctor husband, John Hall. The club is only a short walk from the Royal Shakespeare Theatre, about a block from the river.

Although not administered by the trust association, the **Holy Trinity Church,** one of England's most beautiful parish churches, on the banks of the Avon, is also much visited. Shakespeare was buried here, leaving behind the threat engraved on his tombstone: "and curst be he who moves my bones." Contribution requested from adults wishing to view Shakespeare's tomb is 20p (39¢) for adults, 15p (29¢) for students.

Another attraction on "The High" is **Harvard House,** the former home, built in 1596, of Katherine Rogers, the mother of the founder of Harvard University, John Harvard. A Chicago millionaire purchased it and presented it to the American university, which runs it today.

Nearly every visitor to Stratford wants to attend at least one performance at the **Royal Shakespeare Theatre,** designed in 1932 to stand right on the Avon by Miss Elizabeth Scott (the building was a subject of much controversy). The old Memorial Theatre caught fire and burned down in the 1920s. The long season of the Bard's plays begins in April and lasts until January. Five or six of Shakespeare's dramas and comedies usually operate in repertory. Reservations, of course, should be made in advance, as the theater is popular. Chances are you won't get a good seat (or even a seat) if you should just arrive at the box office.

Windsor

Windsor means two things to an English person: a castle and a college. Windsor Castle, the largest inhabited castle in the world, has been the home of English sovereigns for more than 800 years. And nearby Eton College has been educating future sovereigns along with lesser fry for more than 500.

Windsor Castle stands 21 miles outside London. The train from either Waterloo or Paddington Station does the trip in 50 minutes. Green Line coaches 704 and 705 from Hyde Park Corner take around 1½ hours.

The castle was built by William the Conqueror and completed before his death in 1087. An immense, looming structure, it has distinctly mixed memories for Britain's royalty. King John waited here in seething rage before being forced to sign the Magna Carta by his obstreperous barons in 1215. Here, Queen Victoria's beloved consort Albert died in 1861, turning her into the eternally grieving "Widow of Windsor." The State Apartments are still used at certain times by the present Queen Elizabeth.

When the Royal Standard is up, you know the queen is in residence and her apartments closed to visitors. At other times they can be viewed by the public—the only glimpse of inhabited royal suites you're liable to get. Admission is £1 ($1.95) for adults, 50p (98¢) for children. The rest of the castle—and it's a mighty big rest—is open free from 10 a.m. till sunset.

Eton College, founded in 1440 by King Henry VI, is still the most illustrious "public" (meaning private) school in Britain, and its pupils still wear strange Edwardian garb, top hat and collar, that makes them look like period fashion plates, but carries a helluva load of snob appeal. You can visit the schoolyard and Cloisters free from 2 to 5 p.m.

Two miles beyond Windsor lies the meadow of **Runnymede,** where King John, chewing his beard in fury, signed the Magna Carta. But Runnymede is also the site of the John F. Kennedy Memorial, one acre of hallowed ground presented to the United States by the people of Great Britain.

Two miles southwest of Windsor Castle lie **Windsor Safari Park and Seaworld,** Winkfield Road (tel. Windsor 69841). Even the Royal Borough of Windsor has not been spared the safari craze which has swept the world. The Safari Park and Seaworld are just 23 miles from London. Take the M4 motorway and leave it at Junction 6. The park is on the B3022 road. You can watch the performing dolphins and a killer whale and drive through reserves of lions, tigers, baboons, giraffes, camels, and many other wild animals. Open from 10 a.m., the park has catering facilities, but you can picnic on acres of green. If you have a soft-top car or come on public transport from Windsor, take the safari bus around the reserves. Admission to Safari Park is £2.90 ($5.66) for adults, £2.30 ($4.49) for children. The dolphin and killer whale show, as well as the parrot show and other amusements, are free.

Canterbury

The ancient pilgrimage center in Kent, 56 miles from London, is the site of the cathedral that is the Mother Church of the worldwide Episcopalian movement. By train from Victoria, Charing Cross, Waterloo, or London Bridge Stations, the journey takes 1½ hours. The bus from Victoria Coach Station does it in two to three hours.

Chaucer and his fellow pilgrims went there more than five centuries ago, and the gray West Gate through which they entered still forms the city's main gateway. The goal of their pilgrimage—and that of millions of others—was the magnificent Gothic cathedral, shrine of Archbishop Thomas à Becket, who was murdered there by four knights after their king had asked why no one would rid him of "that turbulent priest."

When the swords hacked into Becket in 1170, **Canterbury Cathedral** was already a century old. Then, as now, it dominates the town, governs its spirit, somehow makes you aware of its presence even when hidden by other buildings.

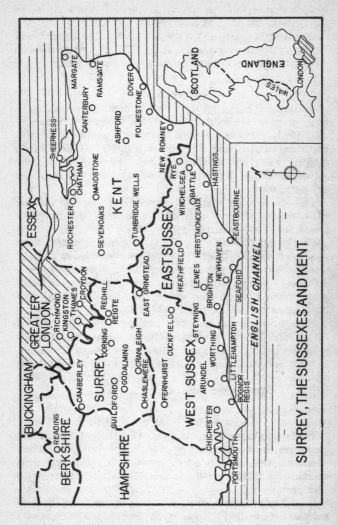

The cathedral is neither as overpowering as Cologne Cathedral nor as awe-inspiring as Notre Dame in Paris. It has a mellow, almost gentle, beauty and a touching simplicity, despite the splendor of the art treasures it houses: the superb stained-glass windows and the opulent tomb of Edward the Black Prince, hero of the "Longbow Battle" of Crécy.

The original church on the site now occupied by the cathedral was erected by St. Augustine in A.D. 597 and became the cradle of English Christianity among the pagan folk of Kent.

Woburn Abbey

The great 18th-century mansion of **Woburn Abbey** is the traditional seat of the dukes of Bedford and the most publicized of all of England's Stately Homes. A wondrous mixture of art gems and carnival gimmicks (it contains paintings by Rembrandt, Holbein, Van Dyck, and Gainsborough, as well as a fun fair and a zoo), the abbey, 44 miles from London, is best visited with an organized tour.

This ancestral seat is run like a cross between a high-class art exhibition and a three-ring circus. The Georgian mansion (which has slept Queen Victoria as well as Marilyn Monroe) contains some $14 million worth of paintings, antique furniture, silver, and tapestries. The Stately Antique Market consists of three streets of period shops selling objets d'art. Surrounding it is a 3000-acre park and zoo with herds of rare deer, European bison, a light railway, pets corner, amusement rides, lake fishing, gardening centers, and legions of sightseers.

Frames runs an excursion that combines Woburn Abbey and the university city of Cambridge. The tour departs from London (11 Herbrand St., W.C.1) at 8:30 a.m. every Sunday throughout the year. The adult fare, including admission fees and the services of a guide, is £13 ($25.35). For reservations, telephone 837-3111. Tube: Russell Square.

Oxford and Blenheim Palace

The famous university town of Oxford, 57 miles from London, can be reached in 1¼ hours by train from Paddington Station. The city is well over a thousand years old, and the earliest of the colleges—St. Edmund Hall, Merton, and Balliol—date from the 13th century.

It's difficult to decide where the university ends and the town begins—the scattered colleges, quads, and chapels blend in with the workaday buildings in a wonderfully harmonious whole, giving every street scene dreaming spires and domes. The two main streets, oddly known as "The High" and "The Broad," are perhaps the most beautiful period thoroughfares in England, set off by the Sheldonian Theatre, the University Church of St. Mary, and the Bodleian Library, one of the most important book collections in the world.

In Broad Street, you'll see a cross marking the spot where England's martyr bishops, Latimer, Ridley, and Cranmer, were burned at the stake during the reign of "Bloody Queen Mary" in 1557.

Oxford University consists of 28 colleges, five of which are for women. Among the more renowned colleges:

Christ Church, known as "The House," was started by Cardinal Wolsey in 1525 and refounded by King Henry VIII in 1546. The college contains the largest quadrangle in Oxford, the Cathedral of the Diocese of Oxford, and a fine Tudor Hall with many portraits. The tower over the main entrance was designed by Sir Christopher Wren and contains the bell called Great Tom which is struck 101 times each evening. Admission is 50p (98¢). For information, telephone Oxford 47607.

Numbering everybody from Wolsey to Wilde among its alumni, **Magdalen** (pronounced "maud-len") was founded by the bishop of Winchester, William of Wayneflete, in 1458. The 15th-century chapel is well worth a visit, as is a 17th-century "screen." After viewing the college, the traditional course of sightseeing is to go on a stroll along **Addison's Walk,** named in honor of the 18th-century poet. The grounds belonging to the park contain a much-publicized deer park.

Ancient **Merton** traces its origins back to 1264. Its library is among the oldest in England, built in the 1370s and containing an astrolabe said to have been owned by Chaucer.

University College on "The High" (tel. Oxford 42681), was founded in 1249. However, legend has it that it was founded by Alfred the Great. The present college buildings were constructed principally in the 17th and 19th centuries. Shelley attended college here, but he was "sent down," or expelled as we say.

The bishop of Winchester founded **New College** in 1379 (the English are fond of calling medieval buildings "new"). Built in the 14th century, its quadrangle was the first one to be designed at Oxford, setting the style for all the rest. In the ante-chapel is exhibited a contemporary sculpture of *Lazarus* by Sir Jacob Epstein. The entrance is on New College Lane.

After you've seen Oxford, take a bus to **Blenheim Palace,** eight miles away at Woodstock. The magnificent palace was presented by a grateful English nation to their most admired warrior, the first duke of Marlborough, in 1704. Later, an even more admired descendant of the duke was born there of an English father and an American mother—and christened Winston Lionel Spencer Churchill. The present duke of Marlborough, Sir Winston's cousin, still lives in the palace.

The palace is open daily from 11:30 a.m. to 5 p.m. from mid-March through October. Adults pay £2.25 ($4.39) and children are charged £1.10 ($2.15). For information, write or phone the Administrator, Blenheim Palace, Woodstock, Oxon (tel. 0993-84325).

Brighton

Britain's favorite seaside resort lies on the Sussex coast, 51 miles from London. Fast trains from Victoria or London Bridge Stations make the trip in 55 minutes. Buses from Victoria Coach Station take around two hours.

Brighton has lost the aura of fashionable wickedness it possessed when the prince regent built his incredible pseudo-Oriental Royal Pavilion there in 1787. Now it's very much a family resort, boasting the warmest sunshine and the best beaches on the British Isles.

Don't bank on actually swimming, however (the English are an excruciatingly hardy lot when it comes to water temperatures), but the seafront promenade and two amusement piers make it a fun town, as well as a beautiful one. Brighton has everything from waxworks and aquariums to three live theaters, every conceivable form of sport, cafés, plush restaurants, five miles of beaches, and the annual London-Brighton Veteran Car Run.

And the town is still a picture of terraced Regency elegance, strangely tranquil after the turmoil along the seafront. At night, the floodlights play on the Royal Pavilion and the floral boulevard.

Hampton Court

Amid rolling green country by the river Thames towers the grandest of all the great palaces built in England during the Tudor period. It was originally intended as the homestead of Cardinal Wolsey, chancellor (meaning prime minister) to King Henry VIII. On second thought, however, the wily cardinal presented it as a gift to his royal master, who then added a few luxurious touches of his own.

You'll see Hampton Court much as it was built more than 400

years ago. Admission in summer to the palace is £1.80 ($3.51) for adults, 90p ($1.76) for children and senior citizens. Off-season prices are lowered to 90p ($1.76) and 50p (98¢), respectively. Recently restored are the Great Kitchens as they were in the 1530s. They cost extra: 40p (78¢) for adults, 20p (39¢) for children. Walk in and see the fantastic Astronomical Clock, made by Nicholas Oursian in 1540. It tells the time, the date, and number of days since the New Year, the phases of the moon, and the times of high water at London Bridge, and was regarded as one of the mechanical miracles of its period. Wander through the royal kitchens, where an ox could be roasted whole, and lounge on the original lawn where King Henry once serenaded his Anne Boleyn—whom he eventually married and then beheaded.

Attached to the original palace there's a later one, designed by Sir Christopher Wren for William of Orange and Queen Mary. Wren built the magnificent formal Fountain Court and the great East Front facing the gardens. Still standing there is the world-famous Great Vine (mentioned in Ripley's "Believe It or Not") which was planted in 1769 and has a main branch now more than 100 feet long. You can also lose yourself in the Maze, cost 10p (20¢). Take Southern Railway direct from Waterloo Station to Hampton Court in 35 minutes.

West Wycombe

In 1735, Sir Francis Dashwood, second baronet, embarked on an ambitious building program in the village of West Wycombe, just 30 miles west of London. Sir Francis, who had a fascination for architecture and design, was responsible for the unusual monuments, the rebuilding of the church, and the complete remodeling of the Dashwood family home. Sitting atop West Wycombe Hill, overlooking the village, is the **Church of St. Lawrence,** crowned by a golden ball. Parts of the church date from the 14th century, but the style was completely changed by Sir Francis. The interior was richly furnished and painted in the style of a third-century sun temple in Syria. From the church tower, you can get a superb view of the village and the surrounding Chiltern Hills. Near the church is the **Dashwood Mausoleum,** a hexagonal monument copied after Constantine's Arch in Rome.

On the slope of the hill is the entrance to the **West Wycombe Caves** (tel. High Wycombe 24411). These winding passages are the result of the mining of a chalk quarry on this site, the product used in building a road out of the village. Sir Francis and his "knights" began to meet here in the mid-18th century to carry on the secret rites of the "Hellfire Club," which included something to do with keeping company with women dressed as nuns, but of "a lively, cheerful disposition." Members of the club included painter William Hogarth and Lord Sandwich.

A visit to West Wycombe wouldn't be complete without a tour of the **Dashwood House.** Behind the many-columned facade are rooms filled with a fine collection of antiques, paintings, and china. George III and Benjamin Franklin were both guests here during Sir Francis's time. West Wycombe Park, a beautifully landscaped garden, provides the perfect setting for this superb example of Palladian architecture.

The village, restored to much of its 18th-century charm, is a treat. You can wander the street, stop for lunch in a public house, or stroll through the four miles of nature trails to explore the surrounding countryside.

West Wycombe is open year round, although there are of course specific hours for the various sights. The caves are open daily from March through September from 1 to 6 p.m., but on weekends only from noon to 4 p.m. the rest of the year. The Dashwood house is only open from June 1 to August 30, Monday to Friday from 2:15 to 6 p.m., but it also opens on Sunday during July and August. Admission to the caves is £1.50 ($2.93) for adults and 75p ($1.46) for children. Admission to the house is £2 ($3.90) for adults and £1 ($1.95) for children, although you can wander the grounds for 80p ($1.56) for adults, 40p (78¢) for children.

Tunbridge Wells

This little Kentish holiday resort was once England's most elegant spa. Some 37 miles inland from London, it can be reached by train from Charing Cross Station in an hour.

Early in the 17th century, someone discovered the medicinal qualities of the chalybeate springs (the "wells" of the name), and the sleepy hamlet was transformed into a high-stepping watering resort for gouty royalty. Its patron saint was the noted dandy "Beau" Nash, who ushered in a stream of free-spending aristocrats and their ladies until "that accursed vogue of sea-bathing" pushed it into a social backwater.

You can still promenade along the Pantiles, a graceful arcade of shops, and try the water once imbibed by George II, the young Queen Victoria, and Edward VII. It even tastes pleasant.

Cambridge

It's one of the world's greatest university towns, its oldest college, **Peterhouse,** having been founded in 1284. The contrast between Cambridge and Oxford is pronounced. Oxford is not only a university town, but an industrial city as well; Cambridge adheres more to the traditional image of an English "town and gown" city.

To begin with, it lies in that part of England known as East Anglia, a bucolic land that embraces Essex and Suffolk, often called "Constable country." Cambridge is 80 miles from Oxford, but only 55 miles northeast of London.

The town boasts 29 colleges for both men and women. A good starting point for your exploration is the corner of Market Hill and King's Parade, the heart of Cambridge. Nearby is Great St. Mary's, the university church. Here, too, is the most brilliant jewel in the Cambridge crown: the 15th-century **King's College Chapel,** considered to be one of the most perfect buildings in the world (stained-glass windows, fan vaulting, lofty spires).

From here, you can walk to most of the colleges along the paths that scholars have followed for seven centuries of academic life. "The Backs," where the grounds of the colleges sweep down to the River Cam, are exciting to see.

Fifteen miles from Cambridge is one of the most magnificent cathedrals of England in **Ely,** that old lady of the "fen country."

Margate

In case the scholastic atmosphere of Cambridge doesn't appeal to you, here is its spiritual opposite. Margate is the largest, jolliest, and noisiest of the so-called Thanet resorts: a cluster of coastal towns in Kent dedicated to the concept of summer fun. The region lies only 74 miles from London—about 100 minutes by rail. And between them the resorts of Margate, Broadstairs, and Ramsgate cover just about every seaside holiday angle— except warm water and surf.

They do, however, get more sunshine than most of the country and offer miles of sandy beaches on which to enjoy it, plus everything that comes under the heading of holiday fun. **Margate** boasts a huge entertainment complex called **Dreamland,** covering 20 acres and embracing a **Safari Park** packed with wild animals. Also here is the **Winter Gardens** complex featuring rock, pop, dance, and comedy stars. The annual events include waterskiing spectaculars, carnivals, a football festival, bathing beauty contests, yachting regattas, and a conglomeration of mechanized thrills from rocket whirlers to rollercoasters.

Ramsgate has a beautiful **Royal Harbor** and **Broadstairs,** the charming and elaborate **Dickens Museum,** complete with Bleak House. In between and round about lie the rustic Thanet villages with windmills, thatched cottages, and ivy-covered churches. Electric trains from London (Victoria Station) run every hour.

Chartwell

Roger Lockyer once wrote, "Chartwell is a dull house, even from some aspects an ugly one, and it contains no collections of fine furniture or paintings, no magnificent ceilings or vaulted roofs. Its one claim to distinction is the quality of its owner—but, then, as Churchill himself said after a narrow vote in the House of Commons, 'One is enough.' "

For many years the former prime minister of Great Britain, its wartime leader, lived at this fairly modest home 1½ miles south of Westerham in Kent (tel. Crockham Hill 368). However, as a descendant of the first duke of Marlborough, he had been born in grander style at Blenheim Palace on November 30, 1874.

Administered by the National Trust, the house is open to the public from March 1 to November 30 on Tuesday, Wednesday, and Thursday from 2 to 6 p.m. On Saturday and Sunday, it is open from 11 a.m. to 6 p.m. Admission to the house and gardens is £1.70 ($3.32) for adults, 80p ($1.56) for children. There's a restaurant, serving snacks, tea, and coffee. From Easter to October, the Green Line coach service (no. 706) runs buses from London to Westerham and on to Chartwell, but on Sunday only.

Cutty Sark, Greenwich

Chapter XI

AND AFTER LONDON . . .

JUST AS PARIS is not France and Rome not Italy, so London is decidedly not Great Britain—or even that portion of it called England.

The city is so overwhelmingly huge that locals as well as visitors tend to mistake it for the entire island. And by doing so, they are depriving themselves of a wide and fascinating range of travel experiences just beyond their doorstep.

Britain is a "tight little island" all right, but packed into that small space is a kaleidoscope of contrasts so varied and multi-patterned that each facet seems to be part of a different country.

There are the harshly beautiful Highlands of Scotland and the sunny Channel Islands with their exotic French flavor; the grim and grimy industrial belt of the north and the smiling orchards of Devon; the Wales of coal pits and slag heaps and the Wales of green meadows and little chapels; the poetic grandeur of Edinburgh and the soot-crusted city giant of Glasgow; the holiday seacoasts of Somerset and the rivet-hammering marine world of the Clyde and Tyne; the velvet lawns of golfing St. Andrews and the "Garden Isle" of Wight . . . all set into the little realm that reaches from Land's End in the south to John O'-Groats in the north.

By U.S. or Canadian standards, the distances involved are mere hops, and railroad service is admirably frequent. You can catch 13 trains per day for the 2½-hour run to Cardiff, capital of Wales. Eight trains daily make the trip to Liverpool in roughly the same time. A rail journey to Edinburgh, the Scottish capital, takes six hours, and you have a choice of seven trains per day.

British Railways, the government body that operates all of the country's railroads, offer a whole series of special concession rates to attract travelers. The same applies to the private bus and interior airline companies.

Now, the only question is—where to?

The following are just a few samples from a truly immense grab bag of holiday fun. They are chosen to give you an idea of the variety available.

Torbay

This is the title bestowed on a lively resort area in Devonshire ("Glorious Devon" to the natives), which embraces the three coastal towns of Brixham, Paignton, and Torquay. Connected by 20 miles of green and golden coastline, warmed by the Gulf Stream and one of the highest sun-rations in Britain, this stretch of sand beaches, hidden coves, tourist hotels, thatch-roofed hamlets, fishing harbors, and entertainment piers can be reached by train from Paddington Station in 3½ hours (train to Torquay).

Rye and Winchelsea

Formerly an island, the ancient town of Rye was chartered back in 1229. "Nothing more recent than a Cavalier's Cloak, Hat and Ruffles should be seen in the streets of Rye," wrote Louis Jennings. Some 65 miles below London, Rye is in Sussex, near the English Channel. Along with neighboring Winchelsea, it was one of the ancient ports of the Cinque Port Confederation.

Once it was a center of smugglers, who sneaked in contraband, stashing it away in the surrounding marshes. After the sea receded, Rye lost its status as a port. The old city today merits exploration by foot, but wear some sturdy shoes as you travel its narrow cobblestoned streets, walking in the footsteps of such men as Henry James who used to live at Lamb House on Mermaid Street.

In the 13th-century **Ypres Tower** is the Rye Museum, and the **Parish Church of St. Mary's** contains a curious clock.

At some point, all visitors drop in at the **Mermaid Inn**, Mermaid Street. Once it was the headquarters of the notorious Hawkhurst Gang, a band of cutthroats. Today it's one of the most mellowed of the old smugglers' inns of England. Everyone from Queen Elizabeth I to George Arliss has slept there. You too can find accommodations, perhaps bedding down in either the Fleur-de-Lys Chamber or the Tudor Rose Chamber. The inn is also a good choice for dining. The dining room, with its linenfold paneling, Caen stone fireplaces, and oak-beamed ceiling, is the

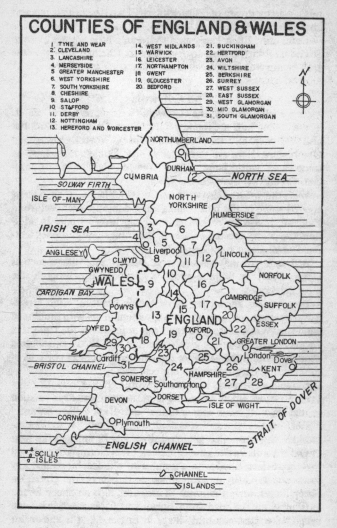

COUNTIES OF ENGLAND & WALES

1. TYNE AND WEAR
2. CLEVELAND
3. LANCASHIRE
4. MERSEYSIDE
5. GREATER MANCHESTER
6. WEST YORKSHIRE
7. SOUTH YORKSHIRE
8. CHESHIRE
9. SALOP
10. STAFFORD
11. DERBY
12. NOTTINGHAM
13. HEREFORD AND WORCESTER

14. WEST MIDLANDS
15. WARWICK
16. LEICESTER
17. NORTHAMPTON
18. GWENT
19. GLOUCESTER
20. BEDFORD

21. BUCKINGHAM
22. HERTFORD
23. AVON
24. WILTSHIRE
25. BERKSHIRE
26. SURREY
27. WEST SUSSEX
28. EAST SUSSEX
29. WEST GLAMORGAN
30. MID GLAMORGAN
31. SOUTH GLAMORGAN

proper background for such typically English food as kidney
soup, poached salmon, and black currant pie.

The sister Cinque Federation port, Winchelsea lies across the
way. In the 19th century, a travel writer said that Winchelsea

was a "sunny dream of centuries ago." That description remains apt today. Once it was sacked by the French, but Winchelsea is peaceful now. Ellen Terry used to live in a little cottage close to Strandgate on the road to Rye. Try to schedule a visit to the 14th-century church to see some interesting tombs.

The Cotswolds

In the 13th century, the Cotswolds were a great wool center. These rolling hills are found principally in Gloucestershire, but also Warwickshire (Shakespeare's shire), Worcestershire, and Oxfordshire. Here are those sleepy little hamlets that enjoy, in some cases, world fame—Moreton-in-Marsh, Chipping Campden, Broadway, Stow-on-the-Wold.

With the wealth derived from Cotswold lambs, their owners erected some of the most outstanding domestic architecture in England, houses or mansions in a honeybrown stone. In addition, the gentry created a series of beautiful stone churches scattered throughout the Cotswolds.

Although you may discover your own favorite village, such as Upper Swell or Shipton-under-Wychwood, **Broadway** is the most celebrated.

Broadway is known for its incredibly beautiful High Street. This street is lined with honey-colored buildings with mullioned windows. While there, you can drop in for tea at the landmark **Lygon Arms,** one of the greatest inns of Old England, standing proudly right in the center of the village. The oldest portions of the building date from the 16th century.

Chipping Campden is another favorite. It lies only 12 miles from Stratford-upon-Avon and is most often visited in relation to that town. It was a winner of the "Best Kept Village Award."

Burford, in Oxfordshire, is the traditional gateway to the Cotswolds. This unspoiled medieval town lies 19 miles to the west of Oxford. It is visited chiefly because of its Norman church and its High Street, filled with a number of old coaching inns. Try to have a typically English lunch at the **Bay Tree Hotel,** on Sheep Street, or at the nearby **Lamb Inn,** also on Sheep Street.

Bibury, on the road from Burford to Cirencester, has been called "the most beautiful village in England." It is known for its **Arlington Row,** a gabled group of 15th-century houses.

Painswick is another contender in the most beautiful village contest. The spire of its 15th-century parish church dominates the village.

Cheltenham is one of England's most fashionable spas, noted for its Regency architecture. Its Promenade has been called "the most beautiful thoroughfare in Britain."

Finally, **Stow-on-the-Wold** is one of the most scenic and most unspoiled market towns in the Cotswolds. You can stop off here en route to Broadway and Chipping Campden. Built at 800 feet above sea level, it is the highest town in the Cotswolds.

Stonehenge

This is Britain's most important prehistoric monument. It's a large oval of megalithic pillars and lintels, lying two miles west of Amesbury and some nine miles north of Salisbury. Stonehenge is believed to be anywhere from 3500 to 4000 years old.

Admittedly, this concentric circle of stones isn't the Pyramids, but, nevertheless, Stonehenge has sparked the imagination of the world. The boulders, especially the bluestones, are believed to have been moved many miles. One report suggests they came from the south of Wales. Of course, legend has it that Merlin delivered the bluestones from Ireland, using clouds as his means of transport.

Romantics in the 18th century suggested fancifully that Stonehenge was the creation of the Druids. But few take that belief seriously.

In the popular book, *Stonehenge Decoded,* its authors speculated that the site was an astronomical observatory—that is, a Neolithic "computing machine" capable of predicting eclipses.

Most visitors to Stonehenge base in Salisbury, described below.

Salisbury

John Constable painted the spire of **Salisbury Cathedral** many times. The building stands 83 miles from London in the West Country. The tower, rising 404 feet, can be seen for miles around.

The cathedral is in the Early English or Gothic style. Construction on the cathedral began in 1220. It was 38 years in the making. The spire dates from the 14th century.

Inside, you can visit the octagonal Chapter House, seeing its fine sculpture, and the Library which has one of the four copies of Magna Carta. Later, you can walk through the Close, containing some 75 buildings in its compound. The attractive town of Salisbury lies in the valley of the Avon River in Wiltshire, and is filled with a number of interesting Tudor inns and tearooms. Thomas Hardy fans know Salisbury as "Melchester," although Anthony Trollope called it "Barchester."

Bath

When Queen Anne made a visit to this spa in 1702, she launched a fashion that was to turn the mineral springs into England's most celebrated spa. Bath lies 115 miles from London in the county of Avon.

It reached its pinnacle of fashion under the dandy, **Beau Nash,** in the 18th century. Creating the settings were the 18th-century architects, John Wood the Elder and his son. They helped design a city of stone gathered from the nearby hills. The final result of this architectural achievement turned Bath into one of England's most harmoniously laid out cities.

This Georgian city on a bend of the River Avon attracted a host of literary and political figures, including Dickens, Nelson, Pitt, and Thackeray. But long before they arrived, Bath was known to the Romans as Aquae Sulis.

Its most important sightseeing attractions are the rebuilt **Assembly Rooms, the Abbey,** the **Pump Room,** and the **Roman Baths.** Bath Abbey, in particular, was built on the site of a much larger Norman cathedral. The present-day structure was launched in 1499.

Finally, 2½ miles outside Bath lies **Claverton Manor,** the first American museum established outside the United States. It presents a glimpse of life as lived by a diversified segment of American settlers until Lincoln's day.

Isle of Wight

A diamond-shaped island dangling below the extreme south coast of England, Wight contains some of the world's most renowned yacht harbors and regularly achieves Britain's (carefully tabulated) record for sunshine.

Cowes, facing the Solent, is a household word to sailing buffs, and Cowes Week one of the greatest regatta turnouts on earth. Yarmouth, a little to the southwest, is another paradise for small yachts people, while Ventnor, the "Madeira of England," is a steeply terraced little resort surrounded by the island's best rambling country. Newport, the island's ancient capital, boasts Carisbrooke Castle, where King Charles I was held prisoner by

Cromwell's Roundheads. Today it is the residence of the governor.

You can reach the island port of Ryde by express train from Waterloo Station, connecting with a ferry steamer at Portsmouth. For a considerably faster and more exciting crossing, try the Hovercraft service from Southampton to Cowes. The craft, looking like a science-fiction engine, skims along on a cushion of air and takes 20 minutes for the trip.

The Channel Islands

Here are more islands but with a subtly different flavor. The little specks of Jersey, Sark, and Guernsey lie closer to France than to England and are, in fact, the only French territories still in Britain's hands after the Hundred Years War ended with the withdrawal of England from the continent. They are not governed from London, but by their own councils, although they owe allegiance to the British sovereign.

It's all wonderfully medieval, but what it boils down to is that the lucky islanders are exempt from British taxes and import tariffs and therefore smoke the cheapest cigarettes and quaff the least expensive liquor in Great Britian. Although thoroughly anglicized by now, they still retain a local patois laced with French (which they talk when they don't want outsiders to eavesdrop), and delight in batches of quaint bylaws. Sark, for instance, permits tractors but no automobiles on the island. During the war, they were the only portions of Britain occupied by the Nazis—and that unintelligible island argot came in very handy for resistance fighters.

You can take a train from Waterloo Station to Southampton (one hour and ten minutes), then a Channel steamer or BUA flight to the islands. Jersey, the largest of them, has claims to fame quite apart from a breed of cows. It offers more than 20 excellent beaches, plus French-style seafood, nightclubs, and cabarets.

Central England

Central England—more often referred to by the catch-all phrase "The Midlands"—contains several widely varied counties or "shires." Their principal touring centers, such as Stratford-upon-Avon or Oxford, have already been dealt with. The others are so virtually unknown to most Americans they qualify as "an offbeat adventure."

This part of England, for instance, offers miles of dreary industrial sections and their offspring, Victorian houses. Yet it's intermixed with some of the island's noblest scenery, such as the Peak District National Park in Derbyshire (Byron said that the scenes here rivaled those of Switzerland and Greece). There are, in short, many pleasant surprises in store for you, from the tulip land of Lincoln in the east to the medieval walled city of Chester in the west.

LINCOLNSHIRE: This eastern county is bordered on one side by the North Sea. Its gaily colored fields of tulips, its marshes and fens, invite a comparison with Holland. The county's homegrown sons include Sir Isaac Newton, John Wesley, and Alfred Lord Tennyson.

In addition to the cathedral city of Lincoln, the busy port of **Boston** on the Witham is ever popular with New Englanders. It was here that the Pilgrim Fathers were initially imprisoned for trying to flee the country. The thing to do in Boston is climb the "Boston Stump," a church lantern tower with an all-encompassing view. The cathedral city of **Lincoln,** 132 miles north from London, was once a stronghold of Caesar's armies. Part of its old Roman wall remains today, as well as the only Roman arch left in England. However, the chief interest is generated by Lincoln Minster, a magnificent cathedral. Workers began its construction in the 11th century, and some of the earliest sections remain standing today. In the library, you'll find a copy—one of the original ones—of Magna Carta.

NORTHAMPTONSHIRE: This sprawling county in the middle of England is rather undistinguished in scenery. Its county town is **Northampton,** an important shoemaking center (a museum of footwear dates back to Roman times). But one of its attractions is of much interest to Americans: **Sulgrave Manor** (tel. Sulgrave 205), the ancestral home of George Washington. It is an almost perfect example of a small Elizabethan manor house, its rooms filled with possessions and pieces of furniture which once belonged to America's first president and his family. The manor is open daily, except Wednesday, from 10:30 a.m. to 1 p.m. and from 2 to 5:30 p.m., April 1 to September 30 (closing at 4 p.m. at other times). It is closed in January. Admission is 70p ($1.37) for adults, 35p (68¢) for children. Incidentally, Sulgrave can be visited by motorists en route from Oxford to Stratford-upon-

Avon. You'll pass through **Banbury** (remember the nursery rhyme of the old Banbury Cross?).

LEICESTERSHIRE: Virtually ignored by modern-day tourists, this eastern Midland county was the home of King Lear and is rich in historical associations. The county town, **Leicester,** is a busy industrial center, but was once a Roman settlement and contains, as well, a 15th-century Guildhall in which Shakespeare is said to have performed. As long as people continue to read Sir Walter Scott's *Ivanhoe,* they will remember **Ashby-de-la-Zouche,** a town that retains a pleasant country atmosphere in spite of the surrounding coal and lead mines. Mary Queen of Scots was imprisoned in an ancient castle here. On the northern border of Leicestershire, seven miles southwest of Grantham, is **Belvoir Castle,** overlooking the Vale of Belvoir, the home of the dukes of Rutland since Henry VIII's time. It contains paintings by Holbein, Reynolds, and Gainsborough, as well as tapestries and magnificent state rooms.

NOTTINGHAMSHIRE: This country is famously linked with Robin Hood's bow and Byron's pen. Of course, Sherwood Forest isn't what she used to be, and those celebrated bandits, Friar Tuck and Little John, are nowhere to be seen. But there are reminders of their spirit. Much of the forest still exists in the so-called Dukeries, a series of large parks scattered throughout the county. At a much later date, the name of Lord Byron enters the picture. **Newstead Abbey,** the former Augustinian priory, nine miles north of Northampton, and later the writer's home, contains a collection of his memorabilia. The gardens are open all year.

DERBYSHIRE: The most magnificent scenery in the Midlands is found within the borders of this county. Sandwiched between Nottinghamshire and Staffordshire, Derbyshire, containing the **Peak District National Park,** is by far the more exciting: waterfalls, hills, moors, green valleys, and dales. The south contains more level land, and the look becomes one of pastoral meadows. The county town is **Derby.**

STAFFORDSHIRE: This county is known throughout the world for its excellence in the ancient craft of pottery, eventually made famous by Josiah Wedgwood, who is properly commemorated in these parts. The county embraces the "Black Country," with its steel and iron works, its coal mines, and smoky, dirty towns. Yet there are features worth exploring. **Litchfield,** in the south, contains the birthplace of Dr. Samuel Johnson, his home now converted into a museum, overlooking the Market Square. In the north is the land of the "Potteries," the Five Towns of Arnold Bennett's novels. **Stoke-on-Trent** now encompasses these towns, whose cone-shaped kilns dot the skyline. **Stafford,** the county town, was the birthplace of Izaak Walton, the British writer and fisherman.

CHESHIRE: This county—famous for a cheese made here—contains the city of **Chester,** England's oldest and best preserved medieval town, complete with a wall which dates from the 14th century. On the banks of the Dee, the city was founded in Roman times, and you can witness here a parade of history of nearly 2000 years' duration. Within its walls are countless half-timbered houses and shops, for which England is so well-known and imitated.

Chester's grand cathedral, a former Benedictine abbey, was built mostly in the 14th century, although earlier portions go back to Norman times. It still possesses many of its monastic buildings, such as a 13th-century chapter house. "The Rows," a double-decker row of shops, one on the street level, another connected by a footway rising above, are a shopper's paradise. You can even shop in the rain.

The city is a convenient point from which to take side trips into Wales, as well as a good stopover en route to the Lake District and Scotland.

SALOP: Formerly known as Shropshire, and immortalized by A. E. Housman's "A Shropshire Lad," this hilly county borders Wales, which accounts for its history of feuds, wars, and bloodshed. It's peaceful today, and you'll remember it as sleepy towns of black-and-white timbered houses. **Shrewsbury,** the county town, on a horseshoe bend of the Severn, is known for its cakes and ale, as well as for being the birthplace of Charles Darwin.

Wales

This western pocket of Britain is almost a separate nation, with its own language, music, and Celtic culture. Wales offers some of the most striking contrasts to be found in the country: the stark coal and iron backdrop of **Port Talbot,** the university city of **Swansea,** and the haunting, incredibly blue and green beauty of rural **Carmathenshire.**

Wales is fishing villages along the rugged Atlantic coast and towering Mount Snowdon, 13th-century **Ruthin Castle,** and the dockland of **Cardiff's "Tiger Bay,"** names that defy pronunciation (Lake Vyrnwy is a mild sample), and chapel hymns with an appeal that transcends all languages.

Folkestone

Close to London, yet a long way from city life, entertaining yet strangely unspoilt, Folkestone combines the charms of a seaside resort with wooded hill surroundings in one thoroughly pleasant package. In case the weather is unsuitable for swimming, there are concerts, variety shows, dancing, and an excellent repertory theater. Trains from Charing Cross Station take just 80 minutes.

Edinburgh

Scotland's capital is—for our money—the most beautiful city in Great Britain, Princes Street the most charming thoroughfare, and the view from the castle the most splendid city panorama anywhere.

Variously known as the "Athens of the North" and "Auld Reekie," Edinburgh is both, depending from which angle you see it. It personifies the Gothic poetry of Sir Walter Scott and the tippling vaudeville rollick of Harry Lauder, the stirring kilt-and-pipe pageantry of the Military Tattoo and the whisky aroma of a thousand old pubs. Edinburgh is history you can touch and walk through in a hundred narrow, steep, enchanting alleys. It's "Bonnie Prince Charlie" riding in on a white charger, as much as the spine-chilling shadows of Burke and Hare, peering around for another candidate for Dr. Knox's anatomy slab.

Your time in this capital city may be limited, and, if it is, then you should see **medieval Edinburgh** if you miss everything else. A visit to what is known as the **Royal Mile** is rewarding. It's composed of Canongate, High Street, and Lawnmarket, moving toward Castle Hill, and leading eventually to the Esplanade. At one end of the Royal Mile is **Edinburgh Castle,** literally dominating the city, on its volcanic rock overlooking Princes Street below.

The castle's oldest surviving building is the tiny chapel of St. Margaret, outside of which sits the five-ton "Mons Meg," a medieval bombard. Inside the castle you can visit the state apartments, where James VI of Scotland (later to be James I of England) was born, the son of Mary Queen of Scots. The buildings are rich in Highland weapons and uniforms, and house the Scottish National War Memorial and United Services Museum. The Crown Chamber shelters the crown jewels, the sceptre, and the sword of state of Scotland.

If you should be in Edinburgh during the Festival, you can inquire at the castle ticket office about volunteer guides who conduct walking parties down the Royal Mile from the Castle Esplanade to the Palace of Holyroodhouse, the headquarters of Queen Elizabeth II whenever she visits the city.

Along the way, several sights will be pointed out to you: St. Giles, Edinburgh's principal church, an imposing Gothic building with spectacular stained-glass windows; the Parliament House, the Law Courts, the City Chambers, and John Knox's House, 45 High St., one of the most interesting of the city's historic buildings, containing many of the reformer's memorabilia; and, finally, the timbered, well-preserved, 16th-century Huntly Museum, on the south side of Canongate.

At the end of Canongate is the old **Palace of Holyroodhouse,** mostly the work of Charles II, although it will forever be known for its association with the tragic reign of Mary Queen of Scots. The castle contains a number of tapestries, mostly Flemish, and additions made by Queen Victoria.

The "new" Edinburgh is to the north of Princes Street, and here you'll find the shops, the stores, the restaurants—all of the conveniences of a modern metropolis. Here, too, are the tartans, the rugs, the cashmeres for which Scotland is known all over the world.

The **Edinburgh International Festival,** major event of the year, occurs in late August, and draws artists from all over the world. In addition to plays, recitals, and concerts, it includes a popular spectacle known as "the military tattoo."

Trains from Kings Cross Station in London take six hours.

The Highlands

This is the Great North of Britain, the breathtakingly dramatic landscape of cold blue lochs (lakes), steep crags, dark gorges, and wind-ruffled heather. Only here do bagpipes sound as they were meant to, and to hear them wailing through a gathering mist is an experience you won't forget in a hurry.

The unofficial Highland capital is **Aberdeen,** the "Granite City," but you have to strike out from there to get the real flavor of the region, or rather regions, as there are West and East and Central Highlands.

The Highlands lack the gentle charm of the south—their beauty has a harsh texture, more grandiose than pretty. The same applies to the climate. Even in midsummer, the Highlands tend to be chilly and moist (Scottish mist), making sweaters and raincoats essential garments.

The BritRail Pass

Probably your best method of traveling about Britain is with one of British Railways' remarkable **BritRail Passes,** which allow you unlimited rail transportation in England, Scotland, and Wales. They're priced at varying levels, depending on the duration of your trip and the class of travel (first class, second class) for which they're applicable. Consult your travel agent *before* you leave for London, as the BritRail Pass can only be purchased in North America.

Piccadilly Circus at Night

Chapter XII

TIDBITS FOR VISITORS

THE FOLLOWING ARE odds and ends which do not fit under our standard chapter headings, but are liable to come in very handy indeed.

Telephone Numbers

All London telephone numbers bear the prefix 01. This is the area code and should only be used when dialing from anywhere *outside* London.

For **Fire, Police,** or **Ambulance,** dial the emergency number 999.

For London region **weather** forecasts, call 246-8091.

For a recorded announcement of **daily events** in London, phone 246-8041.

For the correct **time** from the "Speaking Clock," dial TIM.

If you want to be given an **alarm call** at any particular time, dial INF.

Medical Service

For emergency **medical** treatment, get in touch with your hotel doctor or a hospital Accident and Emergency Department.

Emergency **dental** service: Royal Dental Hospital, 32 Leicester Square, W.C.2 (tel. 930-8831), 9 a.m. to 4 p.m. Outside these hours, call the Accident and Emergency Department of any hospital.

For eye treatment in emergencies: Moorfields Eye Hospital, City Rd., E.C.1 (tel. 253-3411).

All-Night Chemist (Pharmacy)
Boots, Criterion Building, Piccadilly, W.1.

Times and Timing
Britain follows the European 24-hour timetable instead of the American 12-hour shifts. Thus departure times, etc., are given as, say, 19.30 instead of 7:30 p.m. For your own clarity, you simply deduct 12 from every p.m. reading. Britain is also on European time, which means it is six hours ahead of North American Eastern Standard Time, but only five hours ahead of Eastern Daylight Time. And don't forget that there's an additional three hours difference between U.S. East and West Coast time.

Electricity
Britain plugs in on 220-volt electrical current, which is double the American standard 110 volts. Electric shavers, portable irons, etc., will only work with a transformer, except in those thoughtful hotels using adaptable points. Power points, in any case, are one of England's glaring weaknesses. There are never enough of them and—particularly in the smaller hotels—they frequently won't fit American plugs. If possible, bring along an adapter plug for your shaver.

Post and Telegrams
The Post Office at Trafalgar Square stays open all night. To phone a telegram, dial 190 for inland cables, 557 for overseas.

Handy Addresses
American Express, 6 Haymarket, S.W.1 (tel. 930-4411).
U.S. Embassy, 5 Upper Grosvenor St. (tel. 499-9000).
British Tourist Authority, 64 St. James's St., S.W.1 (tel. 499-9325). *930-3488*
West London Air Terminal, Cromwell Road, S.W.7 (tel. 370-4255).
London Transport, 55 Broadway, S.W.1 (tel. 222-1234).

A Summary of Vital Data for London
Certain information, scattered throughout this book, is so important that for easy reference we've set it forth here in short form.

Currency: The unit of currency is the pound, each of which is divided into 100 new pence, written "p." One pound is worth approximately $1.95. As of February 15, 1971, when it adopted a new decimal system, Britain has six coins. The ½p coin is worth approximately 1¢ in U.S. money; 1p equals 2¢; 2p, 4¢; 5p, 10¢; 10p, 20¢; and 50p, 98¢.

Climate: It rains frequently year round in London. But temperatures do not go to extremes: rarely is it hotter than about 80 degrees in summer; just as rarely is it colder than about 35 degrees in winter.

Clothing: In the summer, bring springtime clothes, and be sure to include a raincoat or umbrella for the frequent showers, a sweater or jacket for cool evenings. Wintertime, dress as you would in the northeast United States: warmly.

Tipping: Some hotels and restaurants include a 10% to 15% service charge on the bill, and some add 20% on the bill, eliminating the need for more than spare change as a tip. But be sure to check that service is included. If it isn't, *waiters* get 10% to 15%. *Chambermaids* are often not tipped except for special services. *Bellboys* should get 10p (20¢) per bag, and *cab drivers* are tipped 10p (20¢), a minimum tip for the minimum fare of 50p (98¢), then 15p (29¢) up to a £1 ($1.95) fare. It's pro rata after that. *Barbers* and *hairdressers* should get 20%.

Public Transportation: The *Tube* (subway) is the fastest, and it's clean, well marked, and safe. Fares vary with the distance traveled, usually running between 20p (39¢) for short rides to a high of £1.60 ($3.12) for the outer extremities of London. The average fare in central London is 20p (39¢). *Red buses* service the inner city, *green buses* the outer areas. Fares are cheaper than those on "the tube."

Houses of Parliament

NOW, SAVE MONEY ON
ALL YOUR TRAVELS!
Join Arthur Frommer's $15-A-Day Travel Club

Saving money while traveling is never a simple matter, which is why, almost 20 years ago, the **$15-a-Day Travel Club** was formed. Actually, the idea came from readers of the Arthur Frommer Publications who felt that such an organization could bring financial benefits, continuing travel information, and a sense of community to economy-minded travelers all over the world.

In keeping with the money-saving concept, the membership fee is low—$14 (U.S. residents) or $16 (Canadian, Mexican, and foreign residents)—and is immediately exceeded by the value of your benefits which include:

(1) An annual subscription to an 8-page tabloid newspaper *The Wonderful World of Budget Travel* which keeps you up-to-date on fast-breaking developments in low-cost travel in all parts of the world—bringing you the kind of information you'd have to pay over $25 a year to obtain elsewhere. This consumer-conscious publication also provides special services to readers:

Traveler's Directory—a list of members all over the world who are willing to provide hospitality to other members as they pass through their home cities.

Share-a-Trip—requests from members for travel companions who can share costs and help avoid the burdensome single supplement.

Readers Ask . . . Readers Reply—travel questions from members to which other members reply with authentic firsthand information.

(2) The latest edition of any TWO of the books listed on the following page.

(3) A copy of *Arthur Frommer's Guide to New York*.

(4) Your personal membership card which entitles you to purchase through the Club all Arthur Frommer Publications for a third to a half off their regular retail prices during the term of your membership.

So why not join this hardy band of international budgeteers NOW and participate in its exchange of information and hospitality? Simply send U.S. $14 (U.S. residents) or $16 (Canadian, Mexican, and other foreign residents) along with your name and address to: $15-A-Day Travel Club, Inc., 1230 Avenue of the Americas, New York, NY 10020. Remember to specify which *two* of the books in section (2) above you wish to receive in your initial package of members' benefits. Or tear out this page, check off any two books on the opposite side and send it to us with your membership fee.

FROMMER/PASMANTIER PUBLISHERS Date _____
1230 AVE. OF THE AMERICAS, NEW YORK, NY 10020

Friends, please send me the books checked below:

$-A-DAY GUIDES
(In-depth guides to low-cost tourist accommodations and facilities.)

☐ Europe on $20 a Day	$9.25
☐ Australia on $20 a Day.	$7.25
☐ England and Scotland on $25 a Day	$7.95
☐ Greece on $20 a Day	$7.25
☐ Hawaii on $25 a Day	$8.95
☐ Ireland on $25 a Day	$6.95
☐ Israel on $25 & $30 a Day	$6.95
☐ Mexico on $20 a Day	$8.95
☐ New Zealand on $20 & $25 a Day	$6.95
☐ New York on $25 a Day	$5.95
☐ Scandinavia on $25 a Day	$6.95
☐ South America on $25 a Day	$6.95
☐ Spain and Morocco (plus the Canary Is.) on $20 a Day	$6.95
☐ Washington, D.C. on $25 a Day	$7.25

DOLLARWISE GUIDES
(Guides to tourist accommodations and facilities from budget to deluxe,
with emphasis on the medium-priced.)

☐ Egypt $6.95		☐ Canada	$8.25
☐ England & Scotland $7.95		☐ Caribbean (incl. Bermuda &	
☐ France. $7.95		the Bahamas)	$8.95
☐ Germany. $6.25		☐ California & Las Vegas	$7.95
☐ Italy $6.95		☐ Florida	$6.25
☐ Portugal (incl. Madeira) $7.25		☐ New England	$6.95
		☐ Southeast & New Orleans . . .	$6.95

THE ARTHUR FROMMER GUIDES
(Pocket-size guides to tourist accommodations and facilities in all price ranges.)

☐ Amsterdam/Holland $3.95		☐ Mexico City/Acapulco	$3.95
☐ Athens $3.95		☐ Montreal/Quebec City	$3.95
☐ Boston $3.95		☐ New Orleans	$3.95
☐ Hawaii. $3.95		☐ New York	$3.95
☐ Dublin/Ireland. $3.95		☐ Paris.	$3.95
☐ Las Vegas $3.95		☐ Philadelphia/Atlantic City . . .	$3.95
☐ Lisbon/Madrid/Costa del Sol . $3.95		☐ Rome	$3.95
☐ London $3.95		☐ San Francisco	$3.95
☐ Los Angeles $3.95		☐ Washington, D.C.	$3.95

SPECIAL EDITIONS

☐ How to Beat the High		☐ Museums in New York (Incl.
Cost of Travel $3.95		historic houses, gardens,
		& zoos). $7.95
☐ The Urban Athlete (NYC sports		
guide for jocks & novices) . . . $6.95		☐ Speak Easy Phrase Book (Fr/Sp/
		Ger/It.in *one* vol.) $4.95

☐ Where to Stay USA (Accommodations from $3 to $25 a
night) $6.25

In U.S. include $1 post. & hdlg. for 1st book over $3; 75¢ for books under $3; 25¢ any
add'l. book. Outside U.S. $2, $1, and 50¢ respectively.

Enclosed is my check or money order for $_____

NAME _____

ADDRESS _____

CITY _____ STATE _____ ZIP _____